Inalienable Rights

versus
Abuse

A Commonsense Approach to Public Policy

R. Q. Public

INALIENABLE RIGHTS VERSUS ABUSE
A COMMONSENSE APPROACH TO PUBLIC POLICY

iUniverse books may be ordered through booksellers or by contacting:

iUniverse
1663 Liberty Drive
Bloomington, IN 47403
www.iuniverse.com
1-800-Authors (1-800-288-4677)

Because of the dynamic nature of the Internet, any web addresses or links contained in this book may have changed since publication and may no longer be valid. The views expressed in this work are solely those of the author and do not necessarily reflect the views of the publisher, and the publisher hereby disclaims any responsibility for them.

Any people depicted in stock imagery provided by Thinkstock are models, and such images are being used for illustrative purposes only. Certain stock imagery © Thinkstock.

ISBN: 978-1-5320-1045-3 (sc)
ISBN: 978-1-5320-1046-0 (e)

Library of Congress Control Number: 2016919992

Print information available on the last page.

iUniverse rev. date: 10/31/2017

PRECAUTIONARY DECLARATION

The unique contents of this book have the potential to change life in America for the better. I think it's sad that, in regard to public policy, contemporary mainstream journalists seem to focus exclusively on *extreme* political views. So this book will probably not be mentioned on the evening news. Although I wrote this book to and for older American citizens, I think policy makers of any age should read it. The following warning is for policy makers and anyone in a position to influence public policy:

> If you are of at least average intelligence,
>
> if your mind is at least slightly more open than the average conservative,
>
> if you have a conscience,
>
> and if you read and understand this book in its entirety,

you will be compelled to change the status quo in America. That is both a threat and a promise. I guarantee it.

To the common people.
Each common person deserves the same actualized inalienable
rights to life (health), liberty, the pursuit of happiness, and access
to the common good that each uncommon person experiences.

CONTENTS

PREFACE

Whenever the subjects of politics, race, and/or guns are mentioned in a conversation, perhaps you've noticed people shaking their heads as if they wonder, *what has happened to this country?* If asked that question, I could answer it with an analogy. Imagine a huge henhouse being infiltrated by an increasing number of domineering roosters. Imagine that the roosters are getting more abusive and bolder. The hens, in general, don't like being abused. A minority of hens protests passionately. A different minority of hens fears there will be more chaos and disorder if the domineering roosters do not rule the roost. The majority of hens suffer passively, unmoved by the protesters and unaware that their passivity supports the abusive roosters.

I tried to start an informal movement of people in favor of solving the problem of abusive behavior in the United States in ways that support everyone's individual inalienable rights, including the right to benefit from the common good. I named this movement People for Actualizing Individual Rights (PAIR). I eventually decided that writing this book would be more doable than founding a movement.

This book should be read by American citizens and leaders who truly care about this country and who are open to considering solutions to its problems—solutions based on factual information and particular fundamental principles. Before beginning this book, I started participating in conversation salons at different libraries. The discussions at these groups often focus on social/political problems and situations. Most of the participants are those of or near retirement age. These are people who can remember a time when problems and solutions seemed much simpler than they do today.

It is not unusual for someone in a discussion group to express the sentiment that today's problems are just too complicated. It seems to some that solving one problem creates or exacerbates two or more additional problems. This book will appeal to those folks who share that viewpoint.

Inalienable Rights versus Abuse presents solutions based on foundational principles. One of those principles is that everyone is equal at birth. Some people insist that we are not all equal. One person is better-looking than another person. Sally is wealthier than Lou. Sam has more influence than Larry. That is true. People's differences certainly don't make them equal. However, the other principle is that we are all born with the same intrinsic rights. Those include life, liberty, the pursuit of happiness, and access to the common good. We all share those same rights, and in that sense, we are all equal.

Do we all receive the same opportunities to actualize those rights with which we were born? Absolutely not. There lies the root of many of our social problems—but also the source of the solution to many of those problems. If all American citizens were given the opportunities they deserve to actually experience their individual inalienable rights, it would make a positively profound impact on America as well as on the rest of the world. It is abusive for any group, government, or individual to unfairly deprive a citizen of his or her opportunities to experience inalienable rights.

Abusive behavior is a widespread phenomenon in America. This book presents factual information and data that supports that claim. It also presents my personal opinions about some of the facts. I include relevant opinions of other people that differ from my own and views of others with whom I agree. Direct quotations are signified by either quotation marks or indented bold print.

You may never write a book. But if you do, your publisher may want your potential readers to know what qualifies you to write the book. In other words, "Sell yourself." I have never been good at selling myself. I tend to be reserved. I am usually not comfortable in the limelight; thus I've chosen to use a pen name. I appreciate recognition, but I also fear rejection. In other words, I find the idea of proving my qualifications discomforting.

To what does the word *qualifications* actually refer? If I had previously written several books on political science issues, my qualifications to write one more would probably not be questioned. If I had a doctorate in political science with a specialty in public policy, few people would wonder if I was qualified to write a book about public policy. However, the same people may think I was unqualified to write about abuse unless I possessed a degree or two in psychology.

I don't possess any of those degrees. If I did, I don't think I could write this particular book. Formal higher education has a tendency to mold a person's thinking about the subjects studied. The formal study of political science would not have disqualified me from writing this book; however, I believe that with that education, I would not have the same thoughts and insights as I have expressed in this book.

A more relevant question is, what makes me suited to write about abuse and public policy? There are a number of factors. I have been expressing myself through writing for about sixty years, ever since I fancied myself to be a book author of an adventure series at age nine. The articles and letters that I have published in newspapers and online since then could fill a large volume. After high school, I earned a BA in English literature, minoring in philosophy, with the goal of becoming a professional writer.

I have earned a living in various occupations other than writing. Nine years after college, I returned to higher education and attained a certificate for teaching physical education. In the nineties, I decided to get an MA in counseling services. After earning that degree, I completed an MS program in sustainable systems. Subsequent to the latter degree, I worked for almost ten years as a counselor to the seriously mentally ill in residential programs.

Education, experience, research, and lots of thinking help to formulate worthwhile public policy solutions to the problem of widespread abusive behavior. But so does the absence of a few things. The goal of this book is not to help create conditions that are favorable to any particular group. I am not religious or promoting any particular religion. My suggestions for change are not politically expedient. I am neither strictly liberal nor strictly conservative, though I do favor a republican form of government guided by a constitution. If I have a prejudice, it is against abusers. If I have a bias, it is in favor of everyone's rights opportunities.

Another factor that makes me particularly suited to write this book is a combination of curiosity and imagination. Abuse and rights are closely related. Except for curiosity, I may not have become aware of how they relate. I also have always had an active imagination. I could not have written this book without the ability to imagine what a difference it would make if everyone respected everyone's inalienable rights.

I am also persistent in my quest for pragmatic answers. I know a number of people who believe the solution to any problem is positive thinking. They don't seem to believe it is necessary to understand a problem to solve it. Positive thinking has some value. But it is not productive to believe that a golden age is just over the horizon and that all that is necessary to reach it is to expect it. That sort of thinking removes a sense of personal responsibility for immediate concrete actions to rectify the deteriorating social, political, environmental, and public health conditions of this country.

Simple answers to complicated problems appeal to many Americans who are fearful and uninformed. Simple public policy solutions like "smaller government," "expel all illegal immigrants," and "defund the EPA (Environmental Protection Agency)" do not respect universal human rights. Shaking our heads in despair is also counterproductive.

We need to reevaluate the importance of every citizen's opportunities to experience inalienable rights. Not all American citizens are being treated fairly. The more people who reevaluate and who decide to prioritize everyone's rights, the faster the United States of America will become a better, less abusive place for all to live healthfully, freely, and happily.

I did not write this book without assistance. I would like to thank various librarians of the Pittsburgh Carnegie Library system who gave computer assistance when I needed it most. I am also grateful to the Carnegie Library system for hosting the thought-provoking conversation salons in which I have participated. Then there are those friends who read and gave me feedback on various posts on my blog that form the basis of this book. Those friends include Karen Ciccone, Mary Lou Kientz, Dick Lanken, and Norm Wein. I am especially grateful to Sheila Ann Griffin, my significant other, who listened to the whole manuscript at least twice and offered intelligent critiques.

I would also like to acknowledge the accomplishments of the hundreds of people who researched the data on which the content of this book is based and the writers and organizations that wrote about and published books and articles relevant to this book's contents.

INTRODUCTION

If one lived in the flimsiest shack that ever was and it caught on fire, one may decide to let it burn without trying to save it. That does not sound completely unreasonable. If one possessed the greatest house ever built and there was a slow-burning fire inside the walls, it would seem reasonable to act decisively to find the source of the fire and put it out. But if the owner denies that the column of smoke coming out of a hole in the wall is sufficient proof of an actual blaze or if the owner chooses to ignore the fire because the house is still the greatest, some people may think that the house owner is irrational.

This book presents evidence that the United States is on fire. Something is seriously amiss, and it isn't getting better. Perhaps it's been burning for a long time.

Some people will choose to ignore the evidence. Others will choose to doubt the validity of the evidence without disproving it. Others will admit that the country has serious problems but reason that the problems are insignificant because America is still the greatest country in the world. All of us who admit that the country is on fire agree neither about what the exact nature of the conflagration is nor about what is causing it. We don't all agree on a single solution.

It has been challenging to try to explain, even to myself, why I feel so driven to write this book and to get it published. I had a dream last night in which I felt like a middle-aged, pro-military-industrial-complex conservative. It felt real; it felt appropriate and nonconflictual. It felt like I had never thought any differently. It also reminded me of my deceased parents. I was born in 1947, the youngest of four children. My father was considered relatively well educated for our neighborhood, having completed a two-year business college curriculum. He was a white-collar worker, which enabled me to believe we were middle class. Compared to me, my siblings now seem extremely conservative.

We were reared believing that God was in heaven, that white was good, and that nonwhites were inferior, as were poor whites. All one had to do to get ahead was to work hard. Bigger was always better. New technological innovations were always positive. Upper-class white people were better off financially than middle-class white people because wealthier people were generally superior to those less fortunate than them.

We also believed that politicians and public servants were always looking out for our best interest. A person in a position of authority was superior to those over which the person exercised authority. Authority figures deserved respect and obedience. I suspect that the unconscious justification of adults for teaching these things to children was the belief that as long as most people thought that way, law and order could be preserved and confusion and chaos would be kept at bay. This would allow progress to take place. Progress would allow everyone who deserved it to live a good life.

I did not begin to doubt most of the above until my junior year in high school. A select few high school teachers had the courage to sew some seeds of doubt in my mind. The United States was embroiled in Vietnam as I enrolled in college. More courageous teachers, more challenging questions. *Courageous* refers to the daring required to question conservative thinking and values openly in the midst of a conservative community. If it weren't for those courageous teachers, I might still believe what I was taught growing up.

The dream I referred to above allowed me to realize that if I had never questioned my childhood beliefs, believing those things now might seem natural, comfortable, and nonconflictual. It also made me realize that there are probably millions of older Americans who comfortably and unconditionally believe that there is value in resisting diversity. There are millions who believe that the real threat to our society is those who do not accept *their* traditional values and beliefs, who do not think like *they*, the traditionalists, think. I realized that there are probably millions who see themselves as Christian, patriotic, and "right" and who regard people like me as threats to law and order. These traditionalists are the potential target audience that drives me—them, as well as policy makers. Hopefully this book will encourage policy makers, traditionalists, and especially traditionalist policy makers to open their minds just a crack—enough to look at the facts and the possibilities for a better future for *all* of us.

There are those who prefer to reduce every issue to a question of dollars and cents. As long as the economy is "healthy," they think the country is on "solid ground." However, the only economy that has been thriving since 2008 is the economy of the upper class, especially the top 1 percent of earners.

The United States consists of more than three hundred million of us. For the country as a whole to be healthy and the whole country's economy to be healthy, every one of us, its citizens, must be able to afford the opportunity to live healthfully. The fire in our "house" prevents that from happening. I am not the type of person who stands idly by while my country is consumed by flames. I wrote this book to expose the nature of the fire, its causes, and the ways to fight it.

The fire is abuse, and prioritizing everyone's individual inalienable rights is the way to fight the fire. This book describes the problem we face (a culture of abuse), its causes, and its solutions.

My solutions to the problems, which this book addresses, may seem uncompromising. It is more significant, however, that they are *inclusive*. No one choosing to be included is left behind. Government does not and should not have to force anyone to accept the opportunities offered. If there are people who would decline the opportunities to experience their inalienable rights, they should be left to their own devices and face the consequences of that decision. If churches and other nongovernment-funded nonprofit organizations wish to support such people, that is acceptable.

In an ideal world, when such people choose to take advantage of others illegally, the legal system would apprehend and rehabilitate the lawbreakers. That rehabilitation would include human rights instruction based on the principles in this book. If rehabilitation were not possible, the legal system would ideally keep the law-breaking abusers separated from potential targets of their abuses. The connection between high rates of recidivism and lack of job opportunities for lawbreakers seems pretty obvious to me. (Universal employment opportunity is described in chapter 5.) Anyone able and willing to work, including ex-convicts, would be eligible for a job that pays a healthful living wage. This would, in time, result in a dramatic drop in the crime rate and a marked decrease in the number of incarcerated citizens.

Everyone deserves rights opportunities. Politicians seem to take pride in passing legislation that helps thirty million people improve their lives even though ten million are left living in dire straits. The politicians may congratulate themselves, reasoning that without their statesmen-like willingness to compromise, all forty million people would still be disadvantaged. I wonder what Jefferson would think about the idea that compromise has more value than ensuring *everyone's* rights opportunities.

Why is this book significant? The United States was founded as a republic—that is, a political system governed by a constitution designed to protect the rights of members of minorities. The principles of equality and individual inalienable rights have never been fully implemented for *all* the people. How can our political system allow, encourage, and reward individual initiative while preventing those who gain the most power, wealth, and influence from running roughshod over those with less? What can be done to prevent thugs, corporate polluters, dysfunctional politicians, and other authority figures from threatening the rights of other people?

I have heard a number of people say that the country is "divided." I am not sure what that means, but I think this belief might originate from the views of outspoken ultraconservatives being contrasted with the views of outspoken liberal extremists. It seems to me that liberal extremists are portrayed as believing that government should give poor folks all the blessings and conveniences of modern American life without them having to give anything back. It seems that excessive conservatives, while ignoring the subject of poverty, believe that ensuring the prosperity of the upper class is necessary for the middle class to thrive.

Each of these seeming opposites overlooks something essential: America is supposed to be more than a country with democratic elections and a capitalistic economy. That describes many countries in this world. What distinguishes, or *should* distinguish, the United States is our principles of equality and rights. Everyone is born equal and possesses the same inalienable rights, including the right to benefit from the common good.

The significant concepts are *everyone* and *common*. Extremists propose solutions to the country's problems that seem reasonable to them because their proposals help this group or that group. For solutions to America's problems to be reasonable, the answers need to prioritize the significant principles of equality and rights for which this country should stand. Is this either a simple or an easy task? Not at all. However, this book demonstrates that it is an achievable goal.

What is lacking in this country is public policy that prioritizes everyone's individual inalienable rights. This book demonstrates that such public policy not only is in keeping with our traditional foundational national values but also can be pragmatically implemented. It *must* be implemented in order for the Republic of the United States to endure. The alternative is plutocracy and an intensification of the American culture of abuse.

In writing this book, I found that, to express anything definitive and meaningful about rights, abuse, and public policy, it was necessary to impose limits on these topics. Rather than addressing the general issue of human rights, this book focuses on the individual inalienable rights to life, to liberty, to the pursuit of happiness, and to benefit from the common good. This book also spotlights abuses that threaten those rights. The commonsense public policy approaches suggested are those designed to preserve everyone's rights opportunities.

All Americans are not the same. We are NRA members, Republicans, Democrats, evangelicals, new age thinkers, homosexuals, animal lovers, younger, older, defenders of nature, believers in laissez-faire capitalism, believers in Democratic Socialism, feminists, atheists, agnostics, tax resisters, rich, poor, middle class, survivalists, and so forth. It appears to me that what some members of each of these different groups believe would be best for the country as a whole are things that would also benefit *them* or promote their particular cause. In this book I suggest an alternative idea of what is best for the whole country. I explain how changing our behaviors and altering public policy could enable *all* Americans to experience their inalienable rights.

Some members of the different groups mentioned above remind me of a pack of wolves after a successful group hunt. Each member of the pack tries to get as much of the carcass as possible. Of course, the leader of the pack gets first dibs. The weakest/slowest wolves get whatever is left over, if anything. If the weakest/slowest wolves work together, perhaps they can get more to eat. If members of different national progressive-minded nonprofit groups would join together with a common goal, perhaps they could win a bigger share of the American pie for the sake of quality education, greater social and economic justice, purer water, cleaner air, better police and fire protection for the disadvantaged, and the right of everyone to a job that pays at least a healthful living wage.

If such a general joint effort of all progressive groups does not occur, it might be because some national nonprofit organizations depend on wealthy benefactors for their continued financial existence. That fiscal dependence might make those organizations careful not to offend their chief benefactors. People who control the purse strings control the world. This reminds me of a quotation from billionaire Warren Buffet: "There's class warfare, all right, but it's my class, the rich class, that's making war, and we're winning" (Ben Stein, Your Money, *New York Times,* November 26, 2006, http://www.nytimes. com/2006/11/26/business/yourmoney/26every.html).

We are experiencing a multitude of current social, economic, political, health, and environmental problems that are manifestations of abuse. This book exposes different aspects of abuse in the United States and offers concrete alternatives that would allow all of us to experience the rights opportunities we deserve.

The United States is, by far, not the most abusive country in the world. I am an American. As such, my primary concern and desire is to help improve America. Implementing the public policy improvements suggested in this book would, in time, have a positive effect on the citizens of other countries as well.

The factual information in this book is accurate, and I found a lot of the facts I discovered about the United States disturbing—so disturbing that I was unable to remain emotionally detached. Several times I felt compelled to express my concern for the country by ranting at length about particular ideas or problems. Although the ranting may appeal to readers who want more than a dry recitation of facts, it may not appeal to readers who prefer "just the facts." The rants and my subjective assessments of particular subjects are identified as such so that those readers can skip over them.

I expect that there will be some critics, willing or not to admit their own abusive tendencies, who will assert that abusive behavior has been part of the human experience since Cain slew Abel. They may also claim that abusive behavior of ages past was much more common and severe than it is today. They ask, "So why make an issue of abuse?" The answer is simple. No American citizen deserves to live like the lowest wolf in the pecking order. The United States is supposed to be a republic in which the rights of minority members are protected. Abusive behavior, no matter how common or severe, and no matter who suffers from it, is a violation of inalienable human rights.

You may find that some of the chapter topics do not interest you. Skipping chapters will not be a problem as long as you realize that the sum of the chapters demonstrates the existence of a national culture in which abusive behavior is condoned, practiced, and supported daily. If you wish to intelligently disagree with anything in this book, I suggest you read the introduction and the first three chapters. I would also recommend reading the glossary of frequently used terms located in the back of the book.

These are the underlying beliefs and principles on which this book is based:

- Skepticism is a good thing. The factual information or factual examples presented will include the source of information (usually an Internet address), whenever possible. If source is not included in the text, it can be found in the chapter endnotes.

- Controversial questions will not be avoided. For example, suppose you are a health-conscious individual who does not smoke or drink heavily, and your immediate family members are also health-conscious. You enroll your family in a group health insurance plan administered by a company that allows people of at least normal intelligence who voluntarily engage in risky behaviors, such as heavy smoking, drinking, or drugs, to also enroll in the group plan. Your insurance cost will probably be higher because the company will have to pay more claims filed by the risk takers. Is that fair to you?

- Accepting personal responsibility for behavior is important, as is holding others accountable for the effects of their decisions and behavior.

- We are all created equal and deserve to be treated fairly. This book is dedicated to justice—that is, fair treatment of everyone by everyone.

- No one has a right to abuse anyone. Unfair treatment and all forms of abuse should and need to result in appropriate negative consequences for the abuser.

- For there to be universal freedom from abuse, we must all have the opportunity to live healthfully.

- The experiencing or actualization of individual inalienable rights will not, does not, and cannot nullify anyone else's individual inalienable rights.

- All living beings have an intrinsic right to defend themselves (self-defense) when physically attacked.

- Parents are responsible for their dependent children's actions/behavior and well-being.

1

INDIVIDUAL RIGHTS

A. Types of Rights Vary

For the purposes of this book, I define rights as "that which a person has a just claim to; power, privilege, etc. that belongs to a person by law, by nature, or tradition." This is the definition of a *right* from *Webster's New World Dictionary*, 2nd College Edition.

Rights is not a simple subject. This book focuses on *inalienable rights* (see glossary), which are the powers/privileges with which we are all born and which cannot be surrendered or given away. In this book, the terms *rights*, *human rights*, and *individual rights* are used as synonyms of inalienable rights. *Civil* rights are those powers/privileges established by law. *Private property* rights are possibly related more to tradition than the other two types of rights. Property rights have been codified in this country by civil law. There is a discussion of property rights and their relation to inalienable rights at *www.rgpropertyrights.blogspot.com* (R. Geiger, "What about Private Property Rights: Private Property Rights," February 27, 2016).

Examples of civil rights are those rights specified in the Constitution. We, by virtue of being Americans, have the rights to freedom of religion, speech, and the press; rights of assembly and to petition the government for a redress of grievances; the right to keep and bear arms; the right to be free from searches and seizures without warrants; rights in criminal cases; the right to a fair trial; the right to a trial by jury in civil cases where the value in question exceeds twenty dollars; the right

1

not to be burdened by excessive bails, fines, and punishments; the right to a writ of habeas corpus;[1] the right to be free from bills of attainder;[2] the right not to be affected by ex-post facto laws;[3] the right to be free from slavery and involuntary servitude; the right of those of any race or gender who are eighteen years of age or older to vote. These are all civil rights established by law. The Ninth Amendment of the Constitution clearly states that this list of rights is not meant to be exhaustive and does not deny other rights retained by the people.

Why were these particular rights specified? I believe that the civil rights mentioned in the Constitution were responses to what was happening in the country at the time they were adopted. Those rights asserted in the first ten amendments seem to have been adopted in reaction to the way that the British government treated the American colonists prior to the American Revolution. The right to be free from involuntary servitude (the Thirteenth Amendment) was not added until 1865. A critical number of citizens had decided by that time that slavery was immoral and should be abolished by constitutional law.

Civil and criminal legislation can be a powerful determinant of public policy. This book is concerned with *abusive* (see glossary) behavior. I am opposed to any law that either supports or perpetuates abuse of some by others. I favor laws and regulations that discourage abusive behavior and that protect the actualization of everyone's inalienable rights, that is, *rights opportunities* (see glossary).

Sometimes laws seem to support and encourage a change in general social attitudes. For a law to be effective, it must not lack support from the majority of citizens. Prohibition, which lasted from 1920 to 1933, outlawed importing, producing, transporting, and selling of intoxicating liquors. It was eventually repealed because it lost supporters. The War on Drugs is another legislative failure. As with prohibition, illegal drugs make gangs and organized crime organizations wealthier and more powerful. As with 1920s Prohibition, illegal drugs also deprive governments of the revenue they could collect from taxing the same drugs if they were legal.[1]

A purpose of this book is to help change social attitudes toward all abusive behaviors. Social attitudes that more strongly oppose abuse, will support new laws, the enforcement of which will help preserve all rights opportunities.

B. Actualizing Inalienable Rights

There is a significant difference between inalienable rights and civil rights (those established by law). No person, no group, no government can take away or deprive us of that with which we were born (inalienable rights). Enslaved African Americans had an inalienable right to be free before the Emancipation Proclamation and the Thirteenth Amendment. This demonstrates that we can possess inalienable rights without having rights opportunities. We might be deprived of opportunities to experience the rights with which we were born, but we still retain possession of those rights. Before federal law granted African Americans and women the civil right to vote, they did not possess that legal right.

Unlike civil rights, inalienable rights are not dependent on legislation. The opportunities to experience our inalienable rights, however, can be either prohibited or protected by legislation.

Other factors affect our opportunities to experience our rights. For example, the heads of some corporations seem to think that the maximizing of profit should take precedence over some of their customers' rights opportunities. An instance of this involves the Ford Pinto. According to Mark Dowie, in the 1960s, the Ford Motor Company was aware that their Ford Pinto had a defective fuel tank that would burst into flames in certain types of crashes. Ford's cost/benefit analysis found that even though a new safer design would result in 180 fewer deaths, the cost of the new design (eleven dollars per car) would be more expensive than paying for damages due to deaths, injuries, and car replacements.[2] So, what happened to the rights opportunities of those killed and injured in fiery Pinto accidents? Their inalienable right to life was violated by the Ford Motor Company executive's decision not to recall the cars.

Ford is only one of the companies that have violated people's right to life by prioritizing profit over public health. Cigarette companies

3

are another infamous example (see http://topdocumentaryfilms.com/tobacco-conspiracy/). The heads of some coal-powered electricity-generating plants opt to continue spewing toxic chemicals into the air rather than install expensive pollution controls. (See chapter 11 for details.)

We can be deprived of rights opportunities due to circumstances beyond our control. If you are unemployed, and you need money, are willing and able to work, but can't find a decent job that pays at least enough for you to afford to live a *healthful lifestyle* (see glossary), you may be unable to experience your right to live and to pursue happiness. If that happened, you would be deprived of the ability to experience your right to choose to work for a *healthful living wage* (see glossary).

It seems logical that if you possess the rights to live as you choose and to pursue happiness, you should also have, if needed, a decent job that pays at least a healthful living wage. If you are willing and able to work, you are probably not going to be happy existing on government subsidies. In the absence of available work that suits one's aptitude and pays at least a healthful living wage, an able *financially disadvantaged* (see glossary) person's right to live freely and pursue happiness is not actualized.

Disabled and retired citizens who are not receiving what they need to be reasonably healthy through no fault of their own are also being denied their *rights opportunities* (see glossary) to live freely and to pursue happiness.

Rights, be they inalienable or specified by law, are worthy concepts. And they are nothing but concepts until we actually experience them. What follows is a summary of the individual inalienable rights philosophy on which this book is based.

C. Philosophy of Individual Inalienable Rights

- Either one believes in inalienable human rights for everyone or one does not. One believes that life has intrinsic value and that what supports human life is good and what threatens human life is evil, or one does not believe that. Those who don't believe everyone has an equal right to life might be categorized as communists, fascists, terrorists, white supremacists, plutocrats, or oligarchs. Those people are all abusers. It is a futile waste of time and energy to try to reason with or to try to appeal to an abuser's humanity. That is also true of corporations that disrespect human rights. To support, or even to condone, any type of abusive behavior while giving lip service to universal individual rights (e.g., the right to life) is hypocritical. We need to support human rights and stand against abuse.

- In American society, some people think that, because of the size of their bank account, they should have more rights than less fortunate citizens. Then there are those who are less fortunate who think they have the right to break the laws because they have fewer material resources than others. There are those who believe their passion or their sense of righteousness or their desire for thrills or their boredom gives them the right to vandalize or destroy private or public property. This sort of behavior is a violation of the rights of others.

In this book, the term *rights* refers to the individual inalienable rights possessed by everyone, everywhere, and all the time. It does not refer to the so-called rights possessed exclusively by those with either more wealth or more power. The actualizing of anyone's individual rights will not, does not, and cannot nullify anyone else's individual rights. For example, does the power to arbitrarily kill another person give the killer a right to take the other person's life? No, because killing nullifies the dead person's right to life. You don't have a right to interfere with another person's inalienable rights to live, to be healthy, and to be free from abuse. If you wish your own rights to be respected, you need to respect the rights of others.

You may hear some people asserting that businesses have, or should have, certain rights. Corporations, particularly large corporations, typically consist of *groups* of people. Groups do not possess inalienable individual rights. Any rights possessed by corporations, particularly due to the doctrine of corporate personhood, are a product of our legal system. As such, these rights can be taken away by changing the law. Joining a group neither enhances nor detracts from your inalienable rights. Inalienable rights prohibit a group from deciding what the purpose of an individual member's life should be. A group has neither individual rights nor the right to interfere with, threaten, or nullify anyone's rights opportunities.

- There are limits to exercising rights. For example, despite the civil right to free speech, we are disallowed from crying "Fire!" in a crowded theater and from destroying a person's reputation by spreading lies about him or her. If you are a licensed driver, you have the civil right to drive a car. That right does not include flouting the rules that govern driving. If and when someone's rights are violated in a criminal fashion, the violators risk forfeiting some of their rights opportunities for a time as punishment for their crime. Some believe that the punishments for many abusive crimes are not severe enough. On the other hand, there are laws that punish otherwise responsible adults for activities that are not abusive.

- In general, inalienable individual rights and the *common good* (see glossary) do not conflict. We all have an inalienable right to benefit from the common good. We do not have the right to detract from the common good for our own personal benefit.

- We should be free to make wise or unwise choices. An example of a wise decision would be to live as healthfully as possible. An unwise decision would be to behave carelessly and without regard for others' safety and well-being. Any of us can make a legitimate mistake. If a person's or organization's mistake is made repeatedly and overlooked repeatedly, it will have a lasting negative effect. Society and government should neither condone nor enable people and organizations that repeatedly make decisions that negatively affect anyone's rights opportunities.

[1]   Habeas corpus is a writ requiring a person under arrest to be brought before a judge or into court, especially to secure the person's release unless lawful grounds are shown for their detention.

[2]   Bill of attainder is a legislative act declaring a person guilty without a trial and the resulting forfeiture of property and nullifying of civil rights suffered as a consequence of a sentence of death for treason or felony.

[3]   Ex-post facto laws are laws that are designed to outlaw acts already committed before the law was passed and to punish the perpetrators of the already committed acts, which were not illegal at the time.

[4]   Robert Scott, "Prohibition in the United States," 2012, accessed May 1, 2016, http://www.1920-30.com/prohibition/.

[5]   Mark Dowie, "Pinto Madness," *Mother Jones,* September/October 1977, accessed December 1, 2015, http://www.motherjones.com/politics/1977/09/pinto-madness.

2

RIGHTS AND THE COMMON GOOD

Do the goals of the common good and actual opportunities to experience individual inalienable rights ever conflict? Depending on how one defines each term, they probably could be demonstrated to be in conflict in specific circumstances. I define individual inalienable rights as those privileges intrinsically possessed by everyone by virtue of birth. The common good encompasses what is owned, financed, or administered by some level of civil government and that generally benefits everyone, but what most individual citizens could not afford. Such things as the infrastructure, public libraries, public health protection, environmental preservation, courts, law enforcement, national security, firefighting, public education, public parks, public playgrounds, employment security, government fiscal responsibility, caring for the disabled and retired citizens in need, and responsible foreign policy are all aspects of the common good.

Another term for the common good is *general welfare*, an expression found in the Preamble to the Constitution and in Article One, Section Eight of that document. If one googles "general welfare," one finds its meaning seems to be commonly associated with a government's concern for or promotion of the health, safety, morality, and peace of its citizens. Although health and safety are clearly related to welfare or well-being, I don't think that this meaning of the *general* welfare adequately emphasizes the "general" part of the expression. The word *welfare*, by itself, can mean health, safety, morality, and peace of a country's citizens. When you add *general* as a modifier of welfare, it indicates that *welfare* refers to the whole community. This should not be surprising, because the writers of the Constitution were familiar with the wording of the Declaration of Independence.

> **We hold these truths to be self-evident, that all men are created equal, that they are endowed by their Creator with certain unalienable rights, that among these are life, liberty, and the pursuit of happiness.**

That's another thing the common good and inalienable rights have in common: they each apply to *everyone*. The common good is *not* laissez-faire capitalism, unrestricted free enterprise, cut throat competition, or any other practice that enriches the upper one percent and keeps minorities dependent on the handouts of the rich and powerful.

We all have the right to benefit from the common good. According to these definitions, there is no conflict between rights opportunities and the common good.

3

A CULTURE OF ABUSE

What is abuse, and how is it related to human rights? I believe we are all born with the rights to life, liberty, and the pursuit of happiness, as stated in the Declaration of Independence. I also believe we are all born with the right to benefit from the common good. There are a number of factors that determine if we will or will not get actual opportunities to experience rights. Those factors include physical and mental health, income, and autonomy. When forces beyond our control negatively affect our health, our income, or our autonomy, abuse may be occurring.

Webster's New World Dictionary, 2nd College Edition, uses the words *mistreatment, injury, deception, insult,* and *coarse language* in defining abuse. Mistreating, injuring, or deceiving oneself might fit that literal definition. However, this book is not using the term *abuse* to refer to negative behavior toward oneself.

The term abuse, as used in this book, is an action inflicted on others. Not every action that causes pain to others is abusive. To be considered abusive, an action must meet the following three conditions:

1. The action has a negative effect on others such as mistreatment, injury, deception, and so forth.
2. The action is deliberate or negligent.
3. The action is *un*necessary to preserve individual physical health or the common good.

Abuse is an unnecessary injurious action deliberately or negligently inflicted on others. If a driver runs people down, whether he is sober and feeling destructive or under the influence of drugs or alcohol, it would be abusive since this action meets all three conditions mentioned above. Would the subsequent sentencing of the driver to jail time and/ or compulsory rehabilitation be abusive? The temporary restriction of the driver's right to liberty would discourage potentially injurious driving. Such discouragement is necessary to promote and protect public safety, one aspect of the common good. Depriving an injurious driver of his/her liberty does not satisfy the third condition mentioned above and so is not abusive.

A coal-powered electric generating plant might emit some pollutants which negatively affect the health of certain people. If this were the case it would satisfy the first two conditions for being abusive. As long as we need to depend on coal for energy to heat homes and to produce the necessities of life, a coal-burning plant emitting harmful pollutants would not satisfy the third condition, unless the emissions themselves were unnecessary. Refusing to either equip such a plant with the best available technology to contain harmful pollutants or to shut it down, would be abusive.

A coal plant owner's attempts to deceive the public about the dangers of global warming would also be abusive. If the owner's deception was motivated by the desire to continue profiting financially at the expense of environmental quality, an aspect of the common good, it would be especially abusive.

Not all abusive behavior is illegal. An example would be the owner's deception described above. Nor is illegal behavior always abusive. If a person who is literally starving to death steals a loaf of bread from a store, that would be illegal. If the theft was necessary to prevent death by starvation, it would not meet the third condition of an abusive action.

Understanding what is and is not abusive depends on understanding my definition of "common good". Some people might believe that making it illegal for women and black people to vote in national elections would be in the best interest of the common good and would not meet condition three of abusive behavior mentioned above. This

11

belief or claim would be senseless in terms of what I mean by the common good. That meaning is explained in Chapter 2, Rights and the Common Good.

None of us are perfect. I would not be surprised to find that the average person inadvertently and infrequently abuses others in the course of their daily lives. This is perhaps inevitable. The abuses this book addresses, rather than inadvertent and infrequent, are habitual or persistent.

Unnecessarily depriving people of their rights opportunities in a deliberate or abusive manner is a rights violation also referred to as a rights abuse. How are abuse and inalienable rights related in terms of human beliefs, attitudes, and behavior? Some of us believe *everyone* should have opportunities to actually experience inalienable rights. Others persistently support rights abuses against millions of us.

The next section describes a number of such rights abuses.

A. Frequency of Rights Abuses

How common are such rights abuses? Am I making much to do about nothing? Let's see what's been happening in the United States.

1. Child Mistreatment

According to "Child Mistreatment—Facts at a Glance," American state and local child protective services reported that there were about 686,000 children (9.2 per one thousand) who were verified to be individual distinct victims of maltreatment in the United States and Puerto Rico in 2012.[1] That averages out to seventy-seven per hour.

2. School Bullying

According to WEB TABLES, a US Department of Education website, the National Center for Education Statistics survey of students twelve to eighteen years of age reported that 21.5 percent of the students were bullied at school and cyber bullied anywhere during the 2012–13 school year.[2] If you want to better understand this problem, I recommend watching the DVD documentary *Bully*, written by Lee Hirsch and Cynthia Lowen (directed by Lee Hirsch, The Bully Project, released April 27, 2012, http://www.imdb.com/title/tt1682181/).

3. Workplace Bullying

According to the "2014 Workplace Bullying Institute Survey," 20 percent of those surveyed had been bullied at work at some time during their working lives, and 7 percent were currently being bullied. An additional 21 percent of those surveyed, although not victims of bullying, had witnessed workplace bullying.[3]

4. Elder Abuse

The Centers for Disease Control and Prevention's web page "Elder Abuse and Prevention," reports that hundreds of thousands of Americans sixty years of age or older are being maltreated annually.[4] Many other elderly people are afraid to or unable to report abuse.

5. Police Misconduct

The killing of young black men by police seemed to be almost a common occurrence in 2016. Not every shooting seemed justified. The Cato Institute has a National Police Misconduct Reporting Project, founded by David Packman. The project's "Statistical Report" reveals that unjustified killings are not the only examples of abuse by police. Based on credible reports, some of the police officers surveyed had used excessive force; had engaged in forcible nonconsensual sexual activity; had engaged in fraud/theft/robbery; made false arrests; had conducted illegal raids/searches; had violated civil rights; or were dishonest. The officers surveyed may have committed multiple abusive offenses.[5] (See chapter 7 of this book for more discussion of this problem.)

6. Military Sexual Abuse

According to the US Department of Defense's "Fact Sheet: Defense Manpower Data Center (DMDC) Survey," unwanted sexual contact for military women increased in 2012.[6]

7. Landlord Abuse

According to the New York City Housing Authority's "Residential Data Summary Sheets," 175,587 families resided in NYCHA's public housing developments as of January 1, 2014.[7] A *Dateline NBC* story airing on January 5, 2014, focused on two public housing apartments located in poorer neighborhoods of New York City. The story related the difficulties faced by parents with asthmatic children living in those apartments. There was a mold problem in the bathrooms because of leaky pipes, and the presence of mold led to asthmatic episodes for the children. Asthmatic episodes are potentially deadly. The story showed how difficult and time consuming it was for these parents to get the NYCHA to correct the problem.[8] Landlords responding slowly to tenants' complaints about genuine health threats posed by conditions in their buildings is an example of authority abuse.

8. Intimate Partner Violence

The US Centers for Disease Control and Prevention, a federal government agency, published "National Intimate Partner and Sexual Violence Survey, United States, 2011." This survey questioned noninstitutionalized English- and Spanish-speaking people eighteen years of age and older. According to the survey results, 19.3

percent of women and 1.7 percent of men had been "raped in their lifetime." Stalking had happened to 15 percent (18.3 million) of the women and 5.7 percent (almost 6.5 million) of the men. Victimizations by nonrape types of sexual violence affected 43.9 percent of women and 23.4 percent of men.[9]

9. Violent Criminal Abuse

According to the Federal Bureaus of Investigation's (FBI) "Crime in the U.S., 2012, Crime Clock Statistics," a violent crime occurred in the United States in 2012 at an average of every 26 seconds. That included one murder every 35.4 minutes; one forcible rape every 6.2 minutes; one robbery every 1.5 minutes; and one aggravated assault every 41.5 seconds.[10]

10. Property Crimes

Property crimes are those committed "without force or threat of force against the victims," according to the FBI's "Crime in the U.S., Property Crime" web page. These crimes include burglary, larceny-theft, and motor vehicle theft.[11] These are all abusive crimes that involve financial harm and deception. Property crimes nationwide in 2012, even though there were 14 percent fewer than in 2003, were estimated at almost nine million. According to the FBI "Crime in the U.S., 2012, Crime Clock" referenced above, there was a property crime committed every 3.5 seconds in 2012. That included one burglary every fifteen seconds, one larceny theft every 5.1 seconds, and one motor vehicle theft every 43.7 seconds.[12]

11. Crimes of Deception

The Bernie Madoff case is a well-known example of criminal deception. Crimes of deception include fraud, counterfeiting, identity theft, and embezzlement. Although not all crimes of deception are white-collar crimes, many white-collar crimes are crimes of deception. According to the "Transactional Records Access Clearinghouse (TRAC) Reports," there were "7,049 new white collar crime convictions" by the US Department of Justice during fiscal year 2015.[13]

12. Gangs

According to "The FBI 2011 National Gang Threat Assessment—Emerging Trends" report, there were about 1.4 million active street, prison, and outlaw motorcycle gang members in the United States and Puerto Rico, comprising thirty-three thousand gangs. In 2009, there were a total one million active gang members. For the years 2001–10, there were 12,169 complaints of gang violence, which resulted in 23,094 convictions. Gangs were responsible for 48 percent of violent crimes in most jurisdictions. According to the FBI, members of at least fifty-three different gangs had served in or were affiliated with the US military. Although all branches had been infiltrated by gang members, most military personnel gang members and gang member dependents of military personnel were affiliated with the US Army, the Army Reserves, and the National Guard.[14]

13. Human Trafficking

The US Department of Health and Human Services defines human trafficking as "a form of modern-day slavery. It is a crime involving the exploitation of someone for the purpose of compelled labor or a commercial sex act through the use of force, fraud, or coercion."[15] Crime statistics from the FBI in 2014 listed human trafficking as a separate crime. The actual numbers of perpetrators and victims is unknown. The FBI Operation Cross Country has rescued numerous children from traffickers. According to this operation, from 2006 to 2015, more than 4,800 children were rescued from exploitation as prostitutes, and there have been more than 2,000 convictions for those crimes.[16]

14. Crime Costs

A January 1996 research report, "Victim Costs and Consequences: A New Look" by Miller, Cohen, and Wiersema, presented to the US Department of Justice, National Institute of Justice, found the cost of violent and property crimes to victims was $450 billion annually.[17] That amount did not include the costs of most white-collar crimes and cybercrime.

15. Chronic Disease

According to the "Obesity" web page of Trust for America's Health, "Adult obesity rates have doubled since 1980, from 15 to 30 percent, while childhood obesity rates have more than tripled" (Healthy Americans, accessed December 11, 2015, http://healthyamericans.org/obesity/).

The chronic diseases associated with obesity and being overweight had also been increasing, according to the DVD documentary *Fed Up,* directed by Stephanie Soechtig (Katie Couric & Laurie David, released May 9, 2014, http://fedupmovie.com/#/page/home). Narrated by Katie Couric, *Fed Up* suggests that obesity might be more beyond our control than many of us assume. This video suggests that the food industry has persuasively influenced the executive branch of the federal government.

A related topic is food flavoring. I heard a program on WESA Radio recently, which I cannot document at this time. This is not scientifically verified information; I just present it for consideration. The guest on the radio show claimed that the science of creating flavoring for processed foods has advanced to the point that processed foods taste better than unprocessed foods. This authority said that scientifically enhanced flavoring possibly contributes to the obesity problem. Traditionally, before modern food processing, our brains learned to associate pleasing flavors with nutritional value and safe food. We still tend to be repelled by spoiled foods. It might be that our brains are being fooled into thinking high-fat, high-calorie processed foods are better for our bodies than more natural, unprocessed foods.

Another particular area of concern in regard to obesity and other diseases is the toxic man-made substances in our air, in our water, in our food, and in our bodies. *The Story of Stuff* by Annie Leonard contains information about that.[18]

16. Economic Disparity

According to the US Census Bureau's "American Fact Finder," in 2014, of the 117,259,427 households in the country, 6.3 million or 5.3 percent received income and benefits of $200,000 or more; 7.3 percent of the country's households (8.5 million) received less than $10,000 in income and benefits.[19] In other words, 6 million American households each had at least 95 percent more income to live on than each of the poorest 8.5 million households. For more evidence of economic inequality, go to www.savingrepublic.blogspot.com (R. Geiger, "Is the U.S. a Plutocracy? Who Cares?," *Plutocracy Now!* February 8, 2014, sect. A).

17. Influence of Wealth on Politics

For a full discussion of this topic go to that same blog at www. savingrepublic.blogspot.com. This blog explains that our national government is on the verge of, or has already become, a plutocracy. Section B of "Is the U.S. a Plutocracy? Who Cares?" points out that members of Congress are paid an upper-class income. Senators are more responsive to their upper-class constituents than to their lower-class constituents. And many of the decisions that are made by all three branches of the federal government benefit the wealthy, often to the detriment of lower earners. This information is thoroughly documented at that blog site.

18. Poverty

According to Kathleen Short's "The Supplemental Poverty Measure: 2014," the official 2014 poverty rate was 14.8 percent of the US population (an increase of 0.3 percent from 2013).[20] I define poverty as the inability of people to live a healthful lifestyle and/or to prevent health deterioration because of insufficient financial resources. There is a theoretical possibility that some people choose freely to be poor. Voluntary poverty would not be abusive. Poverty imposed on those able and willing to work or who are disabled or of retirement age is abusive.

19. Religious Abuse

There are various forms of religious abuse. Chapter 16 has a section with information about the problem of abuse by religious leaders in the United States. Some people who identify themselves as militant soldiers of Islam also practice abuse. According to a *Business Insider* article by Ben Winsor, as of August 2014, it is estimated that one thousand to three thousand militant jihadists in Syria and Iraq came from Western Hemisphere countries, with at least one hundred originating in the United States.[21]

20. Hate Groups

The Southern Poverty Law Center (SPLC) "Hate Map" web page reports that there were 784 active hate groups in the United States in 2014. "All hate groups have beliefs or practices that attack or malign an entire class of people, typically for their immutable characteristics" (Southern Poverty Law Center, Montgomery, AL, 2014, accessed December 12, 2015, https://www.splcenter.org/hate-map).

B. The Culture of Abuse

As one can see from the above documented information, abuse exists in all sectors of this "land of the free." We find it in business, in government, at every income level, in schools, in churches, in families, in institutions for the elderly, in intimate relationships. Millions in this country are affected by rights abuses in multiple ways. Americans of today are being abused in regard to physical health, environmental quality, and the growing national debt. These problems will also negatively affect future generations. According to the *Merriam-Webster Dictionary and Thesaurus* online, the term *culture* refers to "a way of thinking, behaving, or working that exists in a place or organization."

I believe that the number and frequency of rights abuses justifies my claim that the United States is permeated with a culture of abusive behavior.

C. The Alternative

This section is my subjective assessment of the information presented above. What would the opposite of a culture of abuse look like? The alternative or opposite culture would be one that prioritizes everyone's rights opportunities. What we have in today's America is health, liberty, and the pursuit of happiness for *some* of the people *some* of the time. We deserve a culture that prioritizes the creation and preservation of rights opportunities for *all* of us, *all* the time.

It seems to me that, for the elite, what is great about America is the opportunity for a self-centered few to hoard as much wealth and power as possible to the detriment of the many. If this has not caused a national facsimile of a pecking order, it certainly is supportive of such a phenomenon. In the human pecking order, those who have more perceive those with less as "losers." In the chicken coop or in the wolf pack, those on top couldn't care less whether all the animals get enough to eat. Some of those humans who are perceived as winners justify their indifference with the claim that "losers" *could* get ahead if they would try harder. Unless the losers can reach the winners' status, the winners will still regard them as losers, no matter how hard the losers try or how much they achieve.

Are we capable of creating a fairer system than what determines the fate of chickens or wolves? I believe we have the ability. The political will is another matter.

---

[1] CDC, "Child Maltreatment—Facts at a Glance," 2014, http://www.cdc.gov/violenceprevention/pdf/childmaltreatment-facts-at-a-glance.pdf.

[2] US Department of Education, National Center for Education Statistics, "Web Tables," April 2015, http://nces.ed.gov/pubs2015/2015056.pdf.

[3] "2014 Workplace Bullying Institute Survey," Workplace Bullying Institute, 2014, accessed December 8, 2015, http://workplacebullying.org/multi/pdf/2014-Survey-Flyer-A.pdf.

[4] Centers for Disease Control and Prevention, "Elder Abuse and Prevention," June 2015, www.cdc.gov/features/elderabuse/2a63d75b5459_story.html.

[5] David Packman, *National Police Misconduct Statistics and Reporting Project* (CATO Institute, April 5, 2011), accessed December 9, 2015, http://www.policemisconduct.net/2010-npmsrp-police-misconduct-statistical-report/.

[6] US Department of Defense, "Fact Sheet: DMDC Survey," n.d., accessed December 9, 2015, http://www.sapr.mil/public/docs/research/WGRA_survey_Fact_Sheet.pdf.

[7] New York City Housing Authority Resources, "Residential Data Summary Sheets," January 1, 2014, 1, http://www.nyc.gov/html/nycha/downloads/pdf/res_data.pdf.

[8] "Breathless," pt. 3, *Dateline NBC*, January 6, 2014, accessed December 9, 2015, http://www.nbcnews.com/video/dateline/53992676/#53992676.

[9] Matthew Breiding, Centers for Disease Control and Prevention, "National Intimate Partner and Sexual Violence Survey, United States, 2011," September 9, 2014, http://www.cdc.gov/mmwr/preview/mmwrhtml/ss6308a1.htm?s_cid=ss6308a1_e.

[10] FBI, "Crime in the United States: 2012 Crime Clock Statistics," 2012, https://www.fbi.gov/about-us/cjis/ucr/crime-in-the-u.s/2012/

crime-in-the-u.s.-2012/offenses-known-to-law-enforcement/crime-clock.

[11] FBI, "2014 Crime in the United States: Property Crime," 2014: https://www.fbi.gov/about-us/cjis/ucr/crime-in-the-u.s/2014/crime-in-the-u.s.-2014/offenses-known-to-law-enforcement/property-crime.

[12] "Crime in the United States: 2012 Crime Clock Statistics."

[13] "TRAC Reports," Transactional Records Access Clearinghouse, Syracuse University, 2015, accessed December 10, 2015, https://trac.syr.edu/cgi-secure/product/login.pl?_SERVICE=express9&_DEBUG=0&_PROGRAM=interp.annualreport.sas&p_month=mar&p_year=14&p_topic=80&p_agenrevgrp=&p_distcode=&p_trac_leadcharge=&p_progcat=&p_stat=gu.

[14] FBI, "2011 National Gang Threat Assessment—Emerging Trends," https://www.fbi.gov/stats-services/publications/2011-national-gang-threat-assessment/2011-national-gang-threat-assessment#Key.

[15] US Department of Health and Human Services, Administration for Children and Families, "What is Human Trafficking?" December 29, 2015, http://www.acf.hhs.gov/endtrafficking/trafficking.

[16] Carrie Adamowski, Federal Bureau of Investigation, "FBI Announces Results of Nationwide Human Trafficking Operation," October 15, 2015, https://www.fbi.gov/contact-us/field-offices/philadelphia/news/press-releases/fbi-announces-results-of-nationwide-human-trafficking-operation.

[17] Ted R. Miller, Mark A. Cohen, and Brian Wiersema, *National Institute of Justice Research Report,* January 1996, 6, accessed December 10, 2015, https://www.ncjrs.gov/pdffiles/victcost.pdf.

[18] Annie Leonard, *The Story of Stuff* (New York: Free Press, 2010).

[19] US Census Bureau, "American (Census) Fact Finder," 2014, factfinder.census.gov/faces/tableservices/jsf/pages/productview.xhtml?pid=ACS_14_1YR_DP03&prodType=table.

[20] Kathleen Short, US Census Bureau, "The Supplemental Poverty Measure," September 2015, 4, https://www.census.gov/content/dam/Census/library/publications/2015/demo/p60-254.pdf.

[21] Ben Winsor, "Military and Defense," *Business Insider,* August 27, 2014, accessed December 12, 2015, http://www.businessinsider.com/isis-is-recruiting-westerners-countries-2014-8.

4

SPECIFYING AREAS OF CONCERN

This book focuses on the following areas or issues as they relate to individual inalienable rights:

- the common good
- poverty
- law enforcement
- fiscal activities of the federal government
- foreign policy of the federal government
- the national economy
- energy

- immigration
- student rights
- environmental preservation
- religion
- gun ownership
- privatization
- values
- individual responsibility

Why single out these particular concerns? Each of these areas is related to what we, as citizens, need in order to experience our rights opportunities.

- As chapter 2 notes, we all have the right to benefit from the common good. The benefits of the common good that are maintained and administered by government allow us to live more fully, healthfully, and affordably.
- Poverty—that is, *the inability of people to live a healthful lifestyle and/or to prevent health deterioration because of insufficient financial*

resources—deprives people of the opportunity to experience their rights to life, liberty, and the pursuit of happiness.

- Police misconduct can be abusive; it can have a negative effect on our individual rights.
- Fiscal responsibility of government is necessary for government to have sufficient funds to protect our rights opportunities.
- The federal government's dealing fairly and firmly with foreign nations and peoples helps to preserve our national security, an aspect of the common good.
- An economic recession or depression can have profound negative effects on our opportunities to experience our rights. This is particularly true of those with lower incomes.
- The energy that enables the country to function has profound effects on our inalienable right to life.
- Illegal immigration relates to human rights in a variety of ways.
- The quality of our primary and secondary education can affect our ability to get decent jobs or to qualify for higher education or for vocational/technical training.
- A quality environment allows us to have clean water to drink, pure air to breathe, and good soil for planting food. Such an environment supports human health.
- The issue of religion relates to rights in more ways than just freedom of religion.
- Private gun ownership can have both positive and negative effects on preserving our inalienable rights.
- The privatization of public services at times negatively affects our individual rights and the common good.
- What we value most has an effect on our rights opportunities.
- Each of us can either act responsibly to support human rights or allow those rights to be violated.

Problems encountered in any of these areas can impede our rights opportunities.

5

POVERTY AND CAPITALISM, I

You may wonder, *can we ever eradicate poverty in this country? And what about in the world in general?* Do we, as Americans, have potential power and primary responsibility to solve the problem of poverty in this country or in the whole world? Any country that wants to solve a national problem must focus on the problem *in that country.* In terms of practicality, if we can't solve the problem in this country, how can we possibly solve it in the rest of the world?

This chapter can serve as an example of looking at public policy problems in terms of individual inalienable rights and finding solutions that protect those rights while not violating the guiding principles listed in the introduction.

There are financially disadvantaged people who cannot live healthfully or prevent health deterioration due to lack of a legitimate means of securing healthful lifestyle resources. I define poverty as *the inability of people to live a healthful lifestyle and/or to prevent health deterioration because of insufficient financial resources.* Poverty is not the absence of a healthful lifestyle, but rather the condition of not having the resources needed to live a healthful lifestyle. Adult citizens should not be forced to work nor forced to accept what they don't want; nor should they be forced to expend their financial resources to live healthfully. Adults should be free to choose to be financially disadvantaged. While there are people in financial need who freely choose to decline the offer of sufficient financial resources, poverty, as I define it, will continue to exist. Call that choice *voluntary poverty.* Voluntary poverty is not abusive.

When the financially disadvantaged are deprived of the resources or the legitimate means of attaining the resources they need, that is *involuntary poverty* and is abusive. An example of poverty abuse is the condition of fewer jobs that pay a healthful living wage being available than the number of citizens who possess the ability and willingness to work and who are in need of that income.

This chapter and the next are concerned with solutions to *abusive* poverty or poverty abuse. Those who experience poverty abuse belong to one of four groups.

1. Adults who are able and willing to work, but who lack sufficient resources to live a healthful lifestyle
2. Children (eighteen and under)
3. Those with disabilities
4. Retirees

Some people in each of these four groups experience poverty abuse. The suggested solutions to poverty abuse for each group will differ. The solutions are entitled

- Jobs for the Common Good
- Common Good Program for Disadvantaged Youth
- Common Good Disabilities Program
- Common Good Program for Retirees

A. Jobs for the Common Good

Those who are able and willing to work, but who lack sufficient resources to live a healthful lifestyle, are not necessarily unemployed. Poverty and unemployment are not synonymous. And not everyone who is unemployed is poor. There are many American citizens who work full time but are still poor. Others would be poor if they weren't receiving social safety-net program benefits. There are millions of American citizens who are able and willing to work, but who cannot find a job that pays a healthful living wage. Some people think that under the "right" conditions, free market capitalism would be able to solve the problem of poverty in America. I would welcome the free market's participation in solving the poverty problem, but I object to the creation of the so-called "right" conditions if and when those conditions are characteristic of *laissez-faire* (see glossary) capitalism.

1. Capitalism

Capitalism refers to an economic system in which the means of production are privately owned. The purest theoretical form of capitalism is called laissez-faire. Laissez-faire is a system in which the owners of industry and business dictate the rules of competition, the conditions of labor, the negative effects of their activities on the environment and on public health, the cost and safety of products and services, and other conditions as they please, without government regulation or control.

2. Laissez-Faire and the Robber Barons

There is an online book by Howard Zinn entitled *History Is a Weapon*, the eleventh chapter of which is entitled "Robber Barons and Rebels."[1] The robber barons were people like Carnegie, Rockefeller, Morgan, Frick, and Vanderbilt who became rich and successful—or, more often, richer and more successful—by using advances in industrial technology to build large business enterprises through unscrupulous means. They kept wages low, maintained high prices, choked out competition, and used government subsidies. This took place in America during the late 1800s to the early 1900s and might have been the closest approximation of an actual laissez-faire system the world has experienced.

During this period of the Industrial Revolution, the United States rose to prominence on the world stage. The price of—that is, the effects of—this rise to prominence are as follows:

- The wholly unjust and abusive acquisition of land from Native Americans and the cruel, unjustifiable subjugation and segregation of the tribes to reservations, tracts of land no one else wanted at the time. This was completed by 1870. Why was it done? To attract and then placate more European immigrants with land grants and to guarantee safe passage for the expanding railroad industry.
- The abusive treatment of the working class. This treatment involved unhealthful/unsafe working and living conditions created by factories and mills for low-paid immigrant laborers. Immigrants like the Chinese who built the railroads were forced into virtual slavery due to their wages not exceeding the price of the room and board supplied by their employers. Thousands of workers were killed or injured in labor strikes that attempted to force their employers to treat them more reasonably.[2]
- Then there was the environmental price. One example of this is the passenger pigeon, which was hunted to extinction by 1900 with the aid of the railroads and the telegraph, according to "Why the Passenger Pigeon Went Extinct" by Barry Yeoman.[3] By 1883, nearly all bison in the United States had been killed. They would have died out completely except for the efforts of private citizens unaided by the government, according to "Time Line of the American Bison."[4]

The Industrial Revolution negatively affected many people's individual rights, including the right to benefit from the common good. Some people would like today's captains of business and industry to possess the same power their counterparts possessed during the Robber Baron period. They believe that would improve conditions for lower-income families today. However, during the Robber Baron period, lower-income families suffered more than lower-income families suffer today.

3. Laissez-Faire and Lawsuits

If government regulations of businesses are completely repealed, the heads of large corporations will be able to negatively affect our rights with impunity. If you think that, in the absence of regulations, you will simply and easily be able to secure redress through the court system for damages caused by big business, you should watch the movies *Flash of Genius, The Insider*, or *Erin Brockovich*. You might be able to win a lawsuit against a corporation for environmental/health damages if you have enough time and money. But aren't those who possess enough time and money living in neighborhoods that aren't exposed to illegal dumping of chemical waste or to contamination of groundwater from fracking? People who have enough time and money to sue can afford to feed their families organic food without toxic chemicals and GMOs. Not only are these people not exposed to pollutants and toxins poorer people deal with, they are also better able to strengthen their immune systems through eating better food.

4. The Necessity of Regulations

It seems to me that, left to their own devices, large national and multinational corporations would be incapable of operating without threatening our individual inalienable rights. If that is so, and if human rights are valued, any solutions to problems involving large corporations must include restrictive regulations on businesses designed to protect our individual inalienable rights and the common good from the activities and practices of private enterprise. When regulators make regulations for businesses without understanding the conditions and limitations of those enterprises or make the assumption that one rule can fit all businesses, unnecessary problems can arise. Common sense should be incorporated into the process of forming regulations.

5. Private Enterprise as a Solution to Poverty

In regard to poverty and economic disparity, private industry with the support of the federal government could be part of the solution. I have been hearing about concentrated populations of unemployed/ poor families living in specific areas in many of America's large cities. What could motivate entrepreneurs to locate industrial facilities in those areas? If they did so, they could adopt New York City's Greyston Bakery apprentice program model in regard to hiring/training low-income residents.[5]

To create effective deterrents to poverty, industries in financially disadvantaged areas would need to pay their employees at least a healthful living wage. If the companies facilitated the most cost-effective, healthful lifestyles for their employees and employees' families, the hourly wages paid would be more affordable for the employer. For example, if the employer provided more affordable decent housing, the employee would be able to live a healthful lifestyle with a lower hourly wage.

A potential problem with this approach is competition with imported goods. If an American industry can't sell enough product because the same type of imported product is cheaper, the business won't succeed. The solution to this situation is for the federal government to raise tariffs on those types of imports so that the American product can be sold at a competitive price in the United States. The goal of this approach is to preserve American jobs rather than to increase profits for American businesses.

6. CEO Salaries

Another potential problem contributing to income inequity is the salaries of management. In 2013, the average pay for corporate CEOs (chief executive officers) was 330 times that of the average worker's pay and 774 times higher than minimum wage earners, according to the AFL-CIO's "Executive Paywatch Project."[6] Who pays for the CEO's salary? Where does that extra money come from? Even if we do not purchase anything directly from a corporation that pays its CEO $40 million plus bonuses, some of us probably buy goods and services from companies that ultimately do purchase goods or services from that company, or others like it. The cost of CEO salaries and bonuses is passed down to consumers in the form of higher prices. Those higher prices make it more difficult for some to afford what they need to live healthfully. This is a potential threat to the inalienable rights to life and happiness of those with lower incomes.

The more a company's CEO is paid, the less profit is available with which to make the company more sustainable in terms of energy conservation, decreasing emissions of toxins, and awarding bonuses to their lowest-paid employees. High salaries for CEOs have a negative effect on prices and on the common good.

What should be done? Should Congress legislate caps on CEO salaries? Or would it be better to increase income tax on salaries above a certain level? How about giving companies tax breaks on profits they use to improve the common good? Decreasing factory pollution and increasing energy efficiency are two ways companies could use their profits to support the common good. Congress needs to help solve the problem of poverty in a way that supports the common good.

Ideally, the private business community would step up to the plate and create jobs that pay at least a healthful living wage for financially disadvantaged individuals who are able to work, but who are unemployed or underemployed. American companies keeping billions in profits on foreign soil to avoid American taxes and paying their CEOs 774 times what the lowest-paid company employee makes might be indicative of an unwillingness on the part of private enterprise to help eliminate poverty by creating more jobs that pay at least a healthful living wage.

7. Creation of Jobs for the Common Good

Even if all adult unemployed and underemployed residents of financially disadvantaged areas of every large city were to be given gainful employment by private enterprises, there would still be many financially disadvantaged people living in rural areas and on Native American reservations. To eliminate involuntary poverty in this country for those who are able and willing to work, the government (preferably local, but state or federal, if necessary) could create jobs for the financially disadvantaged unemployed/underemployed/underpaid. These would be "jobs for the common good." The jobs could be designed to support the common good in ways that would utilize the abilities/talents of the hired workers. Those who are skilled could be put to work rebuilding our crumbling infrastructure. Those who are unskilled could receive on-the-job training. Those without specific useful aptitudes would still be able to perform simple tasks like cutting down kudzu or Japanese knotweed (two common invasive species) or sweeping streets and picking up litter.

As a solution to poverty, these jobs should pay a healthful living wage. The hired workers should be free to switch employment to the private sector whenever the desire and opportunity to do so presents itself. There should be a guarantee of government employment for as long as the workers need it, and there should be opportunities to apply for other government position openings. The workers should receive benefits comparable to those of other government workers doing similar jobs, and they should be held to job standards equivalent to other government workers. Repeated failure to meet those standards of performance should be interpreted as an unwillingness to work and result in termination.

8. Determining Eligibility

Who would be eligible for work in the Jobs for the Common Good program? The program would be open only to American citizens. They would have to be able and willing to work, but be financially disadvantaged. Those possessing sufficient resources to continue to live a healthful lifestyle would not be eligible for the jobs program.

9. Phases of Jobs for the Common Good

Phase 1: Ideally, once the jobs program starts, those who are homeless and those who are financially disadvantaged/unemployed would be hired first.

Phase 2: Once phase 1 is operational, those who are working, but who can't afford a healthful lifestyle because of insufficient resources, pay, and benefits, would be eligible for the program.

10. Unwillingness to Work

Guiding Principle 3 (see the introduction) involves taking personal responsibility for one's decisions and actions. If there are financially disadvantaged people who are able to work but who refuse to do so, they are responsible for their plight. Society, in general, and government, in particular, have no obligation to provide for such people. I have no objection to privately funded nonprofit organizations choosing to help these people; government revenue, however, should not support those able but unwilling to work.

B. Common Good Program for Disadvantaged Youth

Children have the same inalienable rights to life, liberty, and the pursuit of happiness as adults. Most children lack the ability/opportunity to earn enough to afford a healthful lifestyle. In an ideal world, a parent(s) would take the necessary steps not to have more children than they can afford to raise in a healthful fashion without depending on subsidies from the government. That is not happening in more than a million households in the United States. The term "extreme poverty" is used to designate those households living on less than two dollars per person per day in a given month before government benefits. According to a 1996 Stanford University study by Schaefer and Edin, there were 663,000 households living in extreme poverty. By mid-2011, there were 1.65 million. The number

33

of children living in those 1.65 million poor households in any given month of 2011 was 3.55 million.[7]

In an ideal world, all parents would be able and willing to give their children the unconditional, positive regard and firm guidance the children need and which they have an inalienable individual right to receive. But we don't live in an ideal world. According to the US Department of Justice, Bureau of Justice Statistics, there were about 680,000 individual, distinct, verified child-maltreatment cases in the United States and Puerto Rico in 2012. Because of statistics like this, I would prefer the Common Good Program for Disadvantaged Youth (CGPDY) be established as soon as possible. However, I believe that implementing the CGPDY before the Jobs for the Common Good program is in place would be impractical and chaotic. Operating the full program will not be practical until a sufficient number of acceptable child-rearing facilities and competent staff are in place.

1. Cost of Child Rearing

According to a USDA study, "Parents Projected to Spend $241,080 to Raise a Child Born in 2012," the cost of rearing a child through high school depends on a number of factors, including the family's socioeconomic status (those with higher incomes spend more on their children than parents with lower incomes) and geography (e.g., living in the southern states tends to be less expensive). In general, housing is the greatest expense of child rearing, and food is the next greatest expense.[8]

The USDA report referenced above states that for a child born in 2012, a family earning less than $60,640 per year can expect to spend a total of $173,490 (in 2012 dollars) on a child from birth through high school.

2. Parental Responsibility

There are separated and divorced parents who don't pay child support. According to a *New York Times* writer, Laurie Tarkan, there are women getting in vitro fertilization (IVF) leading to as many as eight babies born at a time.[9] Children born to parents who cannot support them are not to blame for being born and have the same inalienable rights as any other human being. These children deserve to receive what they need to grow and to be healthy.

It seems to me that the idea of parents being responsible for their children is not as widely accepted as it used to be. It has become a common practice for people to birth children who must be supported by the state. This practice is irresponsible and is not supportive of the common good. You may accuse me of prejudice because I am suggesting that poor parents should not have large families. I don't think I am prejudiced at all. I come from a lower-income background and have never been a parent. I believe that was a responsible decision to make and in the best interest of the common good.

3. Who Should Support Poor Children?

Children whose parents cannot afford to give them what they need to grow and learn and be healthy must often depend on the kindness of taxpayers to provide for them. How many children can we, as taxpayers, afford to support sufficiently? Adequate support of children involves much more than a roof over their heads and three square meals per day. There is a limit to how much we can afford. The government revenue that will be spent on the support of children not yet born could be spent instead to support the common good. A logical solution is to disallow procreation by those who cannot afford to provide for children. This would be in the best interest of the common good and supportive of all our individual inalienable rights. I don't believe American society, in general, is ready to take this action. However, it would be fairer to taxpayers and to children.

4. Government Support of Big Families

How did American government financial support for big families begin? Perhaps it began at the birth of the country. There were many small farms, and the success of those farms depended on cheap labor— that is, lots of children to do chores. Later, as the United States acquired more land, an expanding population occupying the empty American countryside was perceived as positive. This occupation required more people, more farms, more children.

Just because some expert says our country, or the earth in general, can handle more people does not make more of us a desirable thing. More of us means more pollution, accelerated rates of global warming, scarcer fresh water, more crime, more poverty, more chronic disease, higher health costs, more unemployment, more regimentation, more child mistreatment, more bullying, more elder abuse, as well as extinctions of more species due to habitat destruction.

5. The Population Problem

The government does not have the will to tackle and solve the problem of poverty, yet it financially enables citizens to have children they cannot afford. It is unfair to expect taxpayers to financially support the children of those us who don't pay taxes. The government gradually ending financial compensation for those parents who cannot afford to have more children would be in the best interest of the common good of this and future generations and in keeping with the preservation of our inalienable rights. A public education program to encourage population stabilization in the United States would also be beneficial to the common good.

Some people claim that the death rate during this century in the United States is exceeding the birth rate. Despite that, the population of the United States continues to increase. You can see real-time growth of the US and world populations on the U.S. and World Population Clock web page.[10] As of December 2015, the American population exceeded 320 million. Increasing population is no longer a positive thing.

6. Rethinking Child Bearing and Rearing

Our society needs to reconsider what is acceptable in terms of child bearing and rearing. Traditionally, how parents treat children and how a spouse treats his or her partner has been a private matter in this country. More recently, there have been laws enacted against child and spouse abuse. Such abuse has become socially unacceptable in most areas. The government now has more authority and willingness to intervene in family matters when appropriate.

Our society has a vested interest in ensuring that all children are reared in a healthful fashion and by caregivers who strive to give them unconditional positive regard. Not only is that in the best interest of the common good, but every child has a right to that. The Common Good Program for Disadvantaged Youth (CGPDY) is the solution to providing that healthful upbringing with positive unconditional regard for those deprived of it.

Those parents who are either unwilling to try or are incapable of striving to provide their children with unconditional positive regard should not be allowed to parent. Their offspring, however, still deserve to be reared in a healthful manner.

Low-income parents who are earning at least enough to afford a healthful lifestyle for themselves should be allowed to keep the children, unless the parents are abusive or incapable of striving to give their children unconditional positive regard. Under the CGPDY, parents would have to accept a minimum allowance from the government, enough to provide each of their children with a healthful lifestyle. A child care allowance should be offered to low-income parents of young children if both parents work or if there is only one parent in the household.

There might be parents and would-be parents who are able but unwilling to work and who do not possess the financial resources needed to provide a child with a healthful lifestyle. Those parents should not be allowed to procreate or to adopt or to foster parent. Under the Jobs for the Common Good program, people who are able but refuse to work would not be eligible for government financial support. If such people were to have children and were to receive funds under the CGPDY for those children, they would probably use some of those funds to benefit themselves.

When children need to be separated from parents who don't strive to provide what their children need to be healthy, to grow, and to learn, relocating these children to a healthful supportive environment is essential. Certain nonprofit organizations might be ideal for administering effective relocation programs. A government caseworker would be assigned to each relocated child. The caseworker would be responsible for making sure the child is in a safe, healthful environment and that the child's caregiver is focused on giving the child the positive, unconditional regard and firm guidance that he or she needs to grow and learn. Right now the existence of sufficient ideal settings and caregivers is questionable. Little would be gained by implementing the CGPDY before enough of these environments and caregivers become available.

Jobs and child-rearing classes should be available to parents who want their separated children back and who are willing to learn to be responsible parents.

C. Common Good Disabilities Program

The Social Security Disability Employment Policy Resources by Topic (2015) web page reads,

> **For purposes of Social Security disability benefits, a person with a disability must have a severe disability (or combination of disabilities) that has lasted, or is expected to last, at least 12 months or result in death, and which prevents working at a "substantial gainful activity" level.** (n.d., accessed December 16, 2015, http://www.dol.gov/odep/faqs/general.htm) (third question)

Not everyone with a disability is financially disadvantaged. According to the National Center for Law and Economic Justice's "Poverty in the U.S.: A Snapshot" web page, there were 4.3 million Americans aged eighteen to sixty-four living in poverty with a disability in 2012. That was 28.4 percent of all people with disabilities "compared to 12.5 percent (twenty-two million) of financially disadvantaged Americans aged 18 to 64 who did not have disability" (New York, 2015, accessed December 27, 2015, http://nclej.org/poverty-in-the-us.php).

Do some unemployable financially disadvantaged people fail to qualify for Social Security Disability Insurance even though they really need it? I have little doubt that that happens. Do these people at least qualify for public assistance and food stamps? I would hope so. But for those who are financially disadvantaged *and* disabled *and* homeless, I have my doubts. I know that, at least at one time, a person needed to be living in a residence with an address to receive public assistance.

Actually, public assistance or the federal "welfare" program some of us may remember no longer exists. In 1997, welfare was replaced by the Temporary Assistance for Needy Families (TANF) program. Under this federal program, only people with children are eligible to receive assistance. The recipient must get a job within two years or less, depending on the state. And there is a limit of sixty months of eligibility during the recipient's lifetime. For those with a genuine disability who cannot qualify for Social Security Disability, TANF would not be ideal. For more information, check out the web page "Click State to Find TANF Program" (TANF.us, n.d., accessed December 16, 2015, http://www.tanf.us/).

Citizens with either a temporary or permanent disability have a right to what they need to prevent health deterioration and to rehabilitate. It should be the role of government to ensure that those with disabilities get what they need. That includes American veterans disabled by war.

Each citizen with a disability should have a caseworker who ensures that the person has whatever is needed to prevent health deterioration and to rehabilitate, if that is a viable option. The amount of the subsidy would depend on each person's financial resources, income, and needs. Those with disabilities should receive well-balanced, quality meals (minimally processed, preferably organic), exercise (if feasible), hot running water, a warm, safe, healthful living space, quality health and dental care, the help they need to kick health-threatening habits, prescribed medications, and anything else their doctors deem necessary to prevent health deterioration.

D. Common Good Program for Retirees

According to the "Social Security Benefits Amounts" web page, in the present Social Security system, a recipient's monthly award is based on the worker's Average Indexed Monthly Earnings over a period of thirty-five years.[11] This monthly sum is not going to be enough for *every* retiree to live a healthful lifestyle. A Common Good Program for Retirees should be developed to ensure that all who are at full retirement age and older have enough to live a healthful lifestyle.

~~~~~~~

E. Objections

I'm sure there are a variety of objections to my suggestions for ending poverty. You may think the suggested solutions are unaffordable, unconstitutional, socialistic, or contrary to free trade. Or you may protest that you deserve more than what amounts to a healthful living wage. The next chapter addresses those objections.

[1]   Howard Zinn, *History is a Weapon,* ch. 11, n.d., accessed December 13, 2015, http://www.historyisaweapon.com/defcon1/zinnbaron11.html.
[2]   Melissa Worcester, "1900s Poor Working Conditions," Demand Media, 2016, accessed May 4, 2016, http://www.ehow.com/info_8056348_1900s-poor-working-conditions.html.
[3]   Barry Yeoman, "Why the Passenger Pigeon Went Extinct," *Audubon,* May/June 2014, accessed December 13, 2015, http://www.audubon.org/magazine/may-june-2014/why-passenger-pigeon-went-extinct.

4   US Fish and Wildlife National Service, "Time Line of the American Bison," September 4, 2014, http://www.fws.gov/bisonrange/timeline.htm.

5   "Greyston Bakery," Ben and Jerry, accessed December 13, 2015, http://www.benjerry.com/greyston.

6   "Executive Paywatch," AFL-CIO, 2014, accessed December 13, 2015, http://www.aflcio.org/Corporate-Watch/Paywatch-2014.

7   Luke H. Schaefer and Kathyrn Edin, "The Rise of Extreme Poverty in the United States," Stanford University, 2014, 2, accessed December 14, 2015, http://Web.stanford.edu/group/scspi/_media/pdf/pathways/summer_2014/Pathways_Summer_2014_ShaeferEdin.pdf.

8   US Department of Agriculture, "Parents Projected to Spend $241,080 to Raise a Child Born in 2012," August 14, 2013, http://www.usda.gov/wps/portal/usda/usdahome?contentid=2013/08/0160.xml.

9   Laurie Tarkan, "Lowering Odds of Multiple Births," Health, *New York Times,* February 19, 2008, accessed December 15, 2015, http://www.nytimes.com/2008/02/19/health/19mult.html?pagewanted=all&_r=0.

10 US Census Bureau, "U.S. and World Population Clock," n.d., accessed December 15, 2015, http://www.census.gov/popclock/.

11 Social Security Administration, "Social Security Benefits Amounts," n.d., accessed December 16, 2015, https://www.ssa.gov/OACT/COLA/Benefits.html.

6

POVERTY AND CAPITALISM, II

According to Fry and Kochhar's "Income Calculator," the income that divided the middle and lower classes in 2014 was $41,869 for a family of three.[1] If an economic income lower than $41,869 for a family of three is poverty, being poor is probably inevitable for many. However, my definition of poverty is *the inability of people to live a healthful lifestyle and/or to prevent health deterioration because of insufficient financial resources.*

In chapter 5, I suggested solutions to the problem of poverty in the United States. If these solutions are unaffordable, socialistic, or unconstitutional, or would have a negative impact on *free* trade, there might be a possibility that poverty is inevitable.

The sections of this chapter (A–E) are devoted to addressing the objections related to affordability, socialism, unconstitutionality, and free-trade barriers. Lastly I tackle the issue of defining poverty in terms of middle-class living.

A. Affordability

You may believe that there is simply not enough money in the United States to enable all citizens to live healthful lifestyles. A *New York Times* article by Floyd Norris reported that the total private net worth of the United States in 2014 was $81.5 trillion.[2] According to the web page "Total Number of U.S. Households," there were 15.2 million households in the country in 2014.[3] If the total private net worth were divided equally among the country's households, each of our households would be worth about $700,300.

According to the US Census Bureau, the median wage for 2014 was estimated to be $28,851. That means that half the 153,592,754 American earners in 2014 earned $28,851or less. According to Social Security Online's "Wage Statistics for 2014" web page, the total annual reported personal income of earners for 2014 was $6,797,372,805,419.[4] If that amount were divided evenly among all earners, each earner could benefit from and pay taxes on $44,569. That $6 trillion income is a relatively low calculation. Some sources report the national income as being more than twice that amount. For details check out Statistica's web page "Personal income in the United States from 1990 to 2014."[5]

The point is, there is enough wealth in this country for each of us to live well. The problem is the way in which the wealth is distributed. According to "Who Rules America?" by Professor G. William Domhoff, in 2010, 35.4 percent of all private wealth in the country was owned by the upper 1 percent.[6] "Working for the Few," a 2014 OXFAM study, reported that 1 percent of the world's population owns 50 percent of the world's wealth.[7]

1. Jobs for the Poor

In the last chapter, I suggested that private enterprise with government legislative support could build profitable production facilities in financially disadvantaged population pockets of big cities. This would make a major contribution to solving the problem of poverty.

Even if private industry does decide to do its part in solving the poverty problem in large cities, that major contribution would benefit neither those who are poor and living in rural America nor those living on Native American reservations. Whether or not private enterprise is reluctant to help eliminate poverty and make profits at the same time, we need a Jobs for the Common Good program.

2. Cost of a Government Jobs Program

What, in terms of wages, might a Jobs for the Common Good program cost? To be an effective solution to poverty, the program would have to pay the workers it employs enough to afford healthful lifestyles.

How much it costs each of us to live a healthful lifestyle depends on a number of factors. The formula for determining that cost may be a bit complicated, but it would be similar to the formula for determining the amount of public assistance or food stamps for which each applicant is eligible. The cost of living where we live would be one factor. To remain healthy, each of us needs a warm, safe place to live. Average monthly apartment rental costs vary from city to city—from a low of $623 to a high of $4,000, according to Ilyce Glink of *CBS News*.[8] The average apartment rental cost nationwide is $1,200 per month, according to this source.

To be healthy, you must heat your residence and your water supply. The average energy cost for residences in the United States, according to the US Energy Information Administration's "Frequently Asked Questions" web page, is $107 monthly.[9]

A healthful lifestyle should include the option of an organic diet. A *Consumer Reports* study, "The Cost of Organic Food"[10] found that organic foods had an average cost of 47 percent over the same nonorganic foods. According to the USDA's "Official USDA Food Plans," if you are an average American male nineteen to fifty years old, as of August 2014, you could adequately feed yourself on $171 per month.[11] If an organic diet is 47 percent higher, an organic diet would cost you $252 per month.

You need a reasonable amount of exercise to stay healthy. You might get a minimum of healthful exercise through walking or jogging. You can purchase a good pair of jogging or walking shoes through the mail for about ninety dollars. Two pairs could be sufficient for a year.

In regard to dental care, you can purchase a dental plan for about fifty dollars a month. But that will not pay 100 percent of crowns and certain other dental procedures. In regard to health insurance, if you work for the government, your benefits package would probably include medical coverage. National single-payer health insurance (see **Universal Health Care** below) would be ideal for the United States.

So far, if you are an average American male nineteen to fifty years of age, the cost of a healthful lifestyle could be $18,372 a year, or $1,531 a month. The cost of a healthful lifestyle might be lower than that if your rent is only $630 or less per month. But if you live in San Francisco, where the median monthly rent rate is $4,000, you may be unable to afford a healthful lifestyle on $18,372 a year.

The cost of a healthful lifestyle is dependent on the area in which you live. Costs of food, transportation, housing, and health care vary. The federal government keeps track of these costs for different parts of the country. The cost of affordable housing, for example, is based on median family income (MFI). According to the "Median Household Income" web page, the country is divided into one thousand different areas each with its own MFI.[12] The cost of a healthful lifestyle for each of those areas could include the cost of affordable housing for each area.

I can only estimate the total taxpayer cost of wages for a Jobs for the Common Good program. The average yearly wages for a Jobs for the Common Good worker would be $18,372.

3. Phases 1 and 2 of Jobs Program

Ideally, the Jobs for the Common Good program would have two phases. In phase 1, those who are formerly homeless and those who are unemployed/financially disadvantaged would be hired. (See chapter 5 of this book for hiring details.) Once phase 1 is operational, phase 2 would kick in. In phase 2, those who are working, but who cannot afford a healthful lifestyle because of insufficient resources, pay, and benefits—the working poor—would be hired.

Some of the working poor may be employed by businesses that either keep millions in profits in offshore banks or pay their CEOs astronomical salaries. As it is now, the working poor are eligible for food stamps and Medicaid. These safety-net benefits, paid for by taxpayers, are indirectly subsidizing the private businesses that employ the working poor without providing them with paid health insurance, etc. Jobs for the Common Good could solve that problem. Once phase 2 of the program kicked in, the working poor could earn more money in the program. Private businesses that employ the working poor might be motivated to compensate them with pay and benefits exceeding what the workers could earn in the government program. Otherwise, these private businesses might experience a labor shortage. Eliminating social safety-net benefits to the working poor and decreasing the potential numbers of working poor that would otherwise be employed by the government Jobs program would benefit taxpayers.

The Jobs for the Common Good program might also benefit private enterprise by creating a pool of potential employees from which to recruit new hires.

4. Cost of Jobs for the Common Good Program

According to the National Center for Law and Economic Justice's "Poverty in the U.S.: A Snapshot" web page, in 2012 there were twenty-two million poor American adults (aged eighteen to sixty-four) without disabilities.[13] (By 2016 the number had decreased to 20 million.[14]) If the Jobs for the Common Good program employed all twenty-two million at an average annual wage of $18,372, it would cost the government $404.18 billion for their wages. That may seem like a lot. But, according to Michael Tanner of the Cato Institute, the national 2012 cost of fighting poverty for all levels of governments (local, state, and federal) was $952 billion.[15] Some of that amount was spent on children from poor backgrounds, some poor people with disabilities, and some poor retirees.

5. Cost of Common Good Programs for Retirees and the Disabled

Payroll taxes are deducted from every earner's paycheck to pay for Medicare and Social Security. According to an article by Jean Murray, the more one earns, the more is deducted for Social Security, but only for the first \$118,500 of annual earnings.[16] The Social Security fund is running out of money because the federal government borrowed money from it in the past and has not paid it back. Eliminating the \$118,500 limit would allow the Social Security fund to be replenished in a timely fashion. It would also supply sufficient funds to pay for the Common Good Program for Retirees and for the Common Good Disabilities Program. It would also decrease the nearly trillion-dollar annual expense of fighting poverty.

6. Cost of Common Good Program for Disadvantaged Youth (CGPDY)

As stated in the last chapter, it might be best to delay full implementation of the CGPDY program until the Jobs for the Common Good program is firmly established and until the capability for handling the children who would be separated from inadequate home environments is in place. By that time, there might be a substantial decrease in the number of America's disadvantaged youth.

If and when the program is fully implemented, parents of disadvantaged children should be legally responsible for paying back government subsidies used to support their children. The government should seek the recovery of expenses from the parents wherever possible and cost effective. The parents' savings or income should not be dunned to the extent that a healthful lifestyle for either parent would be unaffordable.

Ideally, the CGPDY program would include a public education campaign to promote responsible child bearing. In the United States, this aspect of the CGPDY would not have to wait to be implemented. An effective educational campaign would save taxpayers money in the long run and would help preserve and promote the common good.

7. The Cost of Neglect

Giving those who are homeless decent housing or the ability to afford decent housing is more cost effective than simply ignoring their continued homelessness. An article at PolitiFactcheck.com by Molly Moorhead affirms that it is much cheaper for government to house the homeless and give them support services than to care for the same people living on the streets.[17] Decent housing for those who are homeless combined with the Common Good programs described in the last chapter would benefit everyone. When we cannot afford to live healthfully, there is also a cost to society in terms of increased health care needs, higher health insurance premiums, workdays lost, and lower productivity.

8. Universal Health Care

While so-called Obamacare has benefited a number of people who would otherwise not be covered by insurance for the medical services they need, it has left and will continue to leave millions of Americans without health insurance, according to Physicians for a National Health Program. The following is from their web page "What is Single Payer?"

> **Single-payer national health insurance, also known as "Medicare for all," is a system in which a single public or quasi-public agency organizes health care financing, but the delivery of care remains largely in private hands. Under a single-payer system, all residents of the U.S. would be covered for all medically necessary services, including doctor, hospital, preventive, long-term care, mental health, reproductive health care, dental, vision, prescription drug and medical supply costs.** (n.d., accessed December 27, 2015, http://www.pnhp.org/facts/what-is-single-payer)

The author of this article asserts that, under single-payer health care, modest taxes would replace premium charges, copays, and deductibles.

We would be free to choose our doctors and hospitals, and "95 percent of all households would save money." Employers would not have to pay for their employees' health insurance. This might encourage employers to hire more workers. This description of single-payer insurance seems as if it would better support the **common good** than the present system.

B. Socialism and the American Dream

These proposed solutions to the problem of poverty are no-nonsense practical approaches that allow those in financial need the opportunity to experience their inalienable rights to life and happiness by allowing them the dignity of earning enough to afford a healthful lifestyle. For children, retirees, or people with disabilities and financially disadvantaged, these solutions would give them the opportunity to experience their individual rights to life and happiness by ensuring that they receive what they need to prevent health deterioration.

1. Relative Significance of the American Dream

Few of us would equate these common good solutions with the American Dream. The expression "American Dream" appears neither in the Declaration of Independence nor in the Constitution. The words "unalienable Rights, that among these are Life, Liberty and the pursuit of Happiness," and the words "general Welfare" do appear in these revered documents. Perhaps some people would prefer putting off implementing the solutions to the problem of poverty in favor of waiting for someone to invent or discover a magic formula allowing us all to achieve the American Dream.

2. How Do People Achieve the American Dream?

One may equate the American Dream with financial independence. Financial independence is not a bad thing. In general, most of the tax income that finances the common good comes from those who are the most financially independent. How do Americans achieve financial independence? Is there a formula? Actually there are a number of ways to become financially independent, including the following:

- by birth—by being born into a wealthy family
- by winning a large lottery contest
- by marrying someone wealthy
- by robbing banks or jewelry stores, or through extortion

Some people do get rich in other ways. Those with lucrative jobs or a low cost of living have been able to achieve financial independence through saving and wise spending habits. In an ideal world everyone would have an opportunity to become financially independent through decent and fulfilling work. Those who have started their own successful businesses like to call themselves *self-made*. Some who become financially independent through business start-ups like to believe and would like others to believe that getting rich is simply the result of hard work. Although this is generally admirable, a certain percentage of new businesses fail. Carmen Nobel wrote that, according to Shikhar Ghosh, a senior lecturer at Harvard Business School, the failure rate of new venture-backed business startups depends on how one defines failure. Professor Ghosh's research found the failure rate is 30 to 95 percent, depending on the definition.[18]

There are a number of possible causes of business failures, including poor planning, poor management, unrealistic expectations, and lack of sufficient capital. Any number of things can go wrong. New businesses that fail do not all fail because those who started them did not work hard enough. Some people are wise enough to know they would not succeed in starting a business, no matter how hard they worked at it. That does not mean they are not willing to work hard. Many lower-income people have worked harder all their lives than some who have achieved financial independence. There is more required to achieve the American Dream through business startups than hard work.

Those who succeed in business do so with the cooperation of

others. Hard work does not automatically result in networking skills and contacts. One almost always needs some sort of wealth to start a successful business venture. If one has a family to support, hard work alone might not allow one to accumulate enough wealth to start a business.

Some with lower incomes spend their lifetimes working harder than some multimillionaires and billionaires. Some of the latter do not work at all. There is no direct cause-and-effect relationship between how hard one works and how much money one makes or how rich one becomes.

3. Socialism

Socialism is a system in which the means of production are owned/controlled by the government and in which *all* profits go to the government, which distributes this wealth to its citizens. In our country, the statutory corporate tax rate was 35 percent from 2001 to 2003. What many large companies actually paid was much less than that, according to McIntyre and Nguyen.[19]

Some of us believe the United States is socialistic. But it is not, because the government does not own the means of production and because the government is not taxing business profits at 100 percent. The privately owned means of production and less than 100 percent corporate tax rates ensure that the United States will continue to be capitalistic.

If our only choices were (1) being purely socialistic (100 percent corporate tax rate) or (2) forcing 14 percent of the population to live in involuntary poverty, which condition would we choose? Fortunately, we do not have to choose either. In this book, the solutions to the problem of poverty neither condone nor embrace pure socialism. There is enough wealth in this country to solve the problem of poverty without taxing businesses at 100 percent and without bankrupting billionaires and multimillionaires.

C. Constitutionality

One additional possible criticism of this book's proposed solutions to the problem of poverty in America, particularly the Jobs for the Common Good program, is that the solutions are unconstitutional. I will use the terms *common good* and *general welfare* interchangeably in this section.

1. Providing for the Common Good

Article One, Section Eight of our Constitution states, "The Congress shall have power to lay and collect Taxes, Duties, Imposts and Excises, to pay the Debts and provide for the Common Defence and general Welfare of the United States." This is known as the General Welfare Clause. Section Eight specifies a number of congressional powers and at the end of the section gives Congress the power "to make all Laws which shall be necessary and proper for carrying into Execution the foregoing powers." This is known as the "elastic clause" because it has allowed Congress to expand its constitutional powers.

2. Implied Powers

Does the power to raise funds to provide for the general welfare, a.k.a. the common good, authorize Congress to pass specific legislation to provide for the common good? The answer is that Congress has the *implied* power to implement provisions for the general welfare.

Implied powers are those not specified in the Constitution and that are derived from the power of Congress to make all laws "necessary and proper" to exercise its enumerated (specified) powers. According to a web page on McCulloch v. Maryland, "There is nothing in the Constitution which excludes incidental or implied powers" (2015, accessed February 5, 2016, http://www.lawnix.com/cases/mcculloch-maryland.html).

3. Legal Obligation

Even though Congress has the implied power to spend money to provide for the common good, does that mean it has the legal obligation to do so? I have been assured by a professor of constitutional law that, although power and obligation are not the same thing, in regard to the Constitution, a power to do a thing carries with it the obligation to do that thing. In regard to providing for the general welfare, then, it seems that those who are elected to the legislative and executive branches of our federal government are failing to carry out that duty in a consistent manner.

4. Defining General Welfare

According to the "General Welfare" web page of the Free Dictionary, in the case of *United States v. Butler* (1936), the Supreme Court

> **established that determination of the general welfare would be left to the discretion of Congress. In its opinion, the Court warned that to challenge a federal expense on the ground that it did not promote the general welfare would "naturally require a showing that by no reasonable possibility can the challenged legislation fall within the wide range of discretion permitted to the Congress." The Court then obliquely confided, "[H]ow great is the extent of that range ... we need hardly remark."** (2015, accessed December 28, 2015, http:// legaldictionary.thefreedictionary.com/General+Welfare)

In *South Dakota v. Dole* (1987), the court "questioned whether 'general welfare' is a judicially enforceable restriction at all" (ibid.).

5. Powers of Congress and the Executive

From court rulings noted above, I surmise that members of Congress have the power to raise funds to provide for the common good, and they possess the discretionary power to determine what the common good entails. The Constitution gives members of Congress the implied legal authority to pass legislation to implement aspects of the common good not specified in the Constitution and gives the executive branch the implied authority to enforce the congressional legislation relating to aspects of the common good not specified in the Constitution.

6. The Tea Party and the Common Good

Those who identify as Tea Party members seem to have a strange interpretation of the common good and less than complete respect for individual inalienable rights. According to an article in the *Guardian* by Diane Roberts, Michelle Bachman "advocates abolishing the EPA as soon as God puts the Tea Party in charge" ("The EPA: The Tea Party's next target," August 3, 2011, http://www.theguardian.com/ commentisfree/cifamerica/2011/aug/03/epa-republicans-tea-party). One may wonder if Bachman spent even a New York minute thinking about the more than sixteen thousand EPA employees whose jobs will be "killed" if the EPA is abolished. Thousands more jobs have been created in the private sector by businesses whose purpose is to help industries comply with EPA regulations. Those jobs would also be killed if the EPA is abolished. In August 2013, there were 2.72 million people employed by the federal government. If the Tea Party succeeds in shrinking the federal government, where will those employees that the federal government no longer needs to employ find jobs?

7. Congressional Failure

Everyone having a job, having the ability to afford a healthful lifestyle, and having environmental and public-health protections is part of the general welfare. Keeping some people financially disadvantaged, causing others to lose their jobs, and taking away our environmental and public health protections all violate the duty of Congress to promote the general welfare. Therefore, by not implementing solutions to the problem of poverty, members of Congress not only violate the individual inalienable rights of millions of us, they also fail to carry out their constitutional duty to provide for the common good. Not only is the proposed Jobs for the Common Good program constitutional, it is a way for members of Congress to carry out their constitutional duty.

D. Free Trade

There is a concern that my suggestions for eliminating poverty might interfere with making/keeping international trade agreements. Free trade is a concept that sounds great in theory. The idea is to have no trade barriers, such as tariffs or excise taxes, imposed by countries on one another's goods and services. So if Country A can produce more of a product than the people in Country A need, or if A can sell the product for a higher price in B, and B has a product it can make more money selling in A, it makes sense for Countries A and B to form a trade agreement that eliminates barriers to trade between the two countries.

1. Free-Trade Problems

There are, of course, all sorts of problems that can arise from these arrangements. One example is goods from one country being toxic. The trade agreement might have prohibited the imports of such products, but slipups happen.

And what happens when Country A starts importing products from Country B that are also produced and sold in A, but which are cheaper than A's products? If the citizens of A stop buying A's products in favor of B's cheaper products, the manufacturers in A might go out of business and have to lay off many workers. The majority of consumers in A might like the cheaper imported goods, but the workers in A that lose their jobs are also consumers. If anyone bothered to ask them what they would prefer—cheaper goods or a job—I wonder, what they would say.

Another potential problem that could arise from free trade involves supply. If one country (let's call it Country B), has an abundance of a product or resource that is in demand in other countries belonging to the same trade partnership, the other countries might stop producing the product themselves in favor of importing it from B. If the product or resource (traded good) from B is a nonessential luxury item, no problem. But if the traded good is essential for the health of citizens in the other countries, there is a potential problem. That problem would occur if and when the supply of the traded good flowing from B is interrupted. The interruption might be caused by a megastorm, a major earthquake, or civil unrest.

This potential problem could be avoided if the other consuming countries have stockpiled enough of the traded good from B or if the other consuming countries have maintained their capacity for producing the traded good from B. Otherwise, the health of the citizens in the consuming countries will suffer. This problem could occur between countries without free-trade agreements as well.

2. Who Do Trade Agreements Benefit?

When leaders of business, industry, and government in different countries enter into international trade agreements, their goal is to find ways of exchanging goods and services that are fair to *them*. Fairness to individual workers in their respective countries is not a priority for these business, industry, and government leaders. First and foremost, trade agreement negotiators want to make sure the people at the top benefit from the trade deal. An article by Don Johnson on the Campaign for America's Future website supports the view that trade deals do not benefit workers as much as they benefit big business owners.[20]

One of the most well-known trade agreements is the North American Free Trade Agreement (NAFTA) from 1994. According to an Economic Policy Institute (EPI) Briefing Paper by Robert Scott, experts predicted NAFTA would increase trade surpluses for the United States. A trade surplus occurs when Country A exports goods to

Country B that are worth more than the goods imported from B into A. The country that exports the lower value of goods experiences a trade deficit, which can lead to loss of jobs. The EPI Briefing Paper reported that, after NAFTA was operational, the United States experienced trade deficits with Mexico that displaced 682,900 US workers by 2010. NAFTA had devastating consequences for the Mexican economy as well.[21]

NAFTA's overall effect on life in America is, perhaps, debatable. What is less debatable is that many wealthy Americans are richer today than they were in 1994. How can that be? Hundreds of thousands lost jobs as a result of cheaper goods from Mexico and Canada being bought by US consumers. That suggests that American manufacturers were selling less and therefore making less profit. If you are an American manufacturer who cannot compete with goods from other countries, you have choices. You can invest your money in your foreign competitor's business, or you can move your operation to a country where the expense of manufacturing is cheaper. Either way, you continue to make money. Too bad making money is not that simple for those who, because of NAFTA, lost manufacturing jobs.

3. The Trans-Pacific Partnership Trade Agreement

As of 2015, there is a new trade agreement in the works. The Trans-Pacific Partnership trade agreement (TPPTA) was negotiated in secret for four years. The web page "Stop TPP" (WordPress.com, accessed January 13, 2016, http://stoptpp.org/), which calls the TPPTA "NAFTA on steroids," is a good source for information on how the TPPTA would threaten our individual rights. The thousand-page draft of this agreement has twenty-nine chapters, twenty-four of which have to do with "harmonizing" standards and regulations between participating nations. Many of us believe that means the large corporations are trying to undermine American standards and regulations that support worker safety, environmental quality, and public health. In other words, if this treaty is approved, wave good-bye to the common good and hello to increasing plutocracy.

The way to preserve and promote the common good here and in the rest of the world is for America to remain steadfast and demand that other nations with lower standards that want trade agreements with the United States raise their standards.

4. Acceptable Trade Agreements

If other countries want to enter into agreements with the United States, they should have comparable standards—environmental, public health, work safety, and human rights—*before* the agreement. To believe that other countries will improve *after* entering into an agreement seems naive.

The bottom line is this: International trade agreements are only fair and acceptable when they respect the individual rights of all citizens in the nations involved. In my opinion, the world's eighty-five richest individuals won't like that, because it might cause a slight decrease in the rate at which their net worth grows. Many American businesses would rather the federal government and the states lower regulatory standards so that business owners and stockholders of businesses can get even richer.

Would eliminating poverty upset the plans and ambitions of the rich and powerful to increase their wealth and power through unfair international trade agreements? Undoubtedly. Would this disruption of the plans of the wealthiest make eliminating poverty any less feasible? Not at all.

5. Globalization

One of the concepts used by those in favor of free-trade agreements is globalization. According to *Merriam-Webster Dictionary and Thesaurus* online, *globalization* refers to "the act or process of globalizing: the state of being globalized; *especially*: the development of an increasingly integrated global economy marked especially by free trade, free flow of capital, and the tapping of cheaper foreign labor markets."[22] There seems to be an effort to get people, in general, to believe that the world is getting smaller because of increased transportation and communication speeds. The message is "You live in a global economy. Nothing can change it. Get used to it."

My tendency is to reply, "Don't tell me what to do. Don't tell me what's important." I think it is outrageous and disgusting to walk into an American store, looking for a specific product to find the store carries only the Chinese-made product. That is due, I suspect, to globalization.

Bruce Maxlish, author of "Three Factors of Globalization: Multinational Corporations, Non-Governmental Organizations, and Global Consciousness," points out that globalization refers not just to economics. There is also the idea of people perceiving themselves as belonging to the whole of humanity as opposed to being members of just a particular nation or race or tribe.[23] If globalization involves more peace and prosperity for the world in general, it would seem to be a good thing.

The dark side of globalization is that it has encouraged the growth of multinational corporations, which have, in turn, promoted the expansion of the economic aspects of globalization. A multinational corporation (MNC) is a private for-profit company with headquarters in one country and divisions of that company in one or more other countries. Some examples are Monsanto, Bayer, Exxon Mobile, Nestlé, and Apple. Of Exxon, Maxlish writes, "It clearly is not only wealthier than 70 or so nation-states, but also more powerful."

Globalization seems to be favored by multinational corporations. Some of us believe that MNC leaders have the goal of controlling the whole world in order to enhance their wealth and power. That is not good for anyone, except the upper 1 percent earners who control these multinational corporations. The idea that multinational corporations want to control everything does not seem at all farfetched for those of us who are familiar with the proposed TPPTA and with GMOs. (For more information on GMOs, refer to www.gmoboycott.blogspot. com, R. Geiger, "GMO Right to Know Info Packet," July 8, 2014). Although multinational corporations may have more wealth and more power than some countries, I don't think we should passively accept their dominance, throw in the towel, do their bidding, and just try to make the best of it. These corporations are threatening everyone's rights opportunities.

Corporations will grow ever bigger, more powerful, and more abusive unless the United States stands up to them and demonstrates to the world that governments, with the support of the common people, can preserve and protect the inalienable rights of every citizen. If America fails to do that, the common people of all countries will lose more rights opportunities as the power of the multinationals grows. As the upper class gets richer, the rest of us will get poorer.

E. Poverty versus Middle Class

To what does "middle class" refer? Fry and Kochhar of the Pew Research Institute have an online calculator that can tell you, based on your income and family size, the socioeconomic class to which you belong. This calculation does not include your family's net worth or regional cost of living. According to the calculator, middle-class families/individuals are those with incomes between $41,869 and $125,608.[24]

I have known poor people who felt they deserved to live a middle-class lifestyle with all the modern comforts and conveniences, regardless of their ability/inability or willingness/unwillingness to work. They felt entitled to it and would have been perfectly willing to accept enough government subsidies to enable them to live that way. If you believe the only acceptable alternative to poverty is a middle-class lifestyle paid for by others, you will neither accept my definition of poverty nor be satisfied with my solution to the problem of poverty. My response to that is the following short rant:

If one is a financially disadvantaged person who feels entitled to live a comfortable middle-class lifestyle, that's not a problem. If one gets an education and a lucrative job, that's great. I only have a problem with the minority of financially disadvantaged people who think that those who pay taxes should pay higher taxes so that they, who pay no taxes, can live like middle-class taxpayers. In my opinion, this idea is bizarre, not to mention unreasonable, unrealistic, and arrogant. Unfortunately, that attitude of personal entitlement helps to reinforce the conservative belief that the financially disadvantaged are all lazy, shiftless, and unreliable.

Poverty, as I define it, is not inevitable and is solvable. This country has more than ample financial resources to prevent involuntary poverty in a constitutional—not purely socialistic—manner that preserves *fair* trade practices. Nor does poverty prevention require everyone to live at a minimum middle-class socioeconomic level. But for every citizen to experience his or her individual inalienable rights, it is necessary to eliminate poverty in the United States.

[1] Richard Fry and Rakesh Kochhar, "Are you in the American middle class? Find out with our income calculator," Pew Research, December 9, 2015, accessed February 10, 2016, http://www.pewresearch.org/fact-tank/2015/12/09/are-you-in-the-american-middle-class/.

[2] Floyd Norris, "Household Net Worth Has Rebounded," *New York Times*, September 19, 2014, accessed December 17, 2015, http://www.nytimes.com/2014/09/20/business/household-net-worth-has-rebounded-since-financial-crisis.html.

[3] "Total Number of U.S. Households," Statistic Brain Research Institute, October 3, 2014, accessed December 17, 2015, http://www.statisticbrain.com/u-s-household-statistics/.

[4] US Social Security Administration, "Wage Statistics for 2014," 2016, https://www.ssa.gov/cgi-bin/netcomp.cgi?year=2014.

[5] "Personal Income in the United States from 1990 to 2014 (in Billion U.S. Dollars)," Statistica—The Statistics Portal, 2014, accessed December 27, 2015, http://www.statista.com/statistics/216756/us-personal-income/.

[6] J. William Domhoff, "Wealth, Income, and Power," University of California at Santa Cruz, February 2013, accessed December 27, 2015, http://www2.ucsc.edu/whorulesamerica/power/wealth.html.

[7] "Working for the Few," Oxfam, 2015, accessed December 27, 2015, https://www.oxfam.org/en/research/working-few.

[8] Ilyce Glink, "Top 10 Cheapest U.S. Cities to Rent an Apartment," *CBS News*, July 20, 2013, accessed December 27, 2015, http://www.cbsnews.com/media/top-10-cheapest-us-cities-to-rent-an-apartment/.

[9] US Energy Information Administration, "Frequently Asked Questions," October 21, 2015, http://www.eia.gov/tools/faqs/faq.cfm?id=97&t=3.

[10] "The Cost of Organic Food," *Consumer Reports,* March 19, 2015, accessed December 27, 2015, http://www.consumerreports.org/cro/news/2015/03/cost-of-organic-food/index.htm.

[11] US Department of Agriculture, "Official USDA Food Plans," August 2014, http://www.cnpp.usda.gov/sites/default/files/CostofFoodAug2014.pdf.

[12] US Census Bureau, "Median Household Income," 2015, http://quickfacts.census.gov/qfd/meta/long_INC110212.htm.

[13] "Poverty in the U.S.: A Snapshot," National Center for Law and Economic Justice, 2015, accessed December 27, 2015, http://nclej.org/poverty-in-the-us.php.

[14] Federal Safety Net, "U.S. Poverty Statistics," accessed October 27, 2016, http://federalsafetynet.com/us-poverty-statistics.html.

[15] Michael Tanner "The American Welfare State: How We Spend Nearly $1 Trillion a Year Fighting Poverty—and Fail," Cato Institute, April 11, 2012, accessed July 29, 2016, http://object.cato.org/sites/cato.org/files/pubs/pdf/PA694.pdf.

[16] Jean Murray, "Annual Maximum Social Security Tax—Updated," About.com, November 28, 2015, accessed December 27, 2015, http://biztaxlaw.about.com/od/glossarys/g/socialsecmax.htm.

[17] Molly Moorhead, "HUD Secretary Says a Homeless Person Costs Taxpayers $40,000 a Year," *Tampa Bay Times,* March 5, 2012, accessed December 27, 2015, http://www.politifact.com/truth-o-meter/statements/2012/mar/12/shaun-donovan/hud-secretary-says-homeless-person-costs-taxpayers/.

[18] Carmen Nobel, "Why Companies Fail—and How Their Founders Can Bounce Back," Harvard University, March 7, 2011, accessed December 28, 2015, http://hbswk.hbs.edu/item/why-companies-failand-how-their-founders-can-bounce-back.

19 Robert McIntyre and T. D. Coo Nguyen, "Freeloaders: Declining Corporate Tax Payments in the Bush Years," *Multinational Monitor*, November 2004, accessed July 29, 2016, http://www.multinationalmonitor.org/mm2004/112004/mcintyre.html.

20 Dave Johnson, "When Trade Theories Confront the Real World, the Real World Wins," Campaign for America's Future, August 5, 2015, accessed December 28, 2015, https://ourfuture.org/20150805/when-trade-theories-confront-the-real-world-the-real-world-wins?utm_source=progressive_breakfast&utm_medium=email&utm_campaign=pbreak.

21 Robert E. Scott, "Heading South," Economic Policy Institute, May 3, 2011, pp. 1, 4, accessed December 28, 2015, http://epi.3cdn.net/fdade52b876e04793b_7fm6ivz2y.pdf.

22 *Merriam-Webster Dictionary and Thesaurus* [online], sv. "globalization."

23 Bruce Mazlish, "Three Factors of Globalization: Multinational Corporations, Non-Governmental Organizations, and Global Consciousness," *Global Studies Journal*, GSJ View, March 1, 2012, https://gsj.stonybrook.edu/view/three-factors-of-globalization-multinational-corporations-non-governmental-organizations-and-global-consciousness/.

24 Fry and Kochhar, "Are you in the American middle class?"

7

POLICE CONDUCT AND INDIVIDUAL RIGHTS

Them have been a number of incidents lately involving the deaths of young blacks at the hands of police in circumstances that suggest the police officers might have practiced authority abuse. By *authority*, I mean a person having the power and right to make or enforce laws, rules, orders, regulations, policies, procedures, and the like. Abuse is unnecessarily threatening or violating other people's individual inalienable rights in a deliberate or negligent manner.

Police officers have a difficult job. Society grants to police officers the power and authority "to protect and serve." Without that power and authority, they can't do an effective job. Without police, areas of our cities would dissolve into chaos. A police officer hesitating to use deadly force, in certain instances, will result in one fewer officer to protect and serve. That hesitation might also result in innocent bystander fatalities. The law-abiding public needs to support police officers who are not abusive. They are an essential component of the common good.

What is the extent of abusive police conduct in the United States? The Cato Institute's "2010 National Police Misconduct Statistics and Reporting Project" by David Packman, involved a representative national sample of 6,613 law enforcement officers. It found, based on credible reports, that 23.8 percent of the officers had used excessive force; 18 percent had engaged in forcible nonconsensual sexual activity;

7.2 percent were reported for fraud/theft/robbery; 6.8 percent for false arrest; 4.6 percent for illegal raids/searches; 3.6 percent for civil rights violations; 3.2 percent for dishonesty. The same officers may have been reported for multiple abusive offenses.[1] This reporting project suggests that at least 23.8 percent of police officers nationwide have practiced authority abuse. Although 23.8 percent is a significant figure, it does not support the contention that the majority of police carry out their duties in an abusive manner.

Why do those police who use excessive force do so? There are probably a number of factors, including the following:

- If a police officer feels abused, there is a human tendency to strike back. The officer also has the power to strike back.
- Some officers who were bullied as children may react by becoming bullies themselves and have not learned to cope with challenging situations through other means.
- There is also frustration with the court system, which many people perceive as being too soft on some criminals. A gentleman who had worked as a policeman in Baltimore after leaving the military told me that the police with whom he worked in Baltimore would routinely beat up suspects rather than arrest them. They felt that was a greater deterrent to crime than a trial, which too often resulted in the suspect beating the arrest charge because of a technicality.

It is not always easy to distinguish between the exercise of legitimate power and authority abuse. Police officers have a duty to protect the public from criminals. To arrest suspects with unnecessary force is abusive. Who or what determines how much force is necessary? People who intensely resent any kind of authority figure, if confronted by the police will tend to resist and act less than cooperative. If the police have reason to arrest such a resistant suspect, they will probably have to use more force than if the suspect did not resist. The police have a right to arrest someone for probable cause with enough force to avoid injury to themselves. When a suspect is injured while being arrested, it might be evidence of police brutality. The suspect's injuries might also be a consequence of the suspect's unwise decision to resist arrest.

Some of us resent being scrutinized by the police. Even though I am Caucasian, I was once stopped by the police because they saw me leaving a black neighborhood at night. This was shortly after 9/11, and I was feeling generally positive toward police officers and firefighters at that time. So I did not get outraged although I was very curious as to why I was being frisked. It turned out that they suspected me of being in the black neighborhood to buy illegal drugs. Not being a drug user/pusher, I was surprised by that explanation. Nevertheless, the police were doing their job. Do I have the right to drive in a black neighborhood at night? Yes. Do the police have the right to stop people who are acting suspiciously or illegally? Yes. It is in their job description. That was the last time I went to that neighborhood at night, because I don't want to be stopped, questioned, and frisked.

If we don't want to be scrutinized by the police, it is unwise to act suspiciously or illegally. If we choose to attract the attention of the police or to keep company with those who do, we cannot legitimately claim the police have no right to stop and question us. If we prefer not to get shot by the police, it is probably unwise to act in a threatening manner toward them.

Police officers should be allowed to do their job. If you think you are being abused by the police, it is probably in your best interest to contact a lawyer or neighborhood legal services or the ACLU after the fact, rather than mouthing off in the moment. Returning abuse for abuse is not going to be effective and violates the police officer's inalienable rights.

Any position of authority and power brings with it the ability to engage in abusive behavior. My solution to the general problem of abusive police conduct in this country is for police departments to screen police candidates for abusive tendencies and not to hire those with such tendencies. Also, the police officers with a history of abusive behavior need to be removed from positions of authority.

We have the right to expect due diligence from the police and from all other civil officials. "Due diligence" according to *Merriam-Webster* is "the care that a reasonable person exercises to avoid harm to other persons or their property."

Making it illegal or extremely difficult for us private citizens to recover full financial damages resulting from civil servants' lack of due diligence paves the way for lack of accountability, totalitarianism; and widespread authority abuse by government officials.

---

[1]   David Packman, *National Police Misconduct Statistics and Reporting Project* (CATO Institute, April 5, 2011), accessed December 9, 2015, http://www. policemisconduct.net/2010-npmsrp-police-misconduct-statistical-report/.

8

WASTEFUL GOVERNMENT SPENDING

A. Summary

I could be mistaken, but it seems to me that most elected officials don't seem to think that spending government revenue in a wasteful manner is a significant issue. Although *wasteful spending* (see glossary) involves excessive expenditures, decreasing expenses does not necessarily solve the problem. Government contracts can be a source of waste when they are unnecessary or excessively expensive. Budget reform, making buildings more energy efficient, and eliminating subsidies to big businesses are a few ways government can decrease wasteful spending.

Government has spent billions to try to control specific nonvictimizing behaviors like prostitution and illegal drug use. Yet these "problems" persist. More cost-effective approaches could be implemented. The US military wastes billions that should be spent on improved veteran care and on the common good. Wasteful spending, no matter how small the amount, is abusive to taxpayers.

B. What If He Were *Your* Uncle?

Have you ever imagined what you would think of Uncle Sam if he were a person rather than a country or a country's government? What if Uncle Sam were the brother of your mother or father? Imagine that there is a tradition in your family that your uncle Sam's working relatives will contribute 10 percent of their incomes to support Sam's lifestyle. In return, he maintains a large private park with full amenities that the working relatives and their families are free to use on the weekends.

Lately, the quality of the park has been in a steady decline. Why? Because your uncle spends money as if there is no tomorrow. He pays contractors any price they ask. He owns empty, unoccupied buildings he doesn't need. He supports the child of any woman who claims he's the father, even if he doesn't know the woman. He invests money he doesn't actually have in large corporations. He contributes huge sums to charities. He leaves lights on all over his house, even when he's not home, and leaves the attic windows open during the winter. In other words, Uncle Sam engages in wasteful (unnecessary) spending. And year by year, the problem grows worse as his cumulative debt and the interest due on that debt grows.

Your uncle also has legal representatives who support his bad spending habits and who help him spend more of the money he doesn't actually have. I'm afraid these legal representatives are people who have been so well off financially for so long, they have forgotten how to save money (if they ever knew). They seem indifferent to all the ways Sam is wasting money. But your uncle does pay his legal representatives well. Is there any way in which Sam could exercise improved fiscal responsibility? What if it were possible for him to correct his wasteful habits, pay off his debts, and live comfortably while maintaining that private park with only 5 percent of his relatives' hard-earned wages? If either he or his legal representatives refused to do that, your uncle and his representatives would be behaving abusively toward the family.

C. The Abuse of Wasteful Spending

It is very much the same with wasteful spending by governments. Wasteful spending is abusive because it does not benefit the common good (see chapter 2). Wasteful government spending increases the national debt. In 2012 the debt was $16 trillion. As of December 2015, it had exceeded $18.8 trillion. Tom Murse's "How Much U.S. Debt Does China Really Own?" reports that, in 2015, China owned 8 percent of the US national debt, about $1.2 trillion.[1]

According to the US Treasury Department's "Interest Expense on the Debt Outstanding," the total interest paid on debt by all levels of government in the United States for the 2015 fiscal year was $402,435,356,075.[2] Interest on debt benefits the holder of the debt. By paying billions of dollars in interest to China, the United States is supporting an abusive government that violates the human rights of its citizens. China is also carrying out a campaign of cultural genocide in Tibet, an autonomous country it illegally invaded and occupied in the 1950s. This is another way in which wasteful spending is abusive. Instead of wasting money, the American government could use the money to help pay off our debt to China, thus decreasing our financial support of an abusive regime.

D. Budget Cuts

No amount of tax dollars, no matter how small, is too insignificant to scrutinize, especially when one is in debt to a megabully like China. A more conservative solution to excessive spending is to defund a large program like the EPA or a social safety-net program. That's like a person in debt giving up his car to save money on car payments without thinking about the difficulty and expense of getting to and from work and the grocery store without a vehicle. Wouldn't it make more sense to try to save money by eliminating smaller unnecessary daily purchases? If you spend $2.50 on Starbucks coffee every morning on your way to work, you will expend $650 for daily coffee in a year. That could amount to more than two monthly car payments. Now multiply $2.50 times the number of government employees in this country. If each of them wastes only $2.50 a day, that adds up to hundreds of millions of dollars that could potentially be saved yearly.

Politicians have found an alternative to gutting the biggest program they can find. That solution involves cutting 25 percent of spending in all government departments. But does that guarantee an end to wasteful spending? A department could theoretically waste the same amount of money as it did before the 25 percent cut.

I define waste as unnecessary spending. On a personal level, some people spend money unnecessarily by impulsively purchasing things they don't need. Perhaps wasting money is simply human, and it does help boost the GNP. On a personal level, the individual wasters don't owe China or anyone else trillions of dollars. If they did, they would probably declare bankruptcy. *Declaring bankruptcy that was caused by wasteful spending is completely irresponsible and, perhaps, should be unlawful.* Wasteful spending by someone in debt is senseless. If that is true of individuals, it is also true of organizations, including the federal government. A bankrupt federal government would not be a good thing. So, what steps can be taken now?

E. Government Contracts

There used to be a regular feature on TV news called *The Fleecing of America*. I haven't seen it lately, but the problem of contractors overcharging the government for purchased goods and services remains. The Obama administration has taken positive steps to regain money from overbilling by private companies. I don't know how big that drain on the treasury actually is, but I know that I don't want my tax payments helping to enable private government contractors to become millionaires. A policy that would limit the percentage of profit that private contractors could make from government contracts (20 percent maximum profit may be appropriate) would help control this type of wasteful spending.

For specific examples of wasteful federal government contracts, check out Senator Coburn's annual *Wastebook*.[3] Eliminating funding for the types of projects Senator Coburn describes year after year in his book would save tens of billions of dollars annually.

F. Budget Reform

Government budgeting on all levels needs to be reformed to discourage wasteful spending. As it is now, revenue is divided among individual government agencies and departments. Each department gets a certain allowance for each fiscal year. If the department does not spend the entire allowance, it is supposed to return the balance. The greater that department's returned balance is, the less next year's allowance may be. This encourages each department to spend its entire allowance by the end of the fiscal year, even if that involves throwing a party costing thousands of dollars, allegedly to boost employee morale.[4] There are probably less expensive ways to boost employee morale. Perhaps departments could be motivated to spend money less wastefully. It's a fine thing that the federal government helps states financially with grants and that the states help needy municipalities. It's fine if those states and those municipalities don't need money because of money they have wasted.

G. Energy Efficiency

Another source of wasted tax dollars that goes directly to utility companies is inefficient heating, cooling, and lighting in government buildings. There should be energy audits on all such buildings and requirements for the workers in those buildings to follow the recommendations of the auditors. Leaving windows open in the winter while the heat is left on and leaving lights burning while no one is there—these sorts of practices are wasteful. The same type of audits should be required of any buildings owned by organizations supported by taxpayer dollars.

H. Subsidies to Big Business

A free government handout to certain large industries is another form of wasteful spending. Some call it "corporate welfare." Twenty-eight billion dollars to the oil industry annually may not seem substantial. However, the government also gives millions away to big agribusiness, king cotton, high-speed rail, and others. Why? It may have made sense years ago whenever it started. It doesn't now. Allowing lumber companies to cut trees on public land for a cost that is less than what they would pay for the same trees on private land is a wasteful practice. The government should not be in the business of enabling big, successful businesses to make more profit. For more information check out the Taxpayers for Common Sense website.[5]

I. Drugs and Prostitution

Thinking about all the expense and time and energy that some people have put into eliminating illegal drugs and prostitution from our society, I must wonder if the effort has not been a waste. No matter how much money and manpower is dedicated to these "problems," they will persist. They have been around for thousands of years and will continue to exist no matter how much money is thrown at them. Would illegal drugs and prostitution generate the same amount of interest and number of customers if they were legalized? This question might not be relevant if it weren't for our human tendency to be attracted to that which is forbidden.

Regulating prostitution as they do in Nevada would make it safer from a public health perspective. It would also generate revenue for the government in the form of licenses, fees, and taxes.

Legalizing and regulating all drugs would solve a number of problems. The price of addictive street drugs might be less. With more reasonable pricing, addicts may commit fewer robberies and thefts to support their habit. Revenue for the government in the form of fees and taxes would be collected. Law enforcement could direct more energy to crimes involving victims. Addicts and nonaddicted users of street drugs would be less apt to overdose accidentally. According to the Drug Policy Alliance's "Take Action to End the War on Drugs," the drug war has failed and will continue to fail, costing taxpayers more millions of dollars.[6]

According to "A Drug Policy for the 21st Century," the Obama administration has declared, "Put simply, an enforcement-centric 'war on drugs' approach to drug policy is counterproductive, inefficient, and costly" (The White House, accessed December 28, 2015, https://www.whitehouse.gov/ondcp/drugpolicyreform).

Prisons are overcrowded because of drug arrests.[7] Putting drug users in jail for using drugs does not solve their drug problem, if they even have one. Not everyone who uses recreational drugs has a drug addiction. Addiction, however, is a problem for the addict and for society. Why not make it mandatory for any drug addict convicted of a felony or a misdemeanor to complete a drug-rehab program in addition to whatever sentence the addict receives for the crime? It could also be a condition of parole that the person remain clean and sober. Failure to do so would result in another mandatory rehab program.

J. Eliminating Wasteful Military Spending

A lot is wasted on military spending each year. For specific examples, refer to an article by Gabe LaMonica about Senator Coburn's *Wastebook*.[8] To create jobs in their respective states, some members of Congress see nothing wrong with promoting defense contracts that the Pentagon neither needs nor wants. Job creation is the stated motivation. However, the person or persons who own the military-industrial company that will get the government contract is the party that profits the most. This is an example of elected officials prioritizing partisan politics over the common good. If jobs are the real motivation, why not take that taxpayer money that would be spent unnecessarily and use it to create Jobs for the Common Good (see chapters 5 and 6)? More people who need work could be employed, and everyone would benefit from an enhanced common good. Less money would be needed to finance social safety-net programs.

National defense is an essential part of the common good. All nations have a right to defend themselves if and when they are attacked and to help other nations with which they have mutual defense treaties, if and when those nations are attacked. But to spend money on national defense for systems that will be outmoded by the time they are built or that the Pentagon determines are not necessary detracts from the common good of the nation as a whole and is, therefore, abusive.

Examples of attacks on a country would include the assassination of the president and terrorism perpetrated by foreign powers (9/11 being a specific example). But to send our military forces to invade a country that has not attacked us for the purpose of promoting the "national interests" of the United States is abusive. An example of this is the US invasion of Iraq. A country that possesses enough weapons of mass destruction to destroy all human life on the planet dictating which nations are allowed to possess such weapons and which are not allowed is arrogant and abusive, not to mention somewhat hypocritical.

We are paying a terrible price for our involvement in the Middle East wars. According to an article by Glenn O'Neal on the Med Express news service website, twenty-two veterans commit suicide every day. From 2000 to 2010, "the age-adjusted veteran suicide rate increased by approximately 25 percent while the comparable nonveteran rate increased by approximately 12 percent" ("Suicide rates increasing for both veterans and nonveterans; veterans using VHA services have declining suicide rates," May 4, 2015, accessed December 28, 2015, http://medicalxpress.com/news/2015-05-suicide-veterans-nonveterans-vha-declining.html). More veterans died from suicide during that period than died in combat.

K. The Veterans Administration

Our veterans deserve much better treatment than many receive from the Veterans Administration. The study referenced in the medicalxpress.com article commented that veterans receiving VA services from 2003 on had a lower rate of suicide than those not receiving those services. No explanation was given as to why some veterans who commit suicide did not receive help from the VA. We know from the news that the wait times to receive VA services have not been reasonable.

If the money that goes into the research and development of ever-more-sophisticated weapons systems could be spent on better services for our veterans, perhaps there would be fewer veteran suicides.

L. Money for Weapons versus Money for the Common Good

The United States, China, and Russia don't want one another to gain a weapons development advantage. This is understandable. On the other hand, each country expending time, energy, and expense to develop and acquire ever-more-sophisticated weapons with which to kill the enemy is a drain on valuable resources that should be used to enhance people's common good rather than to destroy it. So why not put as much time, energy, and expense into a weapons-development cessation agreement as is devoted to international trade agreements?

The alleged purpose of trade agreements is to benefit the economies of different countries. If countries could agree to stop developing and acquiring more advanced weaponry, including weaponry in the upper atmosphere and in outer space, it could have a positive effect on the economies of those countries. In the absence of weapons-development competition, countries would have more money to spend on aspects of the common good other than national defense, including better veteran care. Such a treaty would be in the best interest of inalienable rights, because people in all countries have a right to benefit from the common good.

The ways in which governments waste money are many and varied. The "Special Edition Waste Report" by Senator Rand Paul says there is a $43 million compressed natural gas (CNG) filling station in Afghanistan paid for by the US Department of Defense. They built it despite Afghanistan having neither the infrastructure nor the facilities for transporting CNG or automobiles that use CNG. Even if such automobiles were widely available in Afghanistan, the average Afghan could not afford to operate a CNG-powered vehicle.[9]

M. In Conclusion

Wasteful (unnecessary) spending by government, no matter how small, negatively affects our opportunities to benefit from the common good, which is our right. Wasteful spending is fiscally irresponsible and abusive to taxpayers of this and future generations. It benefits the people who are the direct recipients of the spending and those who collect interest on the debt increased by having to borrow more to make up for the wasted funds. Since we are in debt to an abusive power like China, wasteful federal spending also supports abuse in that country.

---

[1] Tom Murse, "How Much U.S. Debt Does China Really Own?" About. com, May 22, 2015, accessed December 28, 2015, http://usgovinfo. about.com/od/moneymatters/ss/How-Much-US-Debt-Does-China-Own.htm.

[2] US Treasury Direct, "Interest Expense on the Debt Outstanding," December 3, 2015, http://treasurydirect.gov/govt/reports/ir/ir_expense.htm.

[3] "'Wastebook' Report Singles out $30B in Federal Spending," *CBS News*, December 17, 2013, accessed December 28, 2015, http://www.cbsnews.com/news/wastebook-report-details-30b-in-questionable-federal-spending/.

[4] Alexander Abad-Santos, "GSA Threw an $800,000 Party and All You Got Was the Bill," *Atlantic Monthly*, April 3, 2012, accessed June 17, 2016, http://www.thewire.com/politics/2012/04/gsa-threw-800000-party-and-all-you-got-was-bill/50663/.

[5] "Eliminate Corporate Welfare," Taxpayers for Commonsense, accessed July 6, 2016, http://www.taxpayer.net/common-sense/eliminate-corporate-welfare#.

[6] "Take Action to End the War on Drugs," Drug Policy Alliance, 2015, accessed January 18, 2016, http://www.drugpolicy.org/action.

[7] Kathleen Miles, "Just How Much the War on Drugs Impacts Our Overcrowded Prisons, in One Chart," Huffington Post, April 3, 2014, accessed June 12, 2016, http://www.huffingtonpost.com/2014/03/10/war-on-drugs-prisons-infographic_n_4914884.html.

8   Gabe LaMonica, "Senator's 'Wastebook' Has Everything that Will Fit in a Pork Barrel," *CNN*, October 22, 2014, accessed January 13, 2016, http://www.cnn.com/2014/10/22/politics/tom-coburn-wastebook/index.html.

9   Senator Rand Paul, "DOD's $43 Million Gas Station Almost Noone Can Use," November 12, 2015, http://www.paul.senate.gov/imo/media/doc/%20Waste%20Report%20Afghan%20Gas%20Station.pdf.

9

FOREIGN POLICY AND HUMAN RIGHTS

oreign policy, an aspect of federal public policy, seems to me to be generally determined by departments within the executive branch of the federal government, with the American president being primarily responsible for American foreign policy. This is a very complicated topic and involves the interaction of politics and politicians from a variety of countries. It seems to me that American foreign policy is often influenced by the interests of certain private American citizens, private enterprises, and multinational corporations. Sections of this chapter are as follows:

A. Annexation of Hawaii
B. Diego Garcia
C. Foreign Hostility and the Overthrow of Legitimate Governments
D. A More Peaceful World
E. Defense Pacts
F. Refining Defense Pact Criteria
G. The American-Israeli Alliance
H. The Right to Peace versus National Unity
I. The ISIS Problem
J. Syria
K. The Nuclear Threat
L. International Trade Agreements
M. Conclusion

A. Annexation of Hawaii

According to the web page "Sanford Ballard Dole," Dole was a private American citizen and cousin of the founder of the Dole Food Company who actively helped to depose the legitimate monarch of Hawaii and in 1893 became the provisional government's president.

> **Ignoring the illegal origins of his own government, he refused President Cleveland's request that Lili`uokalani be restored to the throne. Instead, the Provisional Government declared itself the Republic of Hawai`i and in 1898 Dole went to Washington, D.C. to press for American annexation of the Islands. In 1898, Hawai`i became a United States territory and President McKinley appointed Dole first governor of the territory.** (Info Grafik, 2015, accessed December, 2015, http://www.hawaiihistory. org/index.cfm?fuseaction=ig.page&PageID=407)

B. Diego Garcia

The above is an example of abusive, bullying behavior of Americans toward an indigenous group in the nineteenth century. What happened to the people of Diego Garcia at the urging of and with the full knowledge of the US government occurred in 1971. According to an article by David Vine, "The Truth About Diego Garcia: 50 Years of Fiction About an American Military Base," thousands of natives (Chagossians) of the Chagos Archipelago of the Indian Ocean, were covertly deported to other islands 1,200 miles from where their ancestors had lived since the time of the American Revolution. This mass relocation took place so that the United States could build a navy and air force base on the British-controlled island of Diego Garcia. The Chagossians were forced to leave most of their possessions behind, and no resettlement assistance was given. "More than 40 years after their expulsion, Chagossians generally remain the poorest of the poor in their adopted lands, struggling to survive" (Common Dreams, June 15 2015, accessed December 28, 2015, http://www.commondreams.org/ views/2015/06/15/truth-about-diego-garcia-50-years-fiction-about-american-military-base).

C. Foreign Hostility and the Overthrow of Legitimate Governments

According to Ebrahim Norouzi, in the 1950s, when John Foster Dulles was the Secretary of State, and his brother, Allen Dulles, headed the CIA, the American government orchestrated successful projects to overthrow legitimate governments in Iran and Guatemala for the sake of American corporations.[1]

I suspect these types of repeated abusive actions that negatively and unfairly affect other countries' sovereignty have inspired some of the foreign hostility directed at America and at us Americans. History has shown that the United States has the power to invade a foreign country under the guise of ridding its citizens of a cruel dictator while the real motivation for invasion was to keep that country's oil supply flowing for the sake of America and its allies. America's victory over Saddam Hussein neither convinced all Iraqis to embrace democracy and work together for their common good nor endeared Iraqis to America. Perhaps that had something to do with all the civilian deaths and suffering that resulted from the invasion, not to mention the resulting political instability. Some believe this is all related to an increase in terrorism by Islamic extremists.

D. A More Peaceful World

If we want to live in a more peaceful world where other countries respect America and Americans, the priority of our foreign policy needs to shift to promoting and supporting the individual rights of foreign citizens. That would not be difficult for government leaders who believe everyone, everywhere, under all circumstances possesses the same inalienable rights to life, liberty, the pursuit of happiness, and access to the common good.

E. Defense Pacts

Military agreements with other countries are related to American foreign policy. The United States has an obligation to honor its military commitments to other nations. These commitments include mutual military defense treaties, also known as defense pacts. A defense pact is a type of treaty in which the parties agree to support each other militarily. For example, if Country X is attacked militarily and needs help to defend itself, Country Y agrees to come to the aid of X. This sort of agreement between small noncommunist countries and more powerful countries like the United States offers protection to the smaller countries from megabully governments like China and Russia.

Designating the countries with whom the United States will make defense pacts is an aspect of foreign policy. I suspect that a major factor in making those designations is financial. In other words, how will our economy (i.e., the economy of the upper 1 percent) be affected if the country in question is conquered by an aggressor nation?

F. Refining Defense Pact Criteria

If lasting world peace is ever to occur, American political leaders must realize that peace is directly related to prioritizing the actualization of every foreign and domestic citizen's individual inalienable rights over the economic interests of the rich and powerful. Once that shift in consciousness has occurred, the criteria for selecting countries with which to form defense pacts can be refined.

The United States should not ally itself with any national government that disrespects the individual inalienable rights of its own citizens or with any government that disrespects the individual inalienable rights of citizens in other countries.

Some examples of disrespect for individual inalienable rights by governments are as follows:

- Country A militarily attacking, invading, or occupying Country B when B has not initiated military aggression against A or A's ally
- a country allowing its toxic, radioactive, chemical, or untreated medical waste to be exported to another country or allowing same to be dumped in the ocean
- countries/governments violating treaties designed to preserve the quality of the earth's environment
- governments using revenue to threaten the individual inalienable rights of either its own citizens or citizens of other countries
- governments condoning or supporting the threatening of those rights by any nongovernmental citizen or group, including businesses

If countries that disrespect individual inalienable rights were selectively eliminated as potential defense partners, it would help to reestablish America as an ethical world leader and would discourage abusive behavior in this and in other countries. It would also gain more respect for America from citizens of other nations. In regard to national security, there is more long-term value from this refined approach to foreign policy than from acting pragmatically for the sake of short-term economic gain.

G. The American-Israeli Alliance

It will probably take many years before the world is ready to accept this refinement in American defense-pact policy. By that time, the Israelis and Palestinians might have learned to tolerate each other and respect each other's rights. If one looks at this Middle East conflict through the lens of individual inalienable rights, one sees that Israel has a right to exist as a nation as does Palestine. Palestine, however, does not have the means to exist independently from Israel. Israel supplies the Palestinians with water, electricity, and employment. That needs to change. With international support, waste management could be improved, and desalinization plants (as independent water sources) and electric generation facilities could be built in Palestine. Industries could be established. The Israelis made the desert fertile. The same thing could be done in Palestine. Once Palestine does not have to depend on Israel, the Israelis might not feel a need to threaten the individual rights of Palestinians, and the Palestinians might feel less inclined to attack Israel.

H. The Right to Peace versus National Unity

Resolving violent conflicts between groups of differing ethnicity or religious beliefs within the same country can be achieved in different ways. One way is to have a strong dictator presiding over the country. This solution does not promote citizens' opportunities to experience their individual inalienable rights, so it is not a solution I favor.

Living in peace is a human right. There have been a number of instances in which the right to peace has been secured through the geographical separation of conflicting groups. In 1947, the nation of Pakistan was formed from parts of India to give some Indian Muslims their own country with their own government. For more information, refer to the web page "Why India And Pakistan Were Separated?"[2]

The island of Cyprus is divided by a buffer zone first established in 1964 by the British and ten years later made permanent by the United Nations. The separation is administered by the United Nations Peacekeeping Force in Cyprus (UNPFC). Most Greek Cypriots now live in the southern part of the island, and most Turkish Cypriots live in the north. Each part of Cyprus has a separate government.[3] Another example is a peace treaty in 1953 that officially divided Korea into the communist North and the anticommunist South. There are diverse groups of people who can live more peacefully when separated from one another. In present-day Iraq, there are three main ethnic/religious groups (the Shiites, the Sunnis, and the Kurds), each of which might experience more peace if they each had their own governments and their own geographical boundaries.

I. The ISIS Problem

According to CNN, ISIS is a Sunni militant group with the goal of establishing an Islamic state. In Iraq, ISIS has forced "hundreds of thousands of minorities from their homes," according to Joshua Berlinger's August 8, 2014, article, "Who are the religious and ethnic groups under threat from ISIS?" (August 8, 2014, accessed December 28, 2015, http://www.cnn.com/2014/08/08/world/meast/iraq-ethnic-groups-under-threat-isis/index.html). ISIS fighters are also in Syria and in parts of Africa. An abusive gang of fighters, ISIS threatens individual inalienable rights wherever they go. If ISIS is eventually defeated militarily and there are thousands of surviving militants, what is going to be done with them? Unless something changes, they will probably be returned to their countries of origin. In other words, they will eventually be free to continue to wreak terror throughout the world. This would not support the actualization of everyone's individual inalienable rights.

Trying to destroy the ISIS movement militarily is like trying to put out a grease fire by throwing water on it. Some people may object to giving the followers of ISIS their own country, yet theocracies are not without precedent; the Christians have had Vatican City since the fourteenth century, the Buddhists had Tibet until the 1950s, and the Jews were given Israel. Had the United Nations not created the nation of Israel, perhaps Jewish extremists would still be engaging in what we label terrorism today. I don't know if the majority of Jews objected to violence as a means of securing a homeland. Nor do I know if the majority of the world's Jews even wanted a country to call their own. According to Adherents.com, 21 percent of the world's population is Muslim, whereas only 0.22 percent of the world's population is Jewish.[4]

The international community could conceivably create an Islamic State (IS) from contiguous parts of Syria and Iraq. Ideally, the only residents allowed to remain in the IS would be Muslim terrorists and their supporters. The IS should have set boundaries surrounded by an international buffer zone that would be patrolled by a United Nations peacekeeping force.

The ideal conditions for the creation and existence of the IS would include the following:

- The IS would be free to form its own government without outside restrictions.
- It would be self-sufficient, raising its own food, generating its own power, purifying its own water.
- IS citizens would be prohibited from leaving the IS until such time as the country proves itself to be nonthreatening to the rest of the world.
- The IS would be required to accept any Islamic terrorists, including Al-Qaeda and Taliban fighters captured in other countries and anyone pledging allegiance to violent Islamic radical groups. This would allow the United States to close the Guantanamo prison.
- No firearms or explosives would be allowed to enter the IS.

It may seem that anyone living in the Islamic State would not have any more opportunity to experience his or her inalienable rights to life, liberty, and the pursuit of happiness than prisoners do. This is related to the following Guiding Principle from the introduction: No one has a right to abuse anyone. Unfair treatment and all forms of abuse should and need to result in appropriate negative consequences for the abuser.

J. Syria

I feel reluctant to weigh in on the current military conflict in Syria. It is very complicated. Based on news reports, we know that, Bashar al-Assad, the authoritarian, freely elected president of Syria, has been in power since 2000. His attempt to remain in power in the midst of a civil war has involved attacking/destroying the buildings, infrastructure, and citizens of Syria. There are rebel groups supposedly consisting mostly of Syrian nationals, some of which are sometimes allied with terrorists such as ISIS. Other rebel groups are fighting ISIS and the Assad regime. Then there is the Russian military aid to the Assad regime and the United States aid for the rebels fighting ISIS.

I don't believe other countries should get involved in civil wars. How would we have felt about the British Empire sending a couple thousand British soldiers to aid the Confederacy during our Civil War? However, there is a considerable degree of public sympathy for the innocent people who are suffering and dying in Syria. I believe the noncombatants of this civil war are being used as pawns by all sides. This is a violation of human rights.

Perhaps the United Nations should forcibly establish a temporary ceasefire in Syria while all children in zones of conflict and all willing adult noncombatants would be evacuated from the country. The evacuees would be permitted to return once the conflict has ended. Such a ceasefire and evacuation would be ideally combined with the establishment of the Islamic State described in the previous section. With ISIS removed from the civil war, there would be no need for Russian and American involvement. The Assad regime and the rebels would be free to destroy each other without killing innocents.

K. The Nuclear Threat

Warfare is not conducive to our ability to exercise our inalienable rights, civil rights, and property rights. This was demonstrated by the internment of 120,000 Japanese Americans, mostly American citizens, during World War II.[5]

You may have heard of conspiracy theories that claim that rich people start wars. A theory is just a theory until it is proved. It seems to me that the wealthiest often get wealthier during and immediately after wars and that the power of government leaders to control us increases during wartime.

We seem to have the best chance of experiencing our inalienable rights in peacetime. Once a war ends, life can return to some semblance of normal for the survivors of the victorious side. But what would normal be in the aftermath of a nuclear war? Vast tracts of land and fresh water would be rendered unusable by humans. This would lead to food and water shortages and mass starvation. Millions of survivors would lack adequate health care.

We can tell ourselves there will never be a nuclear war, despite the United States and the Soviet Union having come close to firing nuclear missiles many times.[6] As of 2015, there were nine different countries possessing a total of about sixteen thousand nuclear warheads, according to the Arms Control Association.[7] Then there are states like Iran and North Korea, at least one of which seems to be attempting to become a nuclear power. Besides the dangers of accidents, misunderstandings, and mistakes, there is the possibility of terrorists either purchasing or stealing nuclear weapons. The rapid dismantling of all nuclear warheads everywhere and anywhere is in the best interest of human rights, in my opinion. We should put as much effort and energy into nuclear disarmament treaties as we put into trade agreements and mutual defense treaties.

L. International Trade Agreements

The process of forming trade agreements with other countries is another aspect of foreign policy. My suggestions in regard to international trade agreements are discussed in chapter 6, "Capitalism and Poverty, II," section D ("Free Trade").

M. Conclusion

In regard to all aspects of American foreign policy, the primary goal should be the nonthreatening preservation of human rights of the citizens of other countries. This should *not* involve direct interference with the internal affairs of other countries. The alternative approach is to prioritize the interests and desires of the rich and powerful when making foreign policy decisions. The latter approach will continue to generate ill will toward our country. My approach to foreign policy suggested above will result in more fairness in the world and more peace in the long term. That would be in the best interest of us all.

1   Ebrahim Norouzi, "The Dulles Brothers," Mossadegh Project, April 7, 2010, accessed December 28, 2015, http://www.mohammadmossadegh.com/news/dulles-brothers/.

2   Joydeep, "Why India and Pakistan Were Separated?" Maps of India, 2016, accessed May 7, 2016, http://www.mapsofindia.com/my-india/politics/why-india-and-pakistan-were-separated.

3   United Nations Peacekeeping Mission, "United Nations Peacekeeping Force in Cyprus (UNFICYP)," accessed December 28, 2015, http://www.un.org/en/peacekeeping/missions/unficyp/.

4   "Major Religions of the World Ranked by Adherents," Adherents.com, January 2000, accessed January 6, 2016, http://www.adherents.com/Religions_By_Adherents.html.

5   Eric Foner and John A. Garraty, "Japanese-American Relocation," A+E Networks, 1991, accessed May 8, 2016, http://www.history.com/topics/world-war-ii/japanese-american-relocation.

6   Andrew Evans, "5 Cold War Close Calls," A+E Networks, October 16, 2013, accessed May 8, 2016, http://www.history.com/news/history-lists/5-cold-war-close-calls.

7   "Who Has What at a Glance" Arms Control Association, October 2015, accessed May 8, 2016, http://www.armscontrol.org/factsheets/Nuclearweaponswhohaswhat.

10

THE ECONOMY AND HUMAN RIGHTS

In chapters 5 and 6, "Poverty and Capitalism," the point was made that there is enough wealth in this country to pay for all our health needs. This will continue to be true as long as the economy does not suffer a major problem such as hyperinflation. This chapter is about how the economy can function so that virtually every one of us can experience our individual inalienable rights. Those rights would include the affordability of a healthful lifestyle and the security of that affordability not being threatened by an economic problem such as inflation.

We don't all agree about how the US economy should operate. On one extreme are those who favor laissez-faire, a system in which the owners of capital make all the decisions without government control or oversight. On the other extreme are those who think perpetual economic growth is not only possible, but also desirable, and who think that the government needs to make and follow policies that will bring about unending financial growth. At the same time that the economy is growing, social safety-net programs that will fix everyone's problems should be expanded, the latter believe.

Each extreme is potentially abusive to us citizens, particularly to the poor. This chapter will explain why that is. The topics addressed in this chapter are as follows:

A. Laissez-Faire versus the Welfare State
B. Economic Strategies and Human Rights

C. Perpetual Economic Expansion

D. The Gold Standard

E. Inflation

F. Inflation and Human Rights

G. Return to the Gold Standard?

H. Alternative to the Gold Standard

I. Economic Collapse

A. Laissez-Faire versus the Welfare State

Those with a laissez-faire, *every citizen for himself* philosophy don't believe the government is obligated to support American citizens who are financially disadvantaged. Then there are the welfare-state promoters (welfare statists), who believe the government should spend whatever it takes to provide for the poor. Laissez-faire advocates favor a smaller, weaker central government that would lack the power and authority to protect our opportunities to experience our individual inalienable rights, including the right to benefit from the common good. On the other hand, the welfare statists don't account for the source of the money necessary to expand social programs. Ending deficit spending, paying off the national debt, eliminating wasteful spending (see chapter 8), and raising taxes don't seem to be high on their list of priorities.

B. Economic Strategies and Human Rights

Some American citizens are underemployed, unemployed, or partly employed and are financially disadvantaged even though they are willing and able to perform decent full-time work for a healthful living wage. Neither laissez-faire nor the welfare state strategies can end their deprivation. Each extreme approach to the economy would perpetuate the abuse of involuntary poverty and all its accompanying problems. Giving handouts to those who are financially disadvantaged but able to work is not a humane solution that fulfills the promise of this country to grant each citizen the inalienable right to life, liberty, the pursuit of happiness, and access to the common good. We need to decide which economic strategy is best. Do we prefer (a) perpetual economic expansion, (b) laissez-faire, or (c) the assurance that every one of us who is able to work could earn what we need to live a healthful lifestyle?

C. Perpetual Economic Expansion

My research suggests that perpetual economic growth or expansion is not only unrealistic, but also dangerous to the economy. I suspect the economic plight of Greece in 2015 is an example of a failed attempt at perpetual economic growth. To spend more than one has is never without risk. Some may think that what happened in Greece could not happen here, because our economy is bigger. It might take longer, but we are, in my opinion, heading in that direction. Check out the "US Debt Clock" at http://www.usdebtclock.org/. The debt amount is not decreasing, and there is no plan to stop it from increasing. *The End of Growth: Adapting to Our New Economic Reality* by Richard Heinberg also supports the idea that economic expansion on this planet has reached a limit.[1]

D. The Gold Standard

Alan Greenspan, an American economist who served as chairman of the Federal Reserve of the United States from 1987 to 2006, wrote the article "Gold and Economic Freedom," in which he seems to favor the gold standard. Greenspan also favors laissez-faire economics.[2] I found this article a bit alarming, but also thought-provoking. The gold standard is a monetary system in which a government holds a supply of gold in reserve as a backup. The government issues currency and banknotes and guarantees their value by making them convertible into gold.

According to Greenspan, before World War I, when the US banking system and most of the world's banking systems were based on gold, banks would occasionally lend out as much money as their gold reserves could support. At that point, interest rates on borrowing would rise sharply, new credit would become unavailable, and the country's economy would temporarily decline. These recessions were short and mild compared with the 1932 depression.

E. Inflation

What has happened to the gold standard since the Great Depression? According to www.history.com, "On June 5, 1933, the United States went off the gold standard … Congress enacted a joint resolution nullifying the right of creditors to demand payment in gold" ("June 5, 1933—FDR takes United States off gold standard," 2015, accessed December 29, 2015, http://www.history.com/this-day-in-history/fdr-takes-united-states-off-gold-standard).

According to "What is the History of the Gold Standard?" by Kathy Amadeo, in 1973, the US government "decoupled the value of the dollar from gold altogether" (About, Inc., November 3, 2015, accessed December 29, 2015, http://useconomy.about.com/od/monetarypolicy/p/gold_history.htm). The United States government no longer tries to adhere to a gold standard. Is that a problem for us? According to Alan Greenspan, the federal government now issues bonds or creates bank deposits without any real (tangible) assets to back them up. The bonds and deposits (claims) don't have the real value the holders might think they do. Greenspan stated that, as more and more claims are created without an accompanying increase in real assets to back them up, prices must rise. In other words, without the gold standard, inflation will confiscate—that is, decrease the value of—our savings.[3]

Greenspan expressed this view in 1966. Prices have definitely risen since then. According to the "Live CPI & Inflation" calculator, the inflation rate from 1966 to 2015 was 627.75 percent.[4] Each whole percent represents a one-cent increase. If a pound of pistachios cost one dollar in 1966, you could expect to pay $7.28 for the same quantity in 2015.

F. Inflation and Human Rights

In terms of abuse and human rights, why is inflation significant? If we possess the same inalienable rights to life and the pursuit of happiness, and if the opportunity to be healthy is necessary to life and happiness, then the cost of living a healthful lifestyle is significant. Inflation or hyperinflation can negatively affect the ability of some to afford to live healthfully, particularly if they are on fixed incomes. Inflation doesn't just negatively affect the price of luxury items. It also makes quality food and decent housing less affordable.

Inflation might not be a problem at all if wages and benefits increased at the same rate as inflation. For that increase in wages and benefits to be acceptable, the initial amount of wages and benefits would have to be enough to make healthful living affordable for us all. Then there is the tendency of prices to rise as a function of the rising price of labor. Taxes should also rise as social safety-net program expenses and government employee salaries increase. It would seem simpler to keep inflation at zero rather than raising prices, wages, and taxes.

G. Return to the Gold Standard?

If Greenspan is correct, might a return to the gold standard control inflation? These days, no countries back their total money supply with gold. If the United States were to revert to the gold standard in isolation, other countries with American currency could demand American gold in return for American paper currency. There might be more American paper currency in the possession of other countries than the US government has in reserve supplies of gold.

A return to the gold standard does not seem to be a practical solution to the current problems of deficit spending and inflation in the United States. Perhaps Greenspan was mistaken. Perhaps inflation can be controlled in the absence of the gold standard. The inflation rate from 2008 to 2015 has been lower than 10 percent, which some like to characterize as virtually "flat." My idea of flat is 0 percent.

H. Alternative to the Gold Standard

It might be impractical for the United States to return to the gold standard. But what if there were an alternative to the gold standard? The online author of *Energy Backed Money* described a plan for the US dollar to become "a representative currency backed by electricity in units of kilowatt-hours (kWh)" (Money.com, "Introduction to Energy Backed Money," chap. 5, November, 2009, http://www.energybackedmoney. com/chapter5.html). A monetary standard might help stop inflation, decrease economic disparity, and discourage government from deficit spending, wasteful spending, and increasing the national debt. Those are changes that would promote the common good and that would be in everyone's best interest.

If these changes can take place just as quickly without any sort of standard, no problem. The ultimate measure of any economic reform is how well it ensures the opportunities for each of us to actually experience our human rights. That measure will involve the cost of the products and services that we need to live a healthful lifestyle. Those things include nutritional supplements, quality food, decent housing, energy supply, health care, running or walking shoes, therapeutic devices, therapeutic healing, and rehabilitation services. These things need to be as affordable as possible. Any economic reform that does not achieve this and fails to preserve the common good is unacceptable.

I. Economic Collapse

A few people seem to believe that another economic recession or depression is imminent and that the government is doing nothing to prevent it. Those people suggest that we should all buy guns and a supply of gold. Then there are those who insist that the economy is recovering and point to an almost nonexistent rate of inflation since 2008. They claim there is no need to panic.

Neither of these approaches is in the best interest of the common good. Our economy needs to be reformed in a way that allows each of us to afford a healthful lifestyle. The American economy should be restructured in a way that would prioritize the protection and actualization of our individual inalienable rights. This restructuring needs to end inflation, stop deficit spending, end wasteful spending, pay off the national debt, and ensure that everyone willing and able to work at a decent job has the opportunity to do that.

If we, as a nation, believed in such reform, and if we wanted it to happen, it would be possible. Unfortunately, the alarmists would rather be proved correct. They choose to devote their time and energy to preparing for the worst. The conservatives who believe the economy is recovering don't see reform as necessary because they will continue to do well without reforms. I also wonder whether they actually think that full employment would have a negative effect on the growth of the economy. If they think that, conservatives ought to be willing to better support those who are unemployed.

We deserve economic reform. Who would want a major economic crisis instead?

———————

[1]   Richard Heinberg, *The End of Growth* (Gabriola Island, BC: New Society Publishers, 2011).

[2]   Alan Greenspan, "Gold and Economic Freedom" (1966), Constitution Society, 2004, accessed December 29, 2015, http://www.constitution.org/mon/greenspan_gold.htm.

[3]   Ibid.

[4]   US Department of Labor, "Live CPI & Inflation," December 15, 2015, http://data.bls.gov/cgi-bin/cpicalc.pl.

11

FOSSIL FUELS AND HUMAN RIGHTS, I

T his book addresses the nature of America's culture of abuse and suggests solutions that are supportive of individual inalienable rights. Most of the energy used in this country comes from fossil fuels (petroleum, natural gas, and coal). How these sources of energy are extracted and how they are used affects the inalienable right to life and the common good. This chapter exposes a myriad of health, environmental, and economic disadvantages of using fossil fuels, not only for energy production, but also for the production of certain consumer products.

The following is an outline of the sections of this chapter.

A. **The Trade-Off:** The price we pay for fossil fuel usage and what benefits we could have instead.

B. **Coal:** The benefits of coal usage (heating homes and employment) and its negative effects, such as landscape destruction, coal fires, acid mine drainage, mine subsidence, black lung disease, global warming, acid precipitation, arsenic and mercury pollution, and respiratory illnesses.

C. **Support for Coal-Generated Electricity:** The political resistance to discouraging coal-generated electricity.

D. **Oil and Natural Gas:** The benefit of using oil and natural gas (employment) and its negative effects on our environment and health due to well blowouts, oil drilling, hydraulic fracking, oil spills, plastics waste, dioxin pollution, polystyrene production and disposal, BPA and phthalates, petrochemicals, DDT, skin care products, and oxidizing of gasoline.

E. **The Altered Ecosystem:** The geological period in which those plants and animals whose bodies were converted to fossil fuels lived might not have been conducive to the survival of humans and most other modern living species. This section questions the wisdom of converting our modern environment to be more like that environment of eons past.

F. **The End of Fossil Fuels:** The supply of fossil fuels is limited.

A. The Trade-Off

How are inalienable individual rights related to the environment? Earlier chapters have explained the meaning of rights and specifically *inalienable* individual rights. It has been stated that one of those rights is the right to benefit from the common good. One aspect of the common good is environmental quality. What is a quality environment? It is one with clean air, pure water, uncontaminated ground, and species diversity. As we think about the mass of plastic trash floating in the oceans, the barrels of petroleum leaking from pipelines, the tons of pollutants being spewed into the air, and all the endangered species, we realize that the earth's environmental quality seems to be going downhill and that our rights to enjoy a quality environment and to live healthfully are headed in the same direction.

Imagine a culture in which we knowingly and consciously live with declining environmental quality, less-than-optimum health conditions, and rising health care costs. Why would that seem acceptable? Because most of us have jobs that pay us enough to keep ourselves and our families alive? Because we have been brainwashed into believing that this is all our society can afford? Because we are afraid of losing our jobs if we protest? But if the state of our health were to improve, would we not be that much more productive and would not the cost of health care be that much less?

This chapter will analyze the use of fossil fuels—oil, coal, and natural gas—and their effects on the environment and on human health.

B. Coal

1. The Upside of Coal

People were burning coal to keep warm in the winter before they ever started burning it to generate electricity. Coal is very popular in states that have large coal deposits. Mining coal requires the paid labor of many people. Also, without coal there might not be any DDT, which, depending on how it is used, can be a blessing or a curse. The DDT used to kill mosquitos has saved millions from a painful death via malaria. Coal tar has been used to develop a number of topical medications for different skin diseases, according to a Drugsite Trust website.[1]

2. The Downside of Coal Mining

Although employment is generally a positive condition, and coal mining employs many people, that is not a good reason to ignore the negative aspects of coal mining:

a. Mountaintop Mining

Mountaintop mining involves removing the soil covering a mountain and the forest growing there to get to the coal underneath.[2] This process doubles the effect of global warming. The trees cannot absorb the carbon from the coal they once grew over, because the trees will be dead by the time the coal is burned. As the leaves and wood of the dead forest trees decay, even more carbon will be released into the atmosphere. Mountaintop removal has advantages for the coal companies, but it's a lose/lose proposition for environmental quality and for those of us who will suffer from the negative effects of global warming.

b. Coal Fires

Burning coal beds and refuse banks and underground coal mine fires can last for years. These are sources of pollution that have the potential to affect public health negatively, according to Robert B. Finkelman's "Potential health impacts of burning coal beds and waste banks."[3]

c. Acid Mine Drainage (AMD)

According to an article by J. Raymund Hoffert of the Pennsylvania Department of Health, most coal mines discharge acid-impregnated mine water. Streams and other waterways contaminated with AMD cannot maintain a healthy pH balance. In some cases, algae, insects, and fish are not able to survive in these waterways.[4]

d. Mine Subsidence

Old coal mine shafts, sinkholes, and troughs have resulted in very serious property damage due to mine subsidence.[5]

e. Black Lung Disease

Black lung disease, resulting from the inhalation of coal dust, is also a significant aspect of the downside of coal mining. In 1969, the federal government amended provisions of the law regarding black lung disease compensation. According to a Center for Public Integrity (CPI) article by Chris Hamby, entitled "Black lung surges back in coal country," the deaths of seventy-five thousand Americans were related to black lung disease between 1968 and 2007. After the 1969 law went into effect, the number of black lung cases decreased until the late 1990s, when the incidence of the disease increased.

Many of the newer cases have taken a particularly ugly form. While rates of black lung overall have increased, incidence of the most severe, fast-progressing type has jumped significantly. These cases, moreover, are occurring in younger and younger miners. (Washington, DC, 2012, http://www.publicintegrity.org/2012/07/08/9293/black-lung-surges-back-coal-country)

According to this CPI article, no one seems to know why the incidence of black lung is increasing. The rules regarding exposure are decades old and are allegedly not well enforced by government inspectors. Also, mining conditions and methods have changed. An increased exposure to fine silica dust is one possible explanation.[6]

f. Waste Slurry Ponds

A *Washington Post* article, "Oversight Report of Compaction of Coal Mine Waste Slurry Impoundment Embankments," informs the reader that coal extracted from the earth is "cleaned" of rocks, debris, and heavy metals using water. The resulting mixture of water and impurities is called sludge or slurry. This waste is stored in sludge ponds. Coal sludge ponds are created by damming valleys with earth and rocks. They are sometimes constructed over closed underground coal mines. The reliability of the sludge remaining contained within the ponds is questionable. Continued containment depends on the density of the dam holding back the sludge.[7] Containment may also depend on the resistance of the floor of the sludge pond to breaking through to any underground mines.

This is what caused the Martin County, Kentucky, sludge spill on October 11, 2000. An estimated 306 million gallons of sludge (about thirty times more than the oil spilled by the *Exxon Valdez*) flowed down two different streams, killing all aquatic life in those streams; covered the yards of residents; contaminated the drinking water of thousands; and polluted hundreds of miles of rivers. Was this just an unavoidable accident? The company, Martin County Coal, was aware of a smaller break in the same pond in May 1994.[8] The company neither relocated the sludge to a more secure location nor effectively plugged the underground mine entrances.

How large is the potential hazard? A *Washington Post* article by Juliet Eilperin and Steven Mufson, "Many Coal Sludge Impoundments Have Weak Walls, Federal Study Says," notes, "There are 596 coal slurry impoundments in 21 states, according to the Mine Safety and Health Administration" (April 24, 2013, https://www.washingtonpost.com/national/health-science/many-coal-sludge-impoundments-have-weak-walls-federal-study-says/2013/04/24/76c5be2a-acf9-11e2-a8b9-2a63d75b5459_story.html).

3. The Downside of Coal-Generated Electricity

Having enough electricity on which we can rely is a legitimate concern. But there are other concerns when it comes to burning coal to create that energy:

a. Greenhouse Effect

Fossil fuels contain lots of carbon. When fossil fuels like coal, petroleum, and natural gas are burned, that carbon is released into the air. Most weather scientists agree that there is a positive correlation between the concentration of carbon in the earth's atmosphere and an increase in general atmospheric temperature. The sunlight that reaches earth is converted to heat, and that heat is trapped by atmospheric greenhouse gases like carbon dioxide and methane. The increased carbon compounds in the air act like the glass of a greenhouse that lets light in but traps the heat created by the sunlight inside the greenhouse. The results of higher global temperature include a rise in ocean levels, more violent and frequent storms, forest and brush fires, and crop failures. Despite these effects being quite real and evident, some people deny that this greenhouse effect is real.

b. Acid Precipitation

The greenhouse effect is not the only negative aspect of coal burning. Another is acid precipitation, which includes not only acid rain but also acid fog or mist, acid snow, acid dust, and acid gas. In regard to the different forms of acid precipitation, according to the US EPA's "Overview of the Clean Air Act and Air Pollution,"

> **All of these can be formed in the atmosphere and fall to Earth causing human health problems, hazy skies, environmental problems and property damage ... Sulfur dioxide (SO_2) and nitrogen oxides (NOx) are the principal pollutants that cause acid precipitation ... Power plants burning coal and heavy oil produce over two-thirds of the annual SO_2 emissions in the United States.** (November 17, 2015, accessed December 29, 2015, http://www.epa.gov/clean-air-act-overview)

"Prospects; Acid Rain Costs Money," a *New York Times* article by Kenneth Gilpin, states that economist Thomas Crocker of the University of Wyoming "estimates that damages to materials, forests, lakes and agriculture attributable to acid rain amount to $5 billion annually" (April 26, 1981, accessed December 29, 2015, http://www.nytimes.com/1981/04/26/business/prospects-acid-rain-costs-money.html). This was in relation to the northeastern United States and Canada and was written in 1981.

c. Heavy Metal Pollution

A third downside of coal burning is heavy metal pollution. At the end of 2011, power plants fired by coal and oil were responsible for 62 percent of the arsenic pollution in the country and 50 percent of the mercury pollution, according to the EPA's "Cleaner Power Plants" webpage.[9]

"Adverse Health Effects of Heavy Metals in Children" has more information on the dangers of heavy metals and other chemicals, particularly for children.[10]

d. Fine Particulate Matter

Coal-burning power plants emit fine particulate matter into the air. Inhaling these particulates can negatively affect one's lungs and heart and cause serious illness, according to EPA.[11] The EPA expects an increase in greenhouse gasses (GHG) to result in an increase in particulate pollution and a corresponding increase in premature deaths. The agency states that global mitigation (lessening of 2015 levels of GHG) would "prevent an estimated 13,000 premature deaths in 2050 and 57,000 premature deaths in 2100. Economic benefits to the U.S. of avoided premature deaths are estimated at $160 billion in 2050, and $930 billion in 2100" ("Air Quality," U.S. Environmental Protection Agency, accessed July 30, 2016, https://www.epa.gov/sites/production/files/2015-06/documents/airquality.pdf).

C. Support for Coal-Generated Electricity

Not all fossil fuels are of equal quality. According to National Resources Defense Council (NRDC), coal is the dirtiest source of energy used in this country.[12] The US Energy Information Administration's "Frequently Asked Questions" web page reports that energy produced from burning natural gas results in almost 50 percent less carbon dioxide than does the burning of coal to produce an equal amount of energy.[13]

According to a report from the Union of Concerned Scientists, "Ripe for Retirement: The Case for Closing America's Costliest Coal Plants," as of 2011, 353 out of 1,169 coal generating plants in thirty-one states were ripe for retirement. They were reportedly "old, inefficient, dirty, and no longer economically competitive" (Cambridge, MA, December 2012, accessed December 30, 2015, http://www.ucsusa.org/clean_energy/smart-energy-solutions/decrease-coal/ripe-for-retirement-closing-americas-costliest-coal-plants.html#.WDS9cfQ8bIo).

So why keep them operating? If older coal-powered plants close but are not replaced by new coal-burning plants, we could reasonably expect the price of coal to increase and its demand to decrease—that is, unless the plants that remain open decide to operate, if possible, at a greater capacity than they do now. As the demand for coal decreases, the number of coal-industry jobs will decrease. This is bound to happen eventually if and when all coal has been removed from the ground. But politicians stay in office by keeping the voters from their districts and states happy. The suggestion that we might be better off without the problems related to burning coal—including global warming, mine subsidence, mountaintop removal, instable slurry ponds, coal fires, acid precipitation, and acidic streams—is not politically popular in coal-mining country.

The coal industry does employ many people, some of whom cannot imagine making a living any other way. Let's imagine the United States is one big corporation, and the other countries of the world are competing corporations. In that scenario, coal as a source of energy would not be preferable to solar and wind. Energy production is a business expense. Coal has to be dug out of the ground and transported to refining plants. The refined coal then has to be transported to factories or power plants. It must then be burned. The pollution from the burned coal causes disease and damages property. The whole process of using coal for energy is costly in terms of manpower (labor), the energy consumed, and the resulting health and property damages.

Solar energy can be passively collected from the sun and transported over existing transmission lines to any point where it is needed. It does not cause millions in health and property damages. It does not require much energy or manpower to collect and transmit. In short, if the country was a corporation, wind- and solar-generated electricity would decrease the overhead costs of operation.

One can find charts on the Internet that demonstrate that the energy yield from conventional oil is greater per unit of required energy than an alternative energy source like wind. The chart makers calculate the energy necessary to construct the concrete base of the windmill and its constituent parts. For this calculation to be accurate, I would think the chart maker would have to know how long the average wind turbine is expected to last and the total amount of energy it is expected to produce during its "life." These energy yield comparisons between conventional and alternative forms of energy seem neither particularly helpful nor necessarily accurate.

Yes, solar and wind generation requires fewer jobs than getting power from coal. But if the United States were a corporation, lower overhead expense would mean more profit and would make our nation more competitive.

In regard to American businesses competing in the world marketplace, some people believe that increased automation would have a positive effect on the economy. That makes sense in that labor is the most expensive cost of many businesses. Businesses in other countries pay their workers less, thus enabling those businesses to sell less-expensive products. Less-expensive products make their businesses more competitive. Products produced with automation should theoretically be less expensive than the same products produced by foreign workers earning a fraction of what American workers make.

Because most of the fifty states are not major coal producers, it seems logical to conclude that the coal industry must be supported by many congressional representatives who do not represent these coal-mining states. This may make you wonder why noncoal state representatives favor the use of coal as an energy source. You may also wonder how much of their personal earnings our congressional representatives have invested in the fossil fuel industry. Or you may ask yourself how much money the fossil fuel industry adds to politicians' campaign coffers.

The answers to these questions may suggest that the politicians' claims about being concerned about coal miners losing jobs is not the real reason they support the coal industry and oppose the EPA proposal to limit carbon dioxide from coal-burning electric plants. If our federal representatives really cared about their constituents, they would raise taxes on the very rich, whose fortunes have been enhanced by their investments in the fossil fuel industries. They would use that extra federal income to gainfully employ laid-off coal workers to remediate the environmental damage caused by the last two centuries of coal mining in the United States.

Is this jobs proposal socialistic rather than capitalistic? If *socialism* refers to a system that enhances the common good while prioritizing our individual inalienable rights and capitalism refers to that which financially benefits the upper 1 percent, then, yes, this jobs proposal is socialistic rather than capitalistic. If the upper 1 percent were benevolent dictators using their vast wealth and influence to enhance the common good while protecting our individual inalienable rights, that would be nice. But the goal/ideal of capitalism has nothing to do with what benefits everyone. The goal of capitalism is self-profit, and the ideal is greed. For evidence of this, check out www.savingrepublic.blogspot. com (R. Geiger, "Is the U.S. a Plutocracy? Who Cares?," *Plutocracy Now!* February 8, 2014, sect. A).

There is another possible explanation for the resistance of certain powerful people in our society to the proposed EPA carbon emissions standard for coal-burning power plants. Might it be all about political power? To control the food supply is to control life. What about controlling the energy supply? Alternative sources of energy like wind and solar don't need to be supplied through the grid. Might those who now control the energy industry feel threatened by the possibility of average citizens being able to afford to meet their energy needs without having to purchase fossil fuels?

D. Oil and Natural Gas

1. The Upside of Oil and Natural Gas

Employment in the oil and gas industry has grown faster than employment in the rest of the private sector since 2007, according to the United States Energy Information Administration's "Today in Energy" web page.[14]

An *American Laboratory* article by Mukta Shukla and Ashok Shukla, entitled "A Look into the Petrochemical Industry," states,

> **According to the American Petroleum Institute (API), "The oil and natural gas industry is the backbone of the American economy." This industry provides and supports over 9 million American jobs and adds about $1 trillion to the U.S. economy (about 7.5 percent of GDP), according to the API**. (*American Laboratory* article by Mukta Shukla and Ashok Shukla January 2012, 44, no. 1, accessed December 30, 2015, http://www.americanlaboratory.com/914-Application-Notes/37318-A-Look-Into-the-Petrochemicals-Industry/)

An article by Sheryl Joaquin points out that petroleum must be located, extracted, refined, and shipped. Many waxes and oils made from petroleum must be manufactured and marketed. These activities employ millions of people worldwide.[15]

2. The Downside of Oil and Natural Gas

Despite the positive aspects of petrochemical production and certain helpful products produced from petrochemicals, we should not ignore the negative aspects of petrochemical extraction and use:

a. Blowouts

> A blowout is one hazard of oil and gas wells. According to OilGasGlossary.com's "Hydraulic Fracturing," a blowout is "an uncontrolled flow of gas, oil, or other well fluids into the atmosphere or into an underground formation" (2014, accessed December 30, 2015, http://oilgasglossary.com/blowout.html). A random spark can cause a blowout to ignite. How frequent are

blowouts and similar oil and gas well problems? "Blowouts and Well Control Problems" states that, in Texas, between January 2011 and May 2015, there were ninety-six reported blowouts and well control problems.[16]

b. Environmental Effects of Oil Drilling.

According to the Rainforest Foundation's "Oil" web page, there are a number of possible negative effects of oil drilling on the nearby ecosystem. The pipes used to extract and transport the oil can corrode, resulting in ruptured pipes and contamination of the surrounding land and water. Contamination can also occur from large, unlined, open waste pits. Then there is air pollution from dust and from the burning of the natural gas found in oil fields. Oil spills and illegal dumping can devastate entire ecosystems. The health of those living near oil wells can also suffer ill effects.[17]

c. Oil Spills

According to "More Oil Spilled from Trains in 2013 Than in Previous 4 Decades, Federal Data Show" by Curtis Tate, in 2013, in the United States, rail tankers carrying crude oil spilled more crude than had been spilled "in the nearly four decades since the federal government began collecting data on such spills ... Including major derailments in Alabama and North Dakota, more than 1.15 million gallons of crude oil was spilled from rail cars in 2013, according to data from the Pipeline and Hazardous Materials Safety Administration" (McClatchyDC, Washington, DC, January 20, 2014: accessed December 30, 2015, http://www.mcclatchydc.com/news/nation-world/national/economy/article24761968.html).

According to the *New York Times* web page "Business Day—Energy and Environment," from 1990 to June 2011, more than 110 million gallons of mostly crude and petroleum products were spilled from the nation's mainland pipeline network. You can check out the map of the national pipelines and spill locations on this web page.[18] An article from *Business Insider* by Robert Wile reported that vehicles transporting oil on the roads spilled more than 7.5 million gallons between 1980 and 2003.[19] Then there have been many accidental oil spills into the world's oceans like the *Exxon Valdez* spill in 1989 and the BP Deepwater Horizon drilling rig explosion and spill in 2010.

"How Crude Oil Toxins and Petrochemicals Affect Your Health," by Edward C. on HubPages.com, discusses the dangers to our health posed by spilled oil.[20] Not only do oil spills pose a hazard to our health and the environment, they also are costly to clean up. The National Oceanic and Atmospheric Administration, Office of Response and Restoration, has information on the expense of cleaning up oil spills on its "Oil and Chemical Spills" web page.[21]

d. Effects of Hydraulic Fracking

Hydraulic fracking is a process of forcing millions of gallons of water and sand as well as a number of chemicals into shale rock to break up the rock and release the natural gas or oil trapped there. The possible negative effects of hydro fracking include damage to trees and wildlife from the containment ponds for the fracking wastewater. Destruction of trees to build roads to well sites, noise pollution, air pollution from dust raised by vehicles going to and from the site, leaking well heads, groundwater and well water contamination, fracking-induced earthquakes, and spoiling natural rural landscapes are other environmental problems that can occur. For more information, check out "The Inside Scoop on Fracking in the United States."[22]

e. Plastics

Without oil wells, there would probably not be as much plastic in the world. According to "Impact of Plastics on Human Health and

Ecosystems" at newsmedical.net, "The manufacture of plastics currently accounts for about 8 percent of the world's petroleum use" (AZoM.com, March 20, 2010, accessed January 2, 2016, http://www.news-medical.net/news/20100320/Impact-of-plastics-on-human-health-and-ecosystems.aspx). Although plastics have made our lives easier and added convenience, plastics also have some disadvantages.

f. Plastic Waste

When we are done using plastic products and products containing plastic parts, we tend to throw the products away. But what happens to the plastic we discard? Food, paper, and wood are biodegraded—that is, consumed by microorganisms. This does not happen to plastic waste. So, what do we do with the plastic we no longer want? Some plastics are recyclable. But that does not guarantee that they will not end up in a landfill. According to "Plastic Biodegradation in Landfills" by Galem Killam at Green Plastics.com, plastics are responsible for 20 to 25 percent of the total weight of municipal solid waste in landfills.[23] Some plastic litter, like deflated helium-filled balloons, have been consumed by wild animals, which resulted in their suffering and death, according to Jessica Tucker.[24] Some plastic litter becomes part of the Pacific Ocean's Plastic Trash Island, according to Tia Ghose.[25]

g. Dioxins

Another fate that some plastic waste meets is burning. According to the "Dangerous Health Effects of Home Burning of Plastics and Waste" fact sheet, burning certain plastics, like PVC, emit carcinogenic chemical dioxins into the air. When these toxins fall to earth, animals and plants can absorb them. If humans eat these plants or animals, the dioxins are stored in their body fat. The dioxins can pass through the placenta of pregnant women and enter the fetus. Dioxins resist chemical breakdown and are disruptive to human hormones.[26]

h. Polystyrene

Another problematic plastic is polystyrene, also known by the brand-name Styrofoam. This plastic is made with hydrofluorocarbons (HFCs), which are responsible for depletion of the ozone layer. The ozone layer is a thin layer of gas in the earth's stratosphere that filters out harmful ultraviolet wavelengths of sunlight.

Hydrofluorocarbons are released from polystyrene during the storage, use, and disposal of the finished foam products. Once released, the HFCs gradually rise to the level of the stratosphere, where they form chlorine molecules in the presence of sunlight. The chlorine molecules, which can last for 150 years, destroy ozone molecules.

In the absence of light and water, polystyrene remains unchanged for five hundred years. Recycling of polystyrene is possible but is often not economical.[27] If burned at extremely high temperatures, polystyrene supposedly does not pose a hazard to human health, although it still produces carbon dioxide. Burning at lower temperature, such as in a bonfire, releases toxins into the air. For more information, see EPA's "Ozone Science: The Facts Behind the Phaseout."[28]

i. BPA and Phthalates

According to "Impact of plastics on human health and ecosystems," the newsmedical.net article referred to above, "Two broad classes of plastic-related chemicals are of critical concern for human health—bisphenol-A or BPA, and additives used in the synthesis of plastics, which are known as phthalates." According to "FDA Continues to Study BPA," although we can ingest small amounts of BPA with the food from plastic-lined food containers, and although animal studies have shown potential health concerns, the FDA claims that BPA does not pose a hazard to human health.[29]

The newsmedical.net article mentioned above is concerned about the toxic chemicals that are used to form BPA. It might be that the hormone-disrupting effects of BPA occur only after the chemical bonds of BPA molecules have been broken. According to the article, these bonds can be broken from the repeated washing, heating, or other stressing of polycarbonate plastics.

The Centers for Disease Control and Prevention's "National Biomonitoring Program" web page reports, "Human health effects from exposure to low levels of phthalates are unknown. Some types of phthalates have affected the reproductive system of laboratory animals" (April 21 2015: accessed January 2, 2016, http://www.cdc.gov/biomonitoring/Phthalates_FactSheet.html). This article notes that more research is needed.

The approaches taken by the CDC and the FDA are in opposition to Pope Francis's recommendation as stated in *Laudato Si*. This pope says that where there is reason to believe a serious physical threat might exist, a cautious approach is best, even in the absence of definite proof.[30] This preventive approach would protect our rights to life and to live without unnecessary threats to our health and to environmental quality. In American society, economic interests often take priority over health concerns. The ideal policy would be to keep BPA and phthalates from coming into contact with the food we consume. Simple, really.

j. Petrochemicals

Petrochemicals are chemical substances derived from fossil fuels and used in a variety of products, including cosmetics, processed foods, pesticides, and fertilizers. The *American Laboratory* article by Shukla and Shukla states,

Many of these chemicals are released into the ground, and air, and water and can have adverse effects on our environment and human life. Depending on their use, since petrochemicals can be absorbed through the skin or might be ingested, they can accumulate in human tissues and organs such as the brain and liver and can cause brain, nerve and liver damage, birth defects, cancer, asthma, hormonal disorders, and allergies. (Mukta Shukla and Ashok Shukla, "A Look into the Petrochemical Industry," *American Laboratory*, January 2012, 44, no. 1, accessed December 30, 2015, http://www.americanlaboratory.com/914-Application-Notes/37318-A-Look-Into-the-Petrochemicals-Industry/)

k. Skin Care Products

An article at the Naturally Balmy website, "The Dangers of Petrochemicals," claims that skin care products containing petrochemicals like mineral oil and petroleum jelly "create an unnatural layer of grease over the skin, preventing it from breathing properly as your skin perspires underneath. As a result, sweat and bacteria are trapped underneath, exacerbating conditions such as eczema and creating a false dependency in the long term" (May 16, 2013, accessed January 16, 2016, http://www.naturallybalmy.co.uk/blog/read_75909/the-dangers-of-petrochemicals.htm).

l. Gasoline

Petroleum is used to make asphalt, synthetic rubber, and paraffin wax. But its main use is fuel (gasoline, jet fuel, heating oil). A number of compounds can be distilled from crude oil, including gasoline, diesel fuel, fuel oil, kerosene, lubricating oils, some types of alcohol, benzene, heavy naphtha, and residuum, according to Joaquin.[31]

The population of the world is increasing at a faster rate than the population of the United States. At this writing, our total population is about 4 percent of the total number of people in the world. According to the United States Energy Information Administration's 2104 article "How much gasoline does the United States consume?" about 3.26 billion barrels (one barrel equals forty-two US gallons) of gasoline were consumed.[32]

At least one possible reason we use so much gasoline is that we have more motor vehicles per capita than most of the world's countries, according to Lubrita.com.[33]

According to "How can 6 pounds of gasoline create 19 pounds of carbon dioxide?" at www.fueleconomy.gov, burning that much gasoline produces nineteen pounds of carbon dioxide.[34] The Union of Concerned Scientists (UCS)'s web page "Cars, Trucks, and Air Pollution" states that "in 2013, transportation contributed more than half of the carbon monoxide and nitrogen oxides, and almost a quarter of the hydrocarbons emitted into our air" (December 5 2014: accessed January 2, 2015, http://www.ucsusa.org/clean-vehicles/vehicles-air-pollution-and-human-health/cars-trucks-air-pollution#.Vog3uV7UWSp). Particulate matter, hydrocarbons, carbon monoxide, sulfur dioxide, nitrogen oxides, hydrocarbons, greenhouse gases, and hazardous air toxics are the major pollutants emitted with the exhaust of gasoline-powered vehicles, according to the UCS.

m. DDT

A number of chemicals would not have been produced in huge quantities if it weren't for fossil fuels. For example, "Biting One's Own Tail: The History of Benzene" states, "In 1849, Charles Mansfield perfected a method for extracting benzene from coal tar on industrial scales" (Human Touch of Chemistry, accessed January 2, 2016, http://www.humantouchofchemistry.com/biting-ones-own-tail-the-history-of-benzene.htm).

Benzene is also produced from petroleum. Without fossil fuels, benzene might have never been produced in large quantities.

Without large quantities of benzene, there would not be enough of a derivative called chlorobenzene to produce massive amounts of DDT. Chlorobenzene is an essential ingredient of the pesticide DDT, which was banned from agricultural use in the United States in 1972. Many believe the ban saved our national symbol, the bald eagle, from extinction.

Steven Milloy of Fox News would probably disagree. He presents an argument that DDT was not the culprit in the lethal thinning of bald eagle eggshells. He does not deny that was a problem, but suggests the cause was not DDT. He writes, "The potential culprits are many. Some that have been reported in the scientific literature include: oil; lead; mercury" ("Bald Eagle-DDT Myth Still Flying High," July 6 2006, http://www.foxnews.com/story/2006/07/06/bald-eagle-ddt-myth-still-flying-high.html). This list of alternatives does not let the fossil fuel industry off the hook for possibly contributing to the diminished numbers of bald eagles. Oil is a fossil fuel; lead was added to gasoline until the 1970s; half of mercury emissions come from burning coal. Perhaps it was a coincidence that eagle shells stopped thinning after the DDT ban.

Some people believe DDT should not have been banned from agricultural use in the United States because it is an effective deterrent to mosquitoes that transmit malaria. In fact, DDT is still used to eradicate malaria in other countries. I have no problem with DDT being used to control mosquitos when other methods fail. However, it is not a practical deterrent in certain types of terrain. And in some areas, mosquitos have developed resistance to DDT, according to Liverpool School of Tropical Medicine.[35]

DDT accumulates in the fatty tissues of our bodies and can be passed from mother to child via breast milk. Tripod.com's "DDT—Effects on the Environment" states that "You will die if you have a concentration above two hundred thirty-six mg of DDT per kg of body weight. Concentration of 6–10 mg/kg leads to symptoms like headache, nausea, vomiting, confusion, and tremors" (accessed January 21, 2016, xhawkbio2.tripod.com/ddt/id4.html).

E. The Altered Ecosystem

This section contains some personal speculative ideas that I believe are unique and not scientifically verified. The reader who cares only about factual knowledge should feel free to skip this section.

Many people accept the theory that fossil fuels come from thick layers of marine plankton or land vegetation buried in the ground and exposed to heat and pressure in the earth's crust over millions of years. But what killed the living organisms that were eventually turned into fossil fuels? The massive quantities of sulfur, nitrogen, mercury, arsenic, cadmium, and other toxic heavy metals released during the burning of fossil fuels suggests to me that the amounts of these elements both on and near the earth's surface and in its oceans today are less than the amounts before the formation of fossil fuels.

The plants living millions of years ago might have bioaccumulated these elements over many generations. According to *The Facts on File Dictionary of Ecology and the Environment*, edited by Jill Bailey, bioaccumulation is "the accumulation of pollutants and other toxins in the tissues of living organisms" (New York: Market House Books, 2004, s.v. "bioaccumulation").

Bioaccumulation happens in organisms when more of a toxin is inhaled, absorbed, or ingested than is excreted or metabolized into something nontoxic. Bioaccumulation is a problem for an organism when its tolerance level for the toxin is exceeded. For example, as noted above, if your body accumulates more than 236 milligrams of DDT per kilogram of body weight, your body will die because its tolerance level for DDT would have been exceeded.

Living organisms have tolerance levels for various toxins, including arsenic and mercury. Exceeding those tolerance levels can kill the organisms. I wonder whether the heavy concentrations of certain elements, which were evidently much more common in ecosystems of eons past, led to massive extinctions of whole species, the remains of which eventually became buried deep in the earth. These mass extinctions may have happened repeatedly through the eons; each time, more of the toxic elements would have been sequestered in the dead organisms. To sequester means to separate or to "capture" and store. In this book, sequestration refers to the long-term imprisoning of elements.

Carbon is an element. It exists in a number of forms, including an atom of a molecule of carbon dioxide (CO_2). Plants "inhale" CO_2 through their leaves. The carbon atoms become part of the plant, and the oxygen atoms are "exhaled." The carbon remains sequestered or imprisoned in the plant until the plant dies or is eaten. Trees are efficient sequesters of carbon because of their large size and because they can live for a long time and take a long time to decay. Once a plant dies and decays, the carbon is eventually released from its "imprisonment."

Fossil fuels have been imprisoning carbon and large quantities of heavy metals, nitrogen, and sulfur for millions of years. Each time massive quantities of organic matter were buried deep in the earth, there was less sulfur, nitrogen, heavy metals, and carbon left in the ecosystem. Most species of plants and animals living today did not exist millions of years ago. I wonder whether we could have survived in those more toxic environments of the distant past. Perhaps we should not be surprised if certain species of plants and animals, including us, that did not exist millions of years ago suffer negative effects from the release of formerly sequestered toxins. Those species include honey bees (see "What's killing the honey bees? Mystery may be solved"[36]), monarch butterflies (see "Monsanto blamed for disappearance of monarch butterflies"[37]), bald eagles, and red spruce trees (see "Acid Rain"[38]). Might these not be compared to the proverbial canary in the coal mine?

F. The End of Fossil Fuels

If we keep extracting fossil fuels from the earth, eventually there will be no more left. That is why they are called *nonrenewable* sources of energy. One source I read predicted an end to fossil fuels as our main source of energy by 2050. Walter Youngquist of Negative Population Growth claims that "the ongoing depletion rate of existing oil fields will ensure the end of significant commercial oil production before 2100" ("A Geomoment of Affluence between Two Austere Eras," June 2015, accessed January 3, 2016, http://www.npg.org/wp-content/uploads/2015/07/2015-Geomoment-Forum-Paperrev070715.pdf?utm_source=7%2F7+email+-+corrected&utm_campaign=email+7%2F7+-+revised&utm_medium=email).

Other sources, like the Institute for Energy Research's "North American Energy Inventory," contend that there are enough fossil fuels in North America alone to satisfy the energy needs of the United States at the present rate of use for more than a thousand years.[39] I am not sure how the energy needs of Mexico and Canada figure into this estimate. Also, one may wonder whether that estimate accounts for the fossil fuels *extracted* from the ground of North America but *exported* to other continents. Then there is the issue of cost. The more inaccessible the fossil fuels are and the more difficult it is to refine them, the more the actual cost of fossil-fuel-generated energy escalates.

The estimates vary, but no one is suggesting fossil fuels will supply the energy we need forever. If we keep drilling and mining, we will eventually run out of fossil fuels. How badly and how rapidly we will further disrupt the climate, flora, fauna, and human health before the last of the fossil fuels are consumed remains to be seen.

Pope Francis's *Laudato Si* (Section 106) points out that the earth does not possess infinite energy and natural resources. Acting as though it does will lead to a depletion of nonrenewable resources and to negative effects to which the earth cannot easily adjust.[40]

The next chapter explores possible future energy sources and usage.

1   "Coal Tar Products List," Drugs.com, Drugsite Trust, 2016, accessed June 18, 2016, https://www.drugs.com/search.php?searchterm=coal+tar.

2   "What Is Mountaintop Removal Mining?" Earth Justice, 2015, accessed December 29, 2015, http://earthjustice.org/features/campaigns/what-is-mountaintop-removal-mining#.

3   Robert B. Finkelman, "Potential Health Impacts of Burning Coal beds and Waste Banks," *International Journal of Coal Geology* 59 (July 12, 2004): 19–24, doi:10.1016/j.coal.2003.11.002.

4   J. Raymund Hoffert, "Acid Mine Drainage," *Industrial and Engineering Chemistry* 39, no. 5 (May 1947): 642–646, doi: 10.1021/ie50449a020.

5   Kentucky Department of Insurance, "Mine Subsidence Fund," 2015, http://insurance.ky.gov/static_info.aspx?static_id=23&Div_id=15.

6   Chris Hamby, "Black lung surges back in coal country," Center for Public Integrity, Washington, DC, 2012, http://www.publicintegrity.org/2012/07/08/9293/black-lung-surges-back-coal-country.

7   "Office of Surface Mining: Oversight Report of Compaction of Coal Mine Waste Slurry Impoundment Embankments, I. Executive Summary," *Washington Post,* 2011, accessed January 13, 2016, http://www.washingtonpost.com/wp-srv/politics/documents/Coal-Refuse-Dams-OSM-Compaction-Study.pdf.

8   "Martin County Sludge Spill," Sourcewatch, May 23, 2012, accessed January 13, 2016, http://www.sourcewatch.org/index.php?title=Martin_County_sludge_spill.

9   US EPA, "Cleaner Power Plants," June 10, 2016, https://www.epa.gov/mats/cleaner-power-plants#controls.

10 World Health Organization, "Adverse Health Effects of Heavy Metals in Children," October 2011, http://www.who.int/ceh/capacity/heavy_metals.pdf.

11 US EPA, "Particulate Matter (PM)," September 10, 2015, http://www3.epa.gov/pm/.

12 "Coal is Dirty and Dangerous," Natural Resources Defense Council, January 15, 2009, accessed December 30, 2015, http://www.nrdc.org/energy/coalnotclean.asp.

13 US Energy Information Administration, "Frequently Asked Questions," June 18, 2015, http://www.eia.gov/tools/faqs/faq.cfm?id=73&t=11.

[14]   US Energy Information Administration, "Today in Energy," August 8, 2013, http://www.eia.gov/todayinenergy/detail.cfm?id=12451.

[15]   Sheryl Joaquin, "Petroleum—Its Uses And Benefits," *EzineArticles,* October 10, 2007, accessed December 30, 2015, http://ezinearticles. com/?Petroleum---Its-Uses-And-Benefits&id=775224.

[16]   Railroad Commission of Texas, "Blowouts and Well Control Problems," July 20, 2015, http://www.rrc.state.tx.us/oil-gas/ compliance-enforcement/blowouts-and-well-control-problems/.

[17]   "Oil," Rainforest Foundation, 2015, accessed December 30, 2015, http:// www.rainforestfoundation.org/effects-oil-drilling-0/.

[18]   "Two Decades of Spills," Business Day—Energy & Environment, *New York Times,* September 9, 2011, accessed December 30, 2015, http://www. nytimes.com/interactive/2011/09/09/business/energy-environment/ pipeline-spills.html?_r=1&.

[19]   Robert Wile, "Tanker Trains Spill Far Less Oil than Pipelines or Trucks," *Business Insider,* July 8, 2013, accessed December 2015, http://www. businessinsider.com/oil-spills-by-mode-of-transport-2013-7.

[20]   Edward C., "How Crude Oil Toxins and Petrochemicals Affect Your Health," Hub Pages, June 10, 2010, accessed December 30, 2015, http://hubpages.com/health/ How-Crude-Oil-Toxins-and-Petrochemicals-Affect-Your-Health.

[21]   National Oceanic and Atmospheric Administration, "Oil and Chemical Spills," 2015, accessed December 30, 2015, http://response.restoration. noaa.gov/oil-and-chemical-spills.

[22]   Orit Nathan Mahalal, "The Inside Scoop on Fracking in the United States," Hub Pages, October 28, 2014, accessed December 30, 2015, http://hubpages. com/business/The-Inside-Scoop-on-Fracking-in-the-United-States.

[23]   Galem Killam, "Plastic Biodegradation in Landfills," Green Plastics, December 2, 2015, http://green-plastics.net/posts/45/ plastic-biodegradation-in-landfills/.

[24]   Jessica Tucker, "How Balloon Releases Harm Wildlife," One Green Planet, June 5, 2014, accessed May 12, 2016, http://www.onegreenplanet. org/animalsandnature/how-balloon-releases-harm-wildlife/.

[25]   Tia Ghose, "Plastic 'Trash Islands' Forming in Ocean Garbage Patch," *CBS News,* July 21, 2014, accessed January 2, 2016, http://www.cbsnews. com/news/plastic-trash-islands-forming-in-ocean-garbage-patch/.

[26]   "Dangerous Health Effects of Home Burning of Plastics and Waste," Women in Europe for a Common Future, accessed

November 27, 2016, http://www.wecf.eu/cms/download2004-2005/homeburning_plastics.pdf.

[27] Bertybign, "Can Polystyrene Be Recycled?" Yahoo Answers, 2009, accessed June 11, 2016, https://uk.answers.yahoo.com/question/index;_ylt=A0LEVjksZ1xXMtAAcf8nnIlQ;_ylu=X3oDMTE0anRnZ284BGNvbG8DYmYxBHBvcwMxBHZ0aWQDRkZVSTNDMV8xBHNlYwNzYw--?qid=20091208132516AAIDtM6&p=Can%20polystyrene%20be%20recycled?

[28] US EPA, "Ozone Science: The Facts Behind the Phaseout," August 19, 2010, http://www3.epa.gov/ozone/science/sc_fact.html.

[29] US FDA, "FDA Continues to Study BPA," January 29, 2015, http://www.fda.gov/ForConsumers/ConsumerUpdates/ucm297954.htm.

[30] Pope Francis, "Laudato Si On Care of Our Common Home," May 4, 2015, sect. 186, accessed January 2, 2015, http://w2.vatican.va/content/francesco/en/encyclicals/documents/papa-francesco_20150524_enciclica-laudato-si.html.

[31] Joaquin, "Petroleum—Its Uses And Benefits," *EzineArticles*, October 10, 2007, accessed December 30, 2015, http://ezinearticles.com/?Petroleum---Its-Uses-And-Benefits&id=775224.

[32] US Energy Information Administration, "How Much Gasoline Does the United States Consume?" 2014, http://www.eia.gov/tools/faqs/faq.cfm?id=23&t=10.

[33] "Interesting Statistic, List of Countries by Vehicles Per Capita," Lubrita, 2014, accessed January 2, 2016, http://www.lubrita.com/news/45/671/Interesting-statistic-list-of-countries-by-vehicles-per-capita/.

[34] US Department of Energy, "How Can 6 Pounds of Gasoline Create 19 Pounds of Carbon Dioxide?" (n.d., accessed January 2, 2016, http://www.fueleconomy.gov/feg/contentIncludes/co2_inc.htm.

[35] Liverpool School of Tropical Medicine, "Genetic Secret of Mosquito Resistance to DDT, Bed Net Insecticides Discovered," *Science Daily*, February 24, 2014, accessed May 12, 2016, https://www.sciencedaily.com/releases/2014/02/140224204808.htm.

[36] "What's Killing the Honey Bees? Mystery May Be Solved," *CBS News*, May 14, 2014, accessed January 2, 2016, http://www.cbsnews.com/news/are-pesticides-killing-off-honey-bees/.

[37] "Monsanto Blamed for Disappearance of Monarch Butterflies," *RT News*, January 31, 2014, accessed January 2, 2016, https://www.rt.com/usa/monsanto-roundup-monarch-butterflies-483/.

[38] US EPA, "Acid Rain," February 4, 2012, http://www3.epa.gov/acidrain/effects/.

[39] "North American Energy Inventory," Institute for Energy Research, December 2011, accessed January 3, 2016, http://instituteforenergyresearch.org/wp-content/uploads/2013/01/Energy-Inventory.pdf.

[40] Pope Francis, "*Laudato Si* On Care of Our Common Home," sect. 106.

12

FOSSIL FUELS AND HUMAN RIGHTS, II

The previous chapter revealed a whole variety of disadvantages and abusive effects of using fossil fuels for energy and for the production of various consumer goods. This chapter will explore the potential future effects of energy production and usage in America. The following is an outline of the sections of this chapter.

A. **Alternative Energy:** What are other ways to produce electricity and to fuel motor vehicles? Which sources of energy are better?

B. **Nuclear Energy:** Is it a viable alternative to fossil fuels?

C. **An Ideal Scenario:** Is it possible to transition to alternative energy production and to reverse the effects of fossil fuel use while protecting our individual inalienable rights?

D. **The Actual Scenario:** Are Supreme Court decisions and the influence of the wealthiest citizens preserving the status quo and slowing down the national transition to alternative energy?

E. **Population:** What is the effect of world population growth on global warming?

F. **Toward a Solution:** What can individuals do to support the transition away from the nation's dependence on fossil fuels?

G. **Planning Ahead:** What are the possible negative and positive outcomes of future energy production and usage?

H. **Conclusion:** Are global warming deniers helping to perpetuate the negative effects of climate change? What steps could government take to speed the transition to alternative energy? How can we help?

A. Alternative Energy

Why not leave as many fossil fuels and their sequestered carbon and toxins in the ground as possible while we find other ways to meet our energy needs and while we deal with the excess carbon and other toxins that have already been released? One alternative would be to implement technology that would remove from fossil fuels all sulfur, nitrogen, and heavy metals. This would probably cost billions, however. And to prevent carbon emissions from fossil fuel burning could cost billions more. Of course, planting and nurturing millions of trees would help sequester excessive carbon, but there seems to be little enthusiasm for that.

Another alternative would be to develop renewable, nonpolluting, nontoxic alternate energy sources. There are sources of electricity other than fossil fuels. Most of the electricity we produce now is supplied by fossil fuels. The United States Energy Information Administration's "What is U.S. electricity generation by energy source?" reported that, according to preliminary information, about 4,093 billion kilowatt-hours of electricity were produced in 2014 in our country. Of that electricity, 39 percent was produced from burning coal, 27 percent from natural gas, and 1 percent from petroleum. The other 33 percent came from nuclear (19 percent), hydropower (6 percent), wind (4.4 percent), biomass (1.7 percent), geothermal (.4 percent), and solar (0.4 percent).[1]

It may have been possible to eliminate fossil-fuel-generated electricity in 2014 if 67 percent of the total power generated was unnecessary. Even so, that would have eliminated only 31 percent of greenhouse emissions according to the EPA's "Sources of Greenhouse Gas Emissions."[2] Let's imagine that we need 4,093 billion kilowatt-hours of electricity per year. Could that amount of electricity be provided with a combination of alternative sources like wind turbines, nuclear plants, geothermal, hydroelectric projects like Hoover Dam or the Tennessee Valley Association's Raccoon Mountain (see "Raccoon Mountain Pumped-Storage Plant"[3]), and microwave-induced plasma gasification technology? The latter sounds like a promising method for improving solid-waste management while producing useful energy, according to Bryan Sims's "Microwave-induced plasma gasification technology makes headway."[4] An article by Robert Wilson, "Can You Make a Wind Turbine Without Fossil Fuels?" points out that these types of alternative energy operations require lots of concrete and steel to construct and that making that concrete and steel cannot be achieved without using fossil fuels.[5]

Changing how we produce enough electricity will be challenging. Changing the way road motor vehicles are fueled might be even more challenging. An article by Sheryl Joaquin points out that

> **hydrogen, ethanol, hybrid, and biomass technologies are promising for automobiles and may soon increase efficiency and reduce emissions; but many of these technologies have not yet proven sufficiently profitable to providers or attractive to consumers. Petroleum retains a key advantage because the price of oil remains low compared to forms of energy with lower environmental impacts, like wind and solar power. Unlike hydrogen or even natural gas, oil is easily transportable and there is a vast infrastructure in place to support its use.** ("Petroleum—Its Uses And Benefits," *EzineArticles,* October 10, 2007, accessed December 30, 2015, http://ezinearticles. com/?Petroleum---Its-Uses-And-Benefits&id=775224.)

No technology is perfect. For example, some people object to wind turbines. If you hate all technology, a wind turbine may look as unattractive to you as a belching smokestack. And the spinning blades of wind turbines kill birds that get too close. Governments could refrain from permitting wind turbines in areas where migratory airborne animals travel and in areas where farming depends on bats or birds consuming large numbers of insect pests. We need to compare the downsides of oil, coal, and gas with the downsides of the alternative energy sources.

B. Nuclear Energy

I have been writing about alternative energy sources other than nuclear energy. The US Energy Information Administration classifies nuclear energy as an alternative energy source for electricity generation. This puts it in the same category as solar and wind. But radioactive elements in the earth seem to be more similar to fossil fuels than to the sun or the wind. Uranium is an abundant element and is the fuel for nuclear reactors. It is also the source of geothermal energy.

Humans are not responsible for all pollution from fossil fuels. Crude oil would probably be leaking from the ground in a few spots around the world even if there were no human beings on the planet. Methane would still form in bogs and be emitted from volcanoes. Lightning would still occasionally set fire to a naturally exposed coal seam. Likewise, radon, a radioactive carcinogenic gas, would still be emitted from the earth into the atmosphere. Breathing in radon gas can seriously affect your health. The EPA's "Are we sure that radon is a health risk?" points out that smoking is the only factor that causes more lung cancer than radon.[6]

In terms of preventing radon from entering buildings, the contractor who builds structures may or may not bother to sufficiently seal the foundation against radon infiltration and may or may not vent the basement to prevent a buildup of radon gas. Andrew Alden points out that radon comes from fractured uranium and that "radon is relatively high in uranium-rich rocks such as ancient granites, high-organic shales and coal beds" ("About Radon," About. com, 2016, http://geology.about.com/od/geophysics/a/aboutradon. htm?utm_term=radon%20gas%20in%20homes&utm_content=p1-main-7-title&utm_medium=sem&utm_source=msn&utm_campaign=adid-5f35ca58-c5f2-4cad-9814-bbc8d79e4d95-0-ab_msb_ocode-31640&ad =semD&an=msn_s&am=broad&q=rad).

Uranium that has not been mined can still have a negative effect on human health. For example, if uranium is fractured during an earthquake, the released radon could migrate into buildings, especially ones with cracked foundations. No human would be responsible for that either, unless the earthquake was induced by fracking. What if we had never used uranium to produce energy? Accidents like Fukushima (2011) and Chernobyl (1986) would not have occurred.

According to "Special Report: Accident in Japan" at atomicarchive. com, there have been seventeen major nuclear power plant accidents in the world between December 1952 and November 1999.[7] Some sources report a much higher incidence. The difference in numbers reported can be attributed to the definition of a "major accident."

Some argue that nuclear energy is safer than fossil fuels and all other alternative energy sources because the number of related fatalities per unit of energy produced is fewer for nuclear than other energy sources. But what about our concern for the common good and human health. An issue that the proponents of nuclear energy seem reluctant to address is nuclear waste. It is highly carcinogenic, and certain radioactive isotopes in the waste can last for millions of years. Iodine-129, for example, has a half-life of 15.7 million years, according to Don Dfoofnik at www.answers.com.[8]

According to the Nuclear Energy Industry's (NEI) "Nuclear Waste Management" web page, the federal government shirked its legal obligation to start removing nuclear fuel waste from nuclear power facilities in 1998. The NEI says that the United States Department of Energy is supposed to be developing a long-term storage facility for nuclear power plant waste.[9] Yucca Mountain, Nevada, had been proposed as a site. According to usnews.com writer Paul Bedard, in 2009, President Obama abandoned plans to use Yucca Mountain and formed a task force to explore alternatives.[10] The nuclear waste continues to be generated and stored at "reactor sites in steel-lined concrete pools filled with water, or in airtight steel or concrete-and-steel containers," according to "Nuclear Waste Management" (cited above).

There is also the problem of stored nuclear waste leaking from deteriorating containers into the ground. "Nuclear waste leaking at Hanford site in Washington, again," by John Upton, reports that the Hanford, Washington, nuclear site has been called "America's most contaminated nuclear site." That distinction might be related to its being in operation since the 1940s. The original purpose of the Hanford site was to develop plutonium for the bomb dropped on Hiroshima.[11]

Some people think it is possible to recycle or reuse waste from nuclear power plants to produce more power. At this point, that concept is purely theoretical.

The Greenpeace International article "The Deadly Legacy of Radioactive Waste" discusses nuclear waste handling solutions that different countries have attempted.[12] I'm not an expert, but it seems to me that deep underground would be a good place to put nuclear waste. The challenge is to make sure it stays put for millions of years. That means shielding the waste from the effects of earthquakes, floods, meteor strikes, and theft. I wonder whether that is even possible. Also, I think it might be less potentially hazardous to store the nuclear waste at a variety of sites rather than to concentrate it all in one place. A disadvantage of dispersal might be an increase in the storage cost. Unless the waste disposal problem is solved, nuclear power generation seems no more desirable than coal in terms of human rights.

We need energy to live and to survive. The issue is not which source of energy is the least threatening to our human rights. What we should ask is "How can energy systems be designed to preserve and promote inalienable rights and the common good for everyone's benefit?" The use of energy that kills us, makes us sick, destroys species, and degrades our environment needs to be eliminated and replaced with less destructive energy systems without further delay. Failure to do that prevents everyone from experiencing their individual inalienable rights.

C. An Ideal Scenario

An ideal rational approach would conserve as much energy as possible to preserve fossil fuels. Carbon, heavy metals, sulfur, nitrogen, and fine particulate matter would be prevented from being emitted from the necessary use of fossil fuels. Sequestering carbon dioxide and heavy metals from burning fossil fuels might require additional energy and might not be 100 percent effective, even after spending billions to implement it. The cost of using alternative nonpolluting energy sources needs to be weighed against the expense of sequestering carbon and heavy metals. An article at howstuffworks.com by Brian Merchant questions the practicality of removing carbon dioxide from burning coal to create so-called "clean coal."[13]

Ideally, we would identify and use effective, healthful alternatives to petrochemicals in foods, pesticides, cosmetics, and medications. We would plant millions of trees around the world. We would voluntarily reverse the world's runaway population growth to preserve the quality of human life. This decrease in population would allow more energy to be conserved. We would prioritize finding a reliable, affordable, nontoxic, nonpolluting renewable source of energy that would not rely on fossil fuels for its creation nor for its continuing operation.

Ideally, we would construct more alternative sources of energy, like wind turbines, sooner rather than later. Because the construction of many of these alternative energy production sources will require the use of fossil fuels, it would seem to me that it would be more economical for us to construct alternative sources like wind turbines and geothermal projects (see "Geothermal Heating District"[14]) before fossil fuels get scarcer and their expense escalates. To run out of fossil fuels before sufficient alternative energy sources are in place would be unfortunate. This is especially so if fossil fuels are exhausted before fusion is perfected (more info at http://sploid.gizmodo.com[15]) or some alternative energy generation process not dependent on fossil fuels is discovered.

D. The Actual Scenario

A University of Kentucky study by Garen, Jepsen, and Saunoris for that state's energy department found that as the price of coal, natural gas, and oil increases, the demand for these commodities decreases.[16] If I were asked whether I would be willing to pay more per kilowatt-hour of electricity in return for a higher standard of health and lower health care costs, my reply would be an enthusiastic yes. If you put that question to a manufacturer of expensive, nonessential luxury products, the answer would probably be negative if his or her business uses electricity from coal-powered plants. Why? If the coal-powered plant has to add pollution-controlling technology, the cost of doing that might be passed on to the consumers of the electricity.

If higher electric rates lead to increased expense of production, business owners must either decrease the cost of overhead or increase the prices of the items sold. Otherwise, their profit margins will suffer. Increasing prices might result in a decrease in the volume of products sold. Expensive luxury products are generally not within the price range of lower-income people who suffer the most from coal-powered electricity pollutants.[17] Therefore, increased energy prices are not so much a problem to the financially disadvantaged as they are to businesses. If increased energy prices lead to decreases in toxic pollution, higher fuel prices would have a beneficial effect on the health of the disadvantaged.

Decisions of Supreme Courts dominated by conservatives often benefit those with higher incomes to the detriment of lower-income folks. When trying to limit toxic pollutants like mercury and arsenic from coal-powered plants, the EPA was judged by the Supreme Court to have acted inappropriately. According to CNN Politics writer Ariane de Vogue,

> **In a loss for the Obama administration, the Supreme Court ruled that the EPA unreasonably interpreted the Clean Air Act when it decided to set limits on the emissions of toxic pollutants from power plants without first considering the costs on the industry to do so.** ("Supreme Court: EPA Unreasonably Interpreted the Clean Air Act," June 29 2015, accessed January 4, 2016, http://www.cnn.com/2015/06/29/politics/supreme-court-epa-emissions/index.html)

So, for the sake of keeping costs down (and demand steady or increasing) for coal-powered electricity generators, we citizens of the United States must endure less-than-optimum health conditions and higher health care costs. The Supreme Court's 5–4 decision against the EPA abused our inalienable individual rights to life and happiness.

In 2015, the EPA proposed the Clean Power Plan to reduce pollution from America's coal-generated power plants. Barbara Hollingsworth reported that the United States Senate voted to block this plan in November.[18] This is symptomatic of the culture of abuse in which inalienable individual rights are not actualized for every person.

E. Population

Achieving independence from fossil fuels will depend a lot on the population of the country and the world. More of us will always increase the need for more energy. Fewer of us can get along with less energy. Government policies that either encourage or reinforce population growth are counterproductive. Even if, through some miracle, mining and drilling for fossil fuels stopped, there would still be an excessive amount of carbon in the atmosphere and in the oceans for an extended period. While there is an increased amount of carbon, glaciers and polar ice caps will continue to melt; sea levels will continue to rise; more violent storms will occur; there will be more frequent forest and brush fires; and climactic conditions will continue to shift.

Animals, including humans, inhale oxygen and exhale carbon dioxide. Plants, including trees take in carbon dioxide and expel oxygen. Trees are great at sequestering carbon dioxide. The more of us there are in the world, the more carbon dioxide is exhaled. The fewer trees, the less carbon dioxide is sequestered.

The more of us there are, the more lumber from trees will be used to shelter us. Increased population leads to an increase in food production. Rainforest Concern's web page "Why Are They Being Destroyed?" states that much of the jungle in Central and South America has been burned down to make room for raising inexpensive cattle that are sold to Russia, China, and the United States.

It is estimated that for each pound of beef produced, 200 square feet of rainforest is destroyed ... However,

the land cannot be used for long: the soil is of poor quality and, without the forest, quickly becomes very dry. The grass often dies after only a few years and the land becomes a crusty desert. (2008, accessed January 4, 2016, http://www.rainforestconcern.org/rainforest_facts/why_are_they_being_destroyed/)

Rhett Butler of Mongabay.com points out that since 1978, more than 298,000 square miles of rainforest in the South American Amazon region has been destroyed.[19] This is a continuing trend and is not limited to South America. The more of us there are, the more trees will be needed to absorb the increased carbon dioxide we produce. But more people also increases the need for more food. So more trees will be destroyed to provide additional food. As the waste from the cut trees is burned or decays, more carbon will be released into the atmosphere.

That this is happening in the rainforest is particularly unfortunate. In the more temperate parts of the globe, trees lose their leaves for a number of months each year. When that happens, no sequestration of carbon dioxide occurs. In the tropics, trees don't lose their leaves. Sequestration occurs all year long.

It might be that global warming cannot be stopped without negative population growth—that is, more of us dying than are being born.

F. Toward a Solution

What can we do to change how we meet our energy needs in a way that would preserve more of the common good and our human rights? (See chapter 2, "Rights and the Common Good.") One thing would be to allow the cost of fossil-fuel-generated energy to increase. Without government subsidies and tax breaks to the oil, coal, and natural gas industries, the price of fossil-fuel-generated energy would increase. If compensation for the damage fossil fuel usage does to our environment, our property, and our health were included in the cost of fossil fuels and the energy they produce, the costs of alternative sources of energy would be more competitive.

Another positive step would be to decrease the amount of energy we waste. We Americans waste a lot of energy. Visit a mall or a library on a hot summer day and notice how absurdly low the inside temperature is. I realize that lower temperatures allow some people with asthma to breathe more comfortably. If that lower temperature is achieved with electricity from burning coal, more fine particulate matter is being added to the air. As a result, people with asthma will find it harder to breathe outside air.

Is there anything we as individuals can do on our own? Every little bit of energy you can avoid wasting makes a difference. For example, turning off an electric light no one needs is helpful. For more ideas, go to web pages like "20 Things You Can Do to Conserve Energy."[20] If you live in a state that is deregulated for electricity, you may be able to choose an energy supplier that can give you electricity for your domicile or business from alternative sources like solar and wind. There is a map of deregulated states at http://www.quantumgas.com.[21] Just because you live in a deregulated state does not necessarily mean you will be able to choose your own electricity supplier. For example, if you live in a senior citizen apartment in a deregulated state, every resident may be required to have the same provider.

Also, do some research before choosing an alternative energy supplier. I signed up with a company out of Texas that sold solar/wind generated electricity in Texas. I found out later that they did not sell that electricity to their Pennsylvania customers.

G. Planning Ahead

Consider the saying "Expect the best outcome, but plan for the worst." Americans don't seem to like to plan far ahead. I don't know how many times I heard growing up, "We'll cross that bridge when we come to it." In regard to the energy future of our nation and of the world, I think it unwise to wait until we reach the bridge. Or perhaps there is a plan in place to deal with the complete depletion of fossil fuels, but it is being kept hidden because it ensures the comfort and survival of only top government leaders and the very rich. That would explain why there is not a lot of concern being expressed by government leaders about the eventual and inevitable exhaustion of fossil fuels if the current rate of consumption continues or increases.

What is the worst that can happen in regard to our energy future? If government regulations designed to protect environmental quality are eliminated, our health will suffer because of huge additional emissions of heavy metals, more acid rain, and more exposure to carcinogens. This will, in turn, raise our health care costs. Even if government regulations remain unchanged, more fossil fuels will continue to be burned, and we will continue to be exposed to increasing bioaccumulation of heavy metals, carcinogens, and all the rest. This will result in increasing negative effects on our environment and on our health.

The worst scenario would involve fossil fuel supplies and reserves becoming so depleted that only the rich could afford to heat their homes and keep their family and company vehicles running on gasoline. In the worst outcome, the growth of the alternative energy supply system would not keep pace with the depletion of fossil fuels. There would not be enough fossil fuels left to expand, or even maintain, the existing alternative energy system. This would be unfortunate because, in this worst outcome, an abundant affordable nontoxic energy source whose implementation would not depend on fossil fuels would never be discovered/invented. With fossil fuels too expensive for most people to use and an insufficient supply of clean alternative fuel sources, those without energy would resort to heating their homes and cooking food with whatever wood and plastic they could find. This would result in greater deterioration of the quality of the environment and of human health. In this worst scenario, most people would have fewer opportunities to experience their inalienable rights than they do now.

Can we formulate a plan to avoid the nightmarish worst scenario? What would the best outcome be for our energy future? I think it would be quite positive if someone discovered or developed a simple, affordable, abundant energy source that would not result in hazardous emissions and toxic waste and that would not depend on fossil-fuel-generated energy for its practical application to heating, manufacturing, and transportation needs. In the best-possible scenario, that discovery would be made ASAP, preferably before human life is virtually hanging in the balance because of heavy metal contamination and global warming.

Without the development of the ideal energy source, the best outcome might involve establishing an alternative energy supply system sufficient for the needs of everyone on earth. This would involve a variety of sources like wind and solar for buildings and biomass and hydrogen for transportation. This system has already started and is growing, accounting for 7 percent of electricity generation in our country. We will need fossil fuels to expand the alternative energy supply system. In this best-outcome plan, we would complete the transition to the alternative energy system before the supply of fossil fuels is exhausted. Ideally, we would all lend a hand by conserving energy, by refraining from wasting energy, and by limiting population growth.

The worst scenario described above is unacceptable for anyone who believes that everyone possesses inalienable individual rights.

H. Conclusion

I have been writing about the environmental abuse related to the fossil fuel industry's desire to maintain and increase its profit margins. But each of us also abuses the environment each time we waste electricity. If you change the oil in your car and dump it into the soil or down the sewer rather than recycling it, you are abusing the environment and threatening everyone's right to a quality environment.

The largest environmental abusers, however, include those highest bidders to whom the ownership of coal, oil, and natural gas are awarded. These natural resources have kept carbon, nitrogen, sulfur, and heavy metals (mercury, arsenic, etc.) sequestered in the ground for millions of years. The owners of the fossil fuels are allowed to extract these resources from the earth in whatever way suits them. The raw product is then transported and sold to processors. Sometimes the owner is also the processor. In the extraction, transportation, and processing stages, accidents happen, workers get sick and die, and our environment is negatively affected.

Whenever the processed fossil fuel resource changes hands, a profit is made until the sale of the end product. Examples of the end product are electricity for homes and gasoline for cars. The cheaper the end product the more of it will be consumed. Greater consumption of gasoline and electricity generated from fossil fuels result in more disruption to health, to agriculture, to property, and to the environment. But who expects the original extractors/suppliers of fossil fuels to take financial responsibility for those disruptions?

EPA's "Greenhouse Gas Inventory Report: 1990–2013" states that "in 2013, United States greenhouse gas emissions totaled 6,673 million metric tons of carbon dioxide equivalents" (December 11, 2015, accessed January 4, 2016, http://www3.epa.gov/climatechange/ghgemissions/usinventoryreport.html).That's just for one year and one country. Some believe that nothing negative will happen when that much extra carbon is added to the atmosphere year in and year out, even though an equal amount of carbon is not being sequestered. You don't need to be a scientist to understand the concept of cause and effect: every action has a reaction or consequence. We should not be surprised to see those who don't understand or accept the concept of cause and effect doing the same thing repeatedly and expecting different results each time.

Those who deny that the increase in atmospheric carbon is causing the planet to heat up should consider the other negative effects of burning fossil fuels. The EPA's "Cleaner Power Plants" reports that in 1990, 167 tons of mercury per year was being emitted from power plants, medical incinerators, and municipal waste combustors. Because of EPA regulations imposed on the latter two, the amount of mercury emissions had decreased to fifty-six tons per year by 2005.[22] That is still a lot of poisonous mercury that used to be sequestered, but no longer is. And fifty-six tons per year is continuing to be added to it, fifty-four tons of which come from power plants.

Death and suffering from black lung disease; millions of cases of other lung diseases; tens of thousands of premature deaths; liver, brain, and nerve damage; birth defects; cancer; asthma; hormonal disorders; and allergies express, in part, "the health care burden of fossil fuels." That expression represents those whose lives or health have been sacrificed so that the majority of Americans can enjoy the world's most technologically advanced and financially prosperous society. That which promotes life/health supports our individual inalienable rights. That which threatens life/health detracts from life and thereby threatens the inalienable right to life.

According to Sun Edison's energymatters.com, the solar cell was invented in 1941.[23] The Federal Office of Energy Efficiency and Renewable Energy's web page "History of Wind Energy," reports that wind turbines were producing energy in Vermont during World War I.[24] The question is, why, after seventy-five years, is less than 5 percent of the nation's energy being supplied by wind and solar? Might the answer be that using fossil fuels for most of America's energy made certain influential entrepreneurs many billions of dollars richer than they would otherwise be?

The fossil fuel industry is responsible for the existence of millions of jobs. Do those jobs justify the abuse of millions of the sick and dying and of those millions who have already died prematurely? Alternative energy also creates jobs. Perhaps those jobs will pay less than fossil fuel jobs. Does the prospect of a minority of the national workforce no longer making more money than the average wage earner justify the continuing illness of millions, continuing crop damage, and continuing deterioration of environmental quality?

I'm not suggesting that the use of fossil fuels should immediately cease. That would be a threat to life itself. I do favor weaning the world in general and our country in particular from dependence on environmental- and health-threatening sources of energy and fuel ASAP.

Technological solutions to global warming have been proposed.

Some of these seem akin to covering a greenhouse with aluminum foil to deflect the sun's rays because the air-conditioning unit broke. Excess heat and any air toxins usually expelled by the air-conditioning would still be trapped inside the greenhouse. So, although the sun's rays are no longer reaching the interior of the greenhouse, some life forms in the greenhouse might still be at risk. Fix the air-conditioning; problem solved. Unfortunately, the heat and toxins from the earth's atmosphere and oceans cannot be eliminated by flipping a switch.

The rapid rise in average temperatures of the atmosphere and oceans of our planet might be part of a natural climate shift. That climate shift might not, but probably is, intensified by human activity. Nevertheless, the climate is changing, and this change shows no indication of ending anytime soon. Whether the warming earth is totally, partly, or not at all the fault of human activity, governments need to do everything humanly possible to help us citizens cope with this problem. Federal, state, and local governments need to act sooner rather than later and in a fashion that protects everyone's human rights and preserves as much of the common good as possible.

There are a number of things government agencies, departments, and offices can do to improve the use of energy while preserving our individual inalienable rights. Those things include the following:

- Government employees conserving energy in daily work activities.
- Improving insulation in all heated/cooled government buildings.
- Installing American-made solar-generating panels or geothermal power sources for all occupied government buildings. This would stimulate alternative green energy industry hiring, increase the tax base, help protect our right to life, and probably decrease the cost of domestic solar panels.
- Switching from a fossil-fuel dependent energy source to an alternative electricity supplier (other than nuclear).
- Eliminating government policies that reinforce or encourage people to propagate more than two children.

- Switching government purchases of needed goods and services to American industries and businesses (preferably small businesses) that use less energy and nonthreatening alternative sources of energy.
- Taxing fossil fuels at every step from extraction through processing and using that tax income to fund research and development of alternative green energy. Funding should include research and development of better batteries to store electricity derived from alternative energy sources.
- Making purchases that benefit alternative energy and the environment. Some examples would be purchasing recycled paper products and replacing vehicles fueled by gasoline and diesel with those using alternative energy sources.

Government regulations of private enterprises that protect our inalienable rights and the common good are helpful. Enforcing regulations that do not achieve that end, however, may be a waste of time and resources and may be an unnecessary nuisance to business owners. Environmental legislation can do only so much to protect the common good. Legislation and regulations are not permanent and are vulnerable to scrutiny from the Supreme Court. This scrutiny may not have been negative if some members of the court had not convinced themselves that corporations are people and possess individual rights that supersede the rights of us citizens, who are not corporations. Government and private enterprise too often act with complicity for the benefit of both to the detriment of the common good. Even if that were not so, government regulations would still be inadequate. Technology is changing faster than the government seems able to write and implement new relevant regulations or to revise the old regulations.

Although it is irresponsible and abusive for governments not to do everything possible to help us cope with increasing climate change, we can rely neither on government alone nor on private enterprise to protect our health and the environment. Entrepreneurs are in business to make a profit. It is my opinion that big business cares more about making money than it cares about me or about you. I believe big business, with very few exceptions, always chooses to prioritize profit over environmental quality and public health.

Where does that leave us? With *us*. It's up to each of us. We need to speak out. We need to vote against candidates who are backed by corporations and who favor the status quo. We need to vote with our conscious purchases of goods and services. We can also express our values by conserving energy.

Getting someone else to read this book might help. In a free society, individual citizens have power and, therefore, responsibility. Giving up in hopelessness is not an option. Doing nothing to change the situation is not an option.

[1]   US Energy Information Administration, "What Is U.S. Electricity Generation by Energy Source?" March 31, 2015, http://www.eia.gov/tools/faqs/faq.cfm?id=427&t=3.

[2]   US EPA, "Sources of Greenhouse Gas Emissions," December 11, 2015, http://www3.epa.gov/climatechange/ghgemissions/sources.html.

[3]   Tennessee Valley Authority, "Raccoon Mountain Pumped-Storage Plant," March 27, 2012, http://pbadupws.nrc.gov/docs/ML1222/ML12223A436.pdf.

[4]   Bryan Sims, "Microwave-induced Plasma Gasification Technology Makes Headway," *Biomass Magazine*, February 17, 2011, accessed January 3, 2016, http://biomassmagazine.com/articles/6814/microwave-induced-plasma-gasification-technology-makes-headway/?ref=brm.

[5]   Robert Wilson, "Can You Make a Wind Turbine without Fossil Fuels?" The Energy Collective, February 25, 2014, accessed January 3, 2016, http://www.theenergycollective.com/robertwilson190/344771/can-you-make-wind-turbine-without-fossil-fuels.

[6]   US EPA, "Are We Sure that Radon Is a Health Risk?" n.d., accessed January 4, 2016, https://iaq.zendesk.com/hc/en-us/articles/212104507-Are-we-sure-that-radon-is-a-health-risk-.

[7] Atomic Archive, *Special Report: Accident in Japan,* 2015, accessed January 4, 2016, http://www.atomicarchive.com/Reports/Japan/Accidents.shtml.

[8] Don Dfoofnik, "What is the Half Life of Iodine-129?," Answers, accessed January 4, 2016, http://www.answers.com/Q/What_is_the_half_life_of_iodine-129.

[9] "Nuclear Waste Management," Nuclear Energy Institute, 2016, accessed January 4, 2016, http://www.nei.org/Issues-Policy/Nuclear-Waste-Management.

[10] Paul Bedard, "Reid Celebrates Obama's Yucca Mountain Decision," *US News,* February 26, 2009, accessed January 4, 2016, http://www.usnews.com/news/washington-whispers/articles/2009/02/26/reid-celebrates-obamas-yucca-mountain-decision.

[11] John Upton, "Nuclear Waste Leaking at Hanford Site in Washington, Again," *Grist,* June 24, 2013, accessed January 4, 2016, http://grist.org/news/nuclear-waste-leaking-at-hanford-site-in-washington-again/.

[12] Eds. Jan Beránek, Rianne Teule, and Aslihan Turner, "The Deadly Legacy of Radioactive Waste," Greenpeace, 2010, accessed January 4, 2016, http://www.greenpeace.org/international/Global/international/publications/climate/2010/deadly-legacy-radioactive-waste.pdf.

[13] Brian Merchant, "Is Clean Coal a Long-term Solution to Pollution?" How Stuff Works, 2015, accessed January 4, 2016, http://science.howstuffworks.com/environmental/energy/clean-coal-solution-pollution.htm.

[14] Public Works Department, City of Boise, Idaho, "Geothermal Heating District," 2015, http://publicworks.cityofboise.org/services/geothermal/.

[15] Jesus Diaz, "Lockheed Martin's New Fusion Reactor Might Change Humanity Forever," Sploid, October 15, 2014, accessed May 13, 2016, http://sploid.gizmodo.com/lockheed-martins-new-fusion-reactor-might-change-humani-1646578094.

[16] Dr. John Garen, Dr. Christopher Jepsen, and James Saunoris, "The Relationship between Electricity Prices and Electricity Demand, Economic Growth, and Employment" (draft report) (University of Kentucky, October 19, 2011, 1–2, http://energy.ky.gov/Programs/Data%20Analysis%20%20Electricity%20Model/Gatton%20CBER%20Final%20Report%2010302011.pdf.

[17] Sue Sturgis, "The Unequal Burden of Coal Plant Pollution," Facing South, November 21, 2012, http://www.southernstudies.org/2012/11/the-unequal-burden-of-coal-plant-pollution.html.

[18] Barbara Hollingsworth, "US Senate Votes to Block EPA's Clean Power Plan," CNS News, November 18, 2015, accessed January 4, 2016, http://www.cnsnews.com/news/article/barbara-hollingsworth/us-senate-votes-block-epas-clean-power-plan.

[19] Rhett Butler, "Amazon Destruction," Mongabay, 2014, accessed January 4, 2016, http://rainforests.mongabay.com/amazon/amazon_destruction.html.

[20] "20 Things You Can Do to Conserve Energy," EcoMall, 2016, accessed January 4, 2016, http://www.ecomall.com/greenshopping/20things.htm.

[21] "Deregulation by States," Quantum Gas & Power Services, accessed January 4, 2016, http://www.quantumgas.com/energy_deregulation_map_of_united_states.html.

[22] US EPA, "Cleaner Power Plants," November 28, 2016, https://www.epa.gov/mats/cleaner-power-plants.

[23] "Solar Panel Brief History and Overview," Sun Edison, 2015, accessed January 4, 2016, http://www.energymatters.com.au/panels-modules/.

[24] US Department of Energy, "History of Wind Energy," n.d., accessed January 4, 2016, http://www.energy.gov/eere/wind/history-wind-energy.

13

IMMIGRATION AND HUMAN RIGHTS

A ttitudes toward immigrants vary among Americans. Some object to immigrants from specific countries. Others point out that all Americans are either immigrants or the offspring of immigrants. That is true of most Americans. But it could be argued that black slaves from Africa were not immigrants—at least, not willing immigrants. And there may still be a few full-blooded Native Americans without immigrant ancestors.

Some people point out that immigrants "founded" this nation and made it great. That is one perspective.

Then there is the idea that the country can benefit from allowing immigrants to live and work here if they possess exceptional talent, skill, or expertise. There are also refugees and those who need political asylum. It would be neither expedient nor humane to stop all foreigners from entering the United States. This chapter is not about legal immigrants, asylum seekers, or refugees. It focuses on employment of illegal immigrants, the issue of deportation, and an alternative solution to the problem of illegal immigration.

A. Employing Illegals

Consider the issue of illegal immigrants taking jobs that unemployed citizens could perform. Passel and Cohn of *PEW Research* reported that in 2010, 5.1 percent of workers in the United States were unauthorized immigrants.[1] So, if there were 125 million in the workforce, 5.25 million of those people would have been illegal aliens. The question is, why are so many illegal immigrants employed by American employers? For a detailed answer, refer to the shaded area below. In case you wish to skip over the shaded area, the short answer is as follows:

- demand for low-wage physical labor that many Americans are reluctant to perform
- a developed ethnic job-networking system
- profit, at least in the short term, for American employers who hire illegal immigrants

Immigrants, including millions of unauthorized immigrants, are employed in the United States. Those are jobs that about half of the 9 million citizens who are currently unemployed could theoretically be performing. According to Passel and Cohn, there were 3.5 million unauthorized immigrants living in the United States in 2009. By 2014, there were 11.3 million.[2] Why are there so many illegal immigrants working in the United States? There are a number of possible factors.

One factor is the demand for low-wage physical labor—that is, jobs like housecleaning, landscaping, low-skilled industrial jobs, and harvesting fruits and vegetables. It has been suggested that there are more such jobs than American citizens willing to perform them. It has been estimated that about half of all agricultural workers in the United States are illegal immigrants, according to "Mechanization: California Can Show the Way to End Dependence on Illegal Foreign Labor" by John Vinson.[3] Some believe that if farmers were dependent on American workers to harvest crops, the crops would rot in the fields.

There are a number of articles online about states like Georgia in which crops did "rot in the fields." Law enforcement got tough on illegal immigrants in those states, and the illegal farmworkers left for more tolerant states or went back to their country of origin. Reportedly, most of the American workers recruited to replace the illegals quit after a few days to a few weeks.[4]

I can understand the reluctance of Americans to do low-paying jobs in factories and fields. I worked for a number of years in factories doing repetitive, mind-numbing tasks. I would gladly let a robot or an immigrant do those jobs.

I picked cherries when I was a teenager. We got paid according to how much we picked. Some days I picked quite a lot. When I was tired, however, my performance decreased. I was not consistent enough to make a living harvesting crops. The farmer needs a crew that is going to perform well every day, come rain or come shine. One can imagine that working in the field in the rain is no picnic. The farmer has only so many ladders, so many baskets, and so much room in the truck to pick up and transport the crew. The farmer is going to want the best workers.

Some people believe that immigrants are motivated to work hard in order to avoid having to return to living conditions in their home countries. Those living conditions are supposedly worse than the conditions the immigrants face in this country. Regarding immigrant farmworkers in this country, according to an article by Julianne Glatz, "Working and living conditions for most migrant workers are heartrending. Many live in cardboard shanties, in the open, and even in caves" ("Cheap Food I: Illegal Immigrants," *Illinois Times* Springfield, IL, June 26, 2014, http://illinoistimes.com/article-14108-cheap-food-i:-illegal-immigrants.html).

This does not make the plight of immigrant farmworkers any better, but an article on the Californians for Population Stabilization website by John Vinson claims that only a small percentage of illegal aliens in the United States work on farms. The same article claims that illegals prefer easier jobs than farming and that when they get the opportunity, they leave the farm to perform other jobs. These other jobs are often the same sorts of jobs performed by poorer American citizens.[5] Those poorer citizens must compete directly with immigrants for those jobs.

The Center for Immigration Studies has a comprehensive online article by Phillip Martin about immigration and jobs. Martin describes a network of job information sharing among Mexican immigrants that extends from the States into Mexico.[6] This could be one reason that "Mexicans make up about half of all unauthorized immigrants (58 percent)."[7]

One alternative American growers have to hiring illegal immigrants is the legal guest worker, or H-2A, program. This program does not seem to be limited by quotas—the grower can bring in as many workers as are needed. Most growers don't use the program, however, according to John Vinson's article. This might be because the H-2A program has other limitations, including excessive bureaucratic red tape. Vinson wrote, "One suspects that growers prefer to avoid not only the red tape, but also the requirements under H-2A to meet minimal standards of salary, housing and other amenities for their workers." Another factor that accounts for the large numbers of illegal immigrants is that some American employers prefer illegals.[8]

The article by Phillip Martin reports that employers of illegal immigrants can save labor costs by eliminating fringe benefits like health insurance and pension benefits. Some of these employers fail to make mandatory payments to the government for the illegal employees' Social Security and disability insurance. They reason that saving 20 percent of the wage cost per employee is worth it, because the illegals will probably be afraid to apply for these benefits. "No income taxes are withheld from the farmworkers unless the worker requests withholding, and many nonfarm workers claim large numbers of dependents to minimize the income tax withheld and then fail to file income tax returns."

To avoid withholding income tax, employers can hire workers as independent contractors. Independent contractors are required to make their own tax payments. The employer can also hire workers on a "casual" basis—that is, for fewer than thirty days. Employers are not required to withhold taxes from casual workers. Such workers are sometimes reemployed by the same employer for consecutive months.

Martin writes that employers in industries prone to workplace accidents tend to prefer illegal immigrant workers to avoid the expense of health and safety standards compliance and the expense of strictly observing labor regulations.

According to Martin, immigrants "are concentrated in particular industries, areas, and occupations, and once they gain a foothold, ethnic network recruitment fills job vacancies and excludes unemployed Americans."[9]

Why so many illegal immigrants?

- limited immigration quotas
- demand for low-wage physical labor that many Americans are reluctant to perform
- a developed ethnic job-networking system
- more profit, at least in the short term, for American employers

I don't like the idea of our country having to depend on people from other countries, especially for essential activities like food harvesting. It is also unfair that immigrant farm workers don't have decent living and working conditions and that their labor ages their bodies prematurely. But I do not want the price of our food to escalate either.

Some people with upper-middle-class incomes may think that migrant farmworkers should be paid fifteen dollars per hour. If you were a farmer in this free market economy, would you be willing to give up your annual winter vacation to Europe so that you could pay higher wages to your immigrant farm hands? Or might you try to demand more money for the food you grow? If that attempt was unsuccessful, might you decide you can't afford to continue farming? Upper-middle-class folks in favor of a minimum fifteen-dollars-per-hour wage and who can afford to pay more for their families' food should question what effect higher wages for immigrant farm workers will have on lower-income folks, on people with fixed incomes, and on farmers.

B. The Case for Deportation

Not all unauthorized immigrants in the country are those who crossed the border illegally. There are some whose visas have expired and who stay here anyway.

Some Americans are opposed to deporting any unauthorized immigrants. They think that being here illegally should make no difference, that millions of illegals should be allowed to benefit from the blessings of our country at the expense of Americans who pay taxes. Those free blessings include health care, public assistance, food stamps, American dollars sent back to their home countries, and public education for their children ("about 7 percent of K–12 students had at least one unauthorized immigrant parent in 2012," according to Passel and Cohn). What would we think of an American citizen who illegally entered another country and did those things? Why is it okay for foreigners to rip off the American government and taxpayers? Put another way, since when does desperation or ambition plus boldness plus the ability/willingness to endure physical hardships earn one the license to break the laws of a foreign country?

Illegal immigrants also use up precious resources like fresh water, electricity, fuel, food, and living space. As the immigrants give birth to more children, this consumption increases. According to the previously cited PEW Research report by Passel and Cohn, of the K–12 students who had at least one parent who was an unauthorized immigrant in 2012, 79 percent of those students were born in this country.

Sneaking into someone else's country without authorization is irresponsible. When people act irresponsibly and without accountability, it detracts from everyone's opportunities to experience his or her individual inalienable rights. When people are allowed to get away with breaking the law without accompanying negative consequences, the result is chaotic and detrimental to rights and to the common good. Phillip Martin points out in his article "Illegal Immigration and the Colonization of the American Labor Market" that allowing unlimited numbers of illegal immigrants to enter our country imposes on the United States a social and environmental expense that must be paid by our whole society.[10]

So, what should be done about illegal or unauthorized immigrants in the United States? There are some instances in which deportation seems unreasonable. If a person has lived in this country for at least ten consecutive years, has worked here, paid taxes, has no criminal record, and is willing and able to become a naturalized citizen, American citizenship seems reasonable. Donald Trump would like to deport over eleven million illegal immigrants. He has, so far, presented no detailed practical plan for accomplishing that feat. I suspect it would not be humanely or inexpensively done.

C. An Alternative Solution

I think we should consider alternatives to mass deportation of millions of illegal immigrants. If our economy is truly dependent on illegal immigrant labor, why not make all working illegal immigrants eligible for green cards, with the exception of both those with criminal records and those wanted by the legal authorities of other countries? Many of those immigrants should be deported/extradited anyway.

The green cards granted to illegals would be for permanent, temporary, or seasonal work and would make the immigrants legal residents of this country. To retain their green card status, these immigrants would be required to be employed, to file valid tax returns, and to not break civil or criminal laws. The 140,000 annual limit for employment-based green card holders would have to be waived. This solution would dramatically decrease the number of illegal immigrants, at least temporarily.

If this reform were proposed in the Congress, who would resist this alternative solution? Employers that are abusively/illegally making profits at the expense of illegal immigrants. These employers might claim that without the subsidy of illegal immigrant workers, they would go out of business. If they employed *legal* immigrants, they would have the added business expenses of complying with more laws and regulations, including paying legal minimum wages. If an entrepreneur cannot follow the laws and regulations that preserve the common good and still make a profit—or enough of a profit to satisfy himself or herself—perhaps she or he should not be in that business. With fewer of those businesses around, the number of low-paying jobs for immigrants would decrease, which would, in turn, discourage more illegals from entering the country

Giving green cards to every illegal working immigrant without a criminal record might be more economical than mass deportation of eleven million illegals. Issuing these green cards could result in better wages and working conditions for the lowest-paid immigrants. It might also decrease the number of jobs available to immigrants. For example, if you are employing an illegal immigrant as a housekeeper for six dollars an hour and not paying taxes and worker's comp, you may decide it is too expensive to employ a housekeeper with a green card.

Increased automation—that is, replacing labor-intensive production processes with labor-saving production methods—could help us to become less dependent on the labor of immigrants. I was once opposed to automation because I believed it deprived people of jobs. But if machines can perform the jobs that many Americans are no longer willing to perform, automation would seem to me to be a good thing.

You may think automation is entirely possible when it comes to industrial processes, but agriculture would be different. Fortunately, this is not so. Some farmers have already switched to technologies that improve productivity. John Vinson suggests that automation will be the way we become independent of immigrant farmworkers. He gives examples of existing machinery—grape harvesters, lettuce thinners, tomato pickers, and pistachio harvesters. He believes that technological processes will be developed that will allow machines to pick strawberries with the efficiency of experienced human pickers.[11]

Another partial alternative to immigrant farm workers would be urban farms where we both cultivate and harvest our own fruits and vegetables in return for an investment in the farm. A million such farms in urban settings growing plants that still require stoop labor would help decrease the need for immigrant farmworkers.

D. Conclusion

Some humanitarians think that more jobs for immigrants in this country is a good thing. The total number of people in this world who are poor, who are starving, who are unemployed, and who are without health insurance far outnumber disadvantaged Americans. With that in mind, the three public policy questions that humanitarians need to answer are as follow:

1. *Our fellow Americans* or *the rest of the world's disadvantaged people*: for which group are the citizens of the United States primarily responsible?

2. If we can't afford to provide the opportunities for every American to experience his or her inalienable rights, how can we afford to do that for the rest of the world's needy people?

3. If we can afford to provide the opportunities for disadvantaged Americans to experience their inalienable rights, but we opt instead to support financially needy immigrants, how does that not signal other countries that it is acceptable for them to neglect their own disadvantaged citizens?

---

[1] Jeffrey S. Passel and D'Vera Cohn, "Unauthorized Immigrant Population: National and State Trends, 2010," PEW Research, February 1, 2011, accessed January 4, 2016, http://www.pewhispanic.org/2011/02/01/unauthorized-immigrant-population-brnational-and-state-trends-2010/.

[2] Ibid.

[3] John Vinson, "Mechanization: California Can Show the Way to End Dependence on Illegal Foreign Labor," Californians for Population Stabilization, June 2014, accessed January 4, 2016, http://www.capsweb.org/caps-issues/farm-mechanization-california-can-show-way-end-dependence-illegal-foreign-labor.

[4] Ed Pilkington, "Alabama Immigration: Crops Rot as Workers Vanish to Avoid Crackdown," Guardian, October 14, 2011, accessed May 14, 2016, http://www.theguardian.com/world/2011/oct/14/alabama-immigration-law-workers.

[5] Vinson, "Mechanization."

[6] Phillip Martin, "Illegal Immigration and the Colonization of the American Labor Market," Center for Immigration Studies, January, 1986, accessed January 4, 2016, http://www.cis.org/AmericanLaborMarket%2526Immigration.

[7] Passel and Cohn, "Unauthorized Immigrants."

[8] Vinson, "Mechanization."

[9] Martin, "Illegal Immigration."

[10] Ibid.

[11] Vinson, "Mechanization."

14

PUBLIC EDUCATION AND STUDENT RIGHTS

I am not a professional educator. Counting kindergarten through graduate school, I have a total of about 23.5 years of experience being educated. I remember developing a philosophy of education in college. The goal was to teach children what they need to survive in the real world. Several years later, when I decided to teach physical education, I took a number of courses in general education principles and developed a physical-education teaching theory that emphasized what I called "full physical fitness," a condition that would keep people healthy in the long run while maintaining basic physical skills to deal with emergency situations.

There are many theories about maximizing student learning and about what subjects are most important. Those concerns are not the focus of this chapter. This chapter on education is about individual inalienable rights of students. The following subjects will be addressed:

A. Racial Segregation
B. Equal Education
C. Post High School Education Preparation
D. Improving K–12 Academics
E. School Bullying
F. Teaching Individual Rights
G. Summary

A. Racial Segregation

One would think that the issue of racial segregation in schools would be a thing of the past. According to Wikipedia's "School Segregation in America" web page, making it illegal to send black children to schools attended by white students began with the Jim Crow laws in the South after the Civil War. This is called *de jure* segregation.[1]

According to "Desegregation in the United States" by Tom Head, the Supreme Court outlawed that type of school segregation in *Brown v. the Board of Education* (1954). Chief Justice Earl Warren wrote the ruling, calling education "the most important function of state and local governments." He associated educational opportunity with success in life and asserted that education is a right. Not only did he say education is a right, but that it is a right that must be equally available to all Americans.

> **We come then to the question presented: Does segregation of children in public schools solely on the basis of race, even though the physical facilities and other "tangible" factors may be equal, deprive the children of the minority group of equal educational opportunities? We believe that it does. Separate educational facilities are inherently unequal.** (About.com, 2016, http://civilliberty.about. com/od/raceequalopportunity/tp/Desegregation-History-Timeline.htm.)

This was a rebuttal to the belief that if the quality of schools for minority students were no less than the quality of schools for white students, that was okay. What happened next?

> **The emerging segregationist "states' rights" movement immediately reacts to slow the immediate implementation of *Brown* and limit its effect as much as possible. Their effort will become a *de jure* failure (as the Supreme Court will never again uphold the "separate but equal" doctrine),**

but a *de facto* success (as the U.S. public school system is still profoundly segregated to this day). ("Desegregation," Tom Head)

Until the 1990s, busing was used to achieve racial integration in specific school districts where the minority schools were demonstrably inferior to the white schools. Depending on the court rulings, black students from poor school districts were transported by bus to schools for predominantly white students, white students were bused to schools with predominantly minority students, or both.

Debbie Elliot explains in "Decades Later, Desegregation Still on the Docket in Little Rock," that one result of busing was white flight. This happened in Boston, Little Rock, Arkansas, and in other cities. White families who could afford it moved to the suburbs and established their own schools, leaving the poorer black and white students in the inner cities.[2]

There are a number of other issues connected with busing discussed in an online article "School Desegregation—the Busing Debate." This article points out that not all who oppose busing are against school integration. Some people do not believe busing achieves the desired goal. They point out that minority students tend to stick together when placed in a majority school. Busing does not automatically lead to abolishing racist attitudes in the students involved. If a poorer school district has to purchase or lease more buses, that can detract from educational quality in that school district. "By 2003 the anti-busing viewpoint appeared to have prevailed. During the 1990s federal courts released many school districts from supervision by declaring these districts free of the taint of state-imposed segregation" (Net Industries, 2016, http://law.jrank.org/pages/10024/School-Desegregation-BUSING-DEBATE.html).

Despite the relaxation of busing requirements by the courts, some school districts tried to continue to achieve diversity by using students' race as a factor in assigning students to particular schools. Parents who wanted their children to go to those particular schools, but were denied acceptance on the basis of race, felt this was unfair. In 2007 the Supreme

Court decided in their favor and ruled that it is unconstitutional for race to be a determining factor in school assignments. The Supreme Court did not rule out other methods of achieving racial diversity in schools, like gerrymandering school neighborhood boundaries ("School Desegregation—The Busing Debate").

I don't know what the answer is. Studies have shown that black students do better academically when they are in classes with white students. When white students were bused to black schools, improvements in the black schools occurred. For the sake of equality and rights, there seem to be sound reasons to encourage integration, regardless of how uncomfortable it might feel. I am advocating the encouragement of integration, not the legal requiring of it. Students should not be forced to go to schools outside their districts. A school with student openings should not be required to accept students from outside the district, but if it does, race should not be a factor in excluding any student who wishes to attend. If there are more applicants than openings, a lottery drawing for eligible students might be held.

B. Equal Education

Justice Warren Marshall in 1954 stated that an education "where the state has undertaken to provide it, is a right which must be made available to all on equal terms." I agree with Marshall because everyone is created equal with the inalienable rights to life, liberty, the pursuit of happiness, and access to the common good.

The question then becomes, how do we make sure all students are receiving equal benefits and opportunities? The US Census Bureau web page "Per Pupil Spending Varies Heavily Across the United States," reports that "per pupil spending for the nation was $10,700 during fiscal year 2013, a 0.9 percent increase from 2012, but varied heavily among states with a high of $19,818 in New York and a low of $6,555 in Utah" (June 2, 2015, http://www.census.gov/newsroom/press-releases/2015/cb15-98.html). How can all students be receiving equal benefits with that much variation in spending?

And why the vast difference? The federal government subsidizes public primary and secondary education to some extent. The individual states contribute more than the federal government. But about half the cost of these schools comes from property taxes levied on property owners living in each school district. The percentages of property value levied are determined by each state government. If there is a set percentage for all property in the state, then school districts with more expensive property might receive more money than districts with poorer property owners.

It might help for all schools in the country to be required to spend comparably equal amounts of revenue per student, taking into account the varying costs of living for different areas. Whether or not the same amount of money was being spent on each student, or even on comparable groups of students, it would not guarantee that any of them were getting a quality education, but it would suggest the possibility that all students were getting equal educational benefits. This could theoretically be done if school property tax was eliminated and the revenue for all public K–12 schools came from state/federal government sources.

Whether or not all schools received comparable funding, if they were not required to spend the money in comparable ways, inequities between schools might persist. It would require a vast bureaucracy to ensure that all educational resources and facilities are the same and of equal quality in every school in the nation. Even then, some teachers will be better at teaching particular subjects than other teachers. This will result in inequality of instruction even if all other factors are the same.

Practically speaking, equality in K–12 schools across the nation is simply not achievable. Robotic teachers with identical programming might eventually take the place of human instructors. But all students are unique. They don't all learn at the same rate. Different subjects are easier for different students. Whether or not all students of varying ethnic and racial backgrounds are given the exact same instruction and opportunities, the results are bound to vary among the different students.

Then there is the controversy about achievement gaps in education. Students of a certain gender will score higher on a test of a certain subject than students of another gender. It is the same with race and nationality. Why is the "gap" a problem? Does anyone seriously believe that all students should have the same scores? Why is it a problem that they don't have the same scores? We know that everyone is not good at everything. Every student is different. It would be ideal for all students to be proficient enough in math or whatever to get and hold a job they desire. Some Koreans being more proficient in math than some Americans is not a failure of American education. I don't think achievement gaps are a good reason to hand down educational edicts.

C. Education Preparation after High School

It would be nice for every student to get high scores in every subject and for all students to receive equal educational opportunities. However, these are unrealistic goals. What is realistic in terms of our inalienable individual rights? Without a quality K–12 education, one's opportunities to choose a job, to attain gainful employment, and to earn enough to live healthfully can be severely limited.

The government is not able to make all K–12 instruction equal. What the government should be concerned with is whether high school graduates are experiencing their right to be prepared to get and keep gainful employment or to successfully complete a two- or four-year college education or post–high school technical/vocational training. It is the responsibility of society and, by extension, government, to ensure that all high school graduates actually experience that right. The federal government or state governments need to monitor the progress of high school graduates. The intervention of either state or federal government in local K–12 education is justified when the local system fails to prepare a significant percentage of high school graduates to succeed in gainful employment, college, or vocational/technical training.

D. Improving Education

Equal education and equal test scores are not realistic goals. That does not rule out the possibility and desirability of individual parents, teachers, principals, and school boards working together to improve the academic success of schools. For inspiring real examples of what has been done in different schools see "Five Top Success Stories of 2014" at learningfirst.org.[3]

Lesson Study is a method of improving teacher performance that's been practiced in Japan for decades according to Linda Lutton.[4] It would be good for it to become a common practice in America's schools.

E. School Bullying

One impediment that can profoundly and negatively affect a student's academic success is bullying. My definition of bullying is illegitimately using one's superior intelligence, strength, status, power, position, influence, or aggressive tendencies in ways that intimidate, control, harm, deprive, or take financial advantage of another or others. That definition certainly describes cyber bullying, cruel teasing, rumor spreading, hazing, violent attacks, humiliation, physical abuse, and other forms of student bullying.

I survived twelve years of parochial school. In each of those years, the bullies always outnumbered their selected victims. In addition to the bullies in my classes, I also had to contend with bullies from upper grades during recess and public school bullies on the way to and from school. According to Lessne and Harmalkar's table 1.1 from the "2011 School Crime Supplement (SCS) of the National Crime Victimization Survey" of 24.46 million students twelve to eighteen years of age, 27.8 percent of those students were bullied at school during the 2010–2011 school year.[5] Irene van der Zande's "Bullying Facts and Solutions" at Kidpower.org also supports my contention that school bullying is a big problem.[6]

159

In regard to why bullying in schools persists, it may help to understand the difference between bullies, victims, and those who are neither. The following is an excerpt from the blog www.bullyalertbully. blogspot.com (R. Geiger, "Psycho-Social Aspects," *Bullying——Do We Really Want It to Stop?* pt. 2, July 31, 2012). If you are not interested in learning more about bullying, you can skip the shaded area below.

The social factor that relates to the survival of bullying behavior into adulthood involves society's unconscious acceptance of many forms of bullying and the beneficial effects of bullying on society.

Bullies are people who tyrannize, intimidate, or cause harm to those with less power, strength, or assertiveness. Specific victims targeted for bullying are often members of minority groups or are individuals perceived to be different, weird, strange, or loners.

There are bullies and targeted victims of bullies. And there are people who are not specifically targeted by bullies, don't perceive themselves as being bullied, and don't generally knowingly and intentionally bully others. These people go along to get along, have normal drives and desires, don't rock the boat, and don't question anything as long as it falls within the limits of "normal." In general, these people do not express opposition to bullies. They may even support certain active bullies. They generally feel no sympathy when those who do not conform to their idea of normal are targeted for bullying. They may even hold the unexpressed belief or attitude that those who deviate from the norm need to be punished until they learn to conform.

Once the deviants "get with the program," the majority (i.e., the normals) can feel more comfortable and secure. In other words, normals unconsciously think that if people who choose to be nonconformists are bullied, it's their own fault. This thought allows normals to remain indifferent to the plight of those targeted by bullies for persecution. Although all teachers provide a priceless, indispensable service, I wonder if the majority of elementary and secondary teachers and administrators in this country are not normals. If this is the case, it would help to explain the continuing existence of school bullying.

One significant aspect of student bullying is that it violates students' individual rights; therefore, it is a form of abuse. In schools, bullying also has the side effect of interfering with the right of the bullied student to the best educational experience available.

There are whole websites devoted to the problem of school bullying and what we can do about it. For a better understanding of the problem, especially if you are one who thinks bullying can have positive effects on the victim, I would recommend the DVD documentary *Bully*, written and directed by Lee Hirsch (The Bully Project, released April 27, 2012, http://www.imdb.com/title/tt1682181/). It is my opinion that the problem of bullying in schools will continue as long as the culture of abuse persists.

F. Teaching Individual Rights

Something that would help create better race relations and decrease school bullying would be incorporating inalienable individual rights instruction into all subjects at all primary and secondary school levels. Children who grow up understanding the nature and limits of their personal inalienable rights and those of others will be more apt to respect the rights of other people and expect their own rights to be respected. Such ongoing education could transform the nature of race relations in this country within two generations, virtually eliminate school bullying, and help to solve the problem of economic inequity. The alternative is a continuing culture of abuse.

I am not advocating religious instruction. I am suggesting that the fundamental values of equality and inalienable rights be taught in schools. If you are either a power monger or an abuser, you will think of some sort of objection to this idea. Why? Because you want to preserve your power.

This paragraph and the next are shaded because it contains my somewhat radical, subjective opinion. I believe every child has the right to be educated in terms of reading, writing, arithmetic, and any other knowledge and skill they need to survive. Let's face it. Children either learn values from educators or have the values they already possess reinforced by them. Educators have the power to help prioritize and preserve individual rights and the common good. They also have the power to prioritize and preserve the values of materialism (see chapter 15, B-4), discrimination, prejudice against certain minorities, religious beliefs that justify abuse, and the belief that pragmatism is superior to principles.

Of those two powers of educators, why would I suspect that, in many parts of this country, the latter power has been exercised more consistently than the first power? How about the popularity of the 2016 Republican presidential candidate? Of course, the values taught by educators probably reflect the general values of the community in which they teach. That is an example of democracy in action. But it is not necessarily American or patriotic or in the best interest of the common good. In my opinion, education that teaches values that threaten either individual inalienable rights or the common good should not be subsidized in any way by the federal government. That applies to school lunch programs and college financial aid. Although it is in the best interest of the nation to have a large number of highly educated/trained professionals, it is counterproductive, in terms of the common good, for those people to have proabusive attitudes.

G. Summary

Racial integration of K–12 public schools is a desirable goal. But it should not be realized at the cost of students' right to liberty. Instead of the government putting time and effort into unrealistic goals like equality in education and closing standardized test score gaps, the government should ensure that all high school graduates are prepared for gainful employment or to successfully complete college or vocational/technical training.

Bullying is a problem for many children. It violates their individual rights and interferes with the quality of their education. If we taught individual inalienable rights to students at all grade levels, it would help improve race relations and would help solve the problem of bullying.

[1]   Wikipedia, "School Segregation in the United States," last modified December 31, 2015, accessed January 4, 2016, https://en.wikipedia.org/wiki/School_segregation_in_the_United_States.

[2]   Debbie Elliot, "Decades Later, Desegregation Still on the Docket in Little Rock," National Public Radio, January 13, 2014, accessed January 4, 2016, http://www.npr.org/sections/codeswitch/2014/01/07/260461489/decades-later-desegregation-still-on-the-docket-in-little-rock.

[3]   "Top Five Success Stories of 2014," Learning First Alliance, 2016, accessed November 28, 2016, http://www.learningfirst.org/top-five-success-stories-2014.

[4]   Linda Lutton, "'Lesson Study,' Japanese Strategy for Improving Teachers, Catching On in U.S.," *Huffington Post*, March 11, 2012, accessed January 4, 2016, http://www.huffingtonpost.com/2012/01/10/lesson-study-japanese-str_n_1197229.html.

[5]   Deborah Lessne and Sayali Harmalkar, US Department of Education, "Student Reports of Bullying and Cyber-Bullying: Results from the 2011 School Crime Supplement to the National Crime Victimization Survey," August 2013, table 1, http://nces.ed.gov/pubs2013/2013329.pdf.

[6]   Irene van der Zande, "Bullying Facts and Solutions," Kidpower Teenpower Fullpower International, 2016, accessed January 5, 2016, https://www.kidpower.org/library/article/bullying-facts/.

15

ENVIRONMENTAL QUALITY AND HUMAN RIGHTS

T his chapter examines how the quality of the environment is related to rights, why environmental quality is being threatened, what environmental responsibility entails, and the environmental effects of human population growth.

A. Environmental Quality

What is environmental quality or a quality environment? The TV series *Zoo* is about a virus that causes animals to attack and kill humans. The premise is that, because we humans have driven so many species into extinction and will continue to do so, an environment free of us humans would be a better environment for many species. In fact, my personal subjective view of environmental quality would be nature completely untouched by human influence. The problem with that view is that *nature* refers to the physical world and all living creatures therein. Since we humans are living creatures, no matter how seemingly unnatural we and our creations appear to be, we and our things are technically part of nature.

Quality refers to that which is good. From a philosophical point of view, good is what makes you happy; evil is that which results in unhappiness. Perhaps the greatest good is life, and the greatest evil is death. That which promotes and supports life is good. A quality environment would be one in which life is promoted and supported. For a lion, that might mean an environment in which prey is abundant. For the prey, that might be an environment in which food is plentiful and predators are scarce. Those are subjective perceptions, however. When predators are scarce, herbivores tend to multiply and eventually eat so much that mass starvation is inevitable. This, objectively speaking, is not a scenario characteristic of a quality environment.

This chapter is about how our inalienable individual rights relate to nature. *Nature* refers to the physical world and all creatures living therein. We people are one animal species. In some ways, we are smarter than other creatures. It is that superior intelligence that has enabled us to change the very nature of nature, or at least large aspects thereof. Global warming would be an example of such change.

B. Why Environmental Quality Is Threatened

The earth is warming. The air, the oceans, and the surface of the oceans are all getting warmer. The oceans have been getting more acidic due to increased absorption of carbon dioxide, according to EPA's "Climate Change Indicators in the United States."[1] Man-made chemical pesticides are killing large numbers of bees, butterflies, other insects, and small aquatic life forms on which fish feed.[2] The thinning ozone layer allows more cancer-causing solar radiation to reach the earth's surface.[3] These are some of many examples of how the quality of our environment is being threatened.

Why are all these problems not being solved? A quality environment is an aspect of the common good, from which we all have the right to benefit. (See chapter 2, "Rights and the Common Good.") How do those responsible for the problems that negatively affect environmental quality justify threatening people's rights to life, to the pursuit of happiness, and to the common good? What is the source of people's indifference and insensitivity when it comes to how they treat nature? There are five possible answers.

1. Ignorance

Ignorance, or lack of awareness, plays a role in the human behavior that negatively affects our environment and our health. Even the most concerned person, albeit uninformed, can unconsciously and unintentionally harm the environment. Consider the use of energy. If one is poor and receiving energy assistance, one may think nothing of leaving outside lights on twenty-four hours a day. And how many times do able-bodied people use the handicap doors to enter and leave a shopping mall? These doors are clearly designated and close more slowly than the other three or four pairs of entrance/exit doors. When the handicap doors are used, the amount of heat in the winter and cool air in the summer that escapes to the outside is greater than what would escape if the regular doors were used. In many areas of the country, electric power is produced from the burning of coal. I imagine that the handicap doors in thousands of malls across the nation are used hundreds of times per day by those who are able-bodied. This results in a considerable amount of unnecessary pollution.

There are many ways in which people harm the environment without being aware. One example is releasing helium balloons. Some of these balloons, once they return to earth and become litter, kill animals that mistake them for food.[4]

It is possible for us to threaten the survival of endangered species without realizing it by purchasing products made from those species. Many of us probably purchase products made from crops or animals grown on land that once supported a rainforest habitat. Examples of these products are soybeans and palm oil.[5]

2. Denial

Humans are adding a virtual witch's brew of humanly invented synthetic chemicals to the ecosphere (air, water, and land) that were never there before, including genetically modifying plants and animals, and releasing vast quantities of mercury, arsenic, sulfur, and carbon that have been locked up in the earth for longer than we humans have been walking on the planet. (See chapter 11, "Fossil Fuels and Human Rights, I.") Some acknowledge these activities are occurring and believe they should continue to occur indefinitely without restrictions. They believe these activities negatively affect neither environmental quality nor human health. The shaded area below is devoted to a short rant about this belief.

I would expect that people who are intelligent enough to understand the law of cause and effect would at least accept the *possibility* of negative effects. Denial thinking is irrational and ignorant. Such thinking by professional decision makers is dangerous. Those deniers in positions of power are authoritarian leaders who have not gotten or have ignored the memo that says unnecessarily threatening our individual rights to drink pure water and breathe clean air might be expected in communist and fascist countries, but such threats are not acceptable in a democratic republic.

3. Religion

It is interesting to me that so-called primitive or hedonistic cultures that regarded different aspects of nature like the sun or a volcano as sacred were not hell-bent on taming and subjugating nature. They seemed to be more skilled in working *with* nature than the cultures responsible for the Industrial Revolution. There were exceptions. Archeology and anthropology reveal that some technologically undeveloped cultures devastated ecological balance in their locales. However, these cultures did not bring us the Industrial Revolution and its accompanying worldwide environmental consequences.

One difference between primitive cultures that lived more in harmony with their environment and the culture that made global warming a reality was that the latter had Genesis 1:26,[6] or their interpretation thereof, to justify their treatment or mistreatment of the earth. In that Bible verse, that is part of the *first* story of the Creation in the book of Genesis, God says to let man have dominion (power) "over all the earth." There is no mention of the fall from grace in the first Creation story. It would seem that God made that statement about dominion *before* Eve was seduced by the serpent into eating the forbidden fruit.

In the second Creation story, after man's fall from grace, God tells Adam "cursed is the ground for thy sake; in sorrow shalt thou eat of it all the days of thy life; thorns also and thistles shall it bring forth to thee" (Genesis 3:17–18). I believe that whatever power over the earth that God seemed to give man in Genesis 1:26 was taken away from humans as punishment for Adam's disobedience ("original sin" in Catholic parlance). This is not a popular interpretation of Genesis. Many people seem to prefer to believe that earth belongs to humans and that it is ours to do with as we please.

Pope Francis, in his encyclical "*Laudato Si*: On Care for Our Common Home,"[7] tries to correct the false belief that we humans have no responsibility for environmental quality. Some authoritarian political leaders of this country said Pope Francis should stick to religion and not speak from a scientific perspective. For more detailed information, refer to the blog www.mylaudatosiblog.blogspot.com (R. Geiger, "The Pope, the Environment, and the Politicians," September 18, 2015).

4. Materialism

In exploring the source of human indifference to environmental quality, the value system of the Western world, which I have labeled *materialism*, must be examined. For a full discussion of materialism, refer to the blog www.savingrepublic.blogspot.com (R. Geiger, "Is the U.S. a Plutocracy? Who Cares?" sect. D, *Plutocracy Now!* February 8, 2014). In short, materialism is a value system in which material things are of the utmost importance as a means for attaining material possessions—that is, money. Materialism is a value system that justifies greed, selfishness, and doing whatever is necessary to make more money. Trashing earth to make a profit is acceptable behavior from a materialistic perspective. Violating individual inalienable rights to increase profit margins is okay for a materialist. The values of materialism are supportive neither of our individual human rights nor of the common good.

Some corporate environmental polluters deliberately violate environmental regulations to increase profits, particularly when the potential gain in profit is greater than the fine that would be levied if they are caught. More unnecessary poisoning of the environment results in a greater incidence of human disease. Corporate environmental bullies rationalize that more environmental regulations will cost more, thus preventing them from expanding their businesses and hiring more people. More workers may produce more unnecessary pollution. More pollution will result in more human sickness and higher health care costs. Corporate bullies seem to be reluctant to accept responsibility for such increases in unnecessary human suffering. But, of course, responsibility is not relevant to the philosophy of materialism.

Corporate bullies do not believe they are responsible for preserving wild, unspoiled natural spaces for present and future generations. If corporate bullies believed they could make a sufficient profit by building a dam that would flood the last unspoiled natural area on earth, they wouldn't hesitate to do so.

Destroying unspoiled natural spaces deprives most of us of our intrinsic right to enjoy unspoiled nature without having to travel extensively to find it. Poisoning the environment causes more sickness and higher health care costs. For people who believe in materialism, profit is more important than both environmental quality and human health.

5. A Desire to Make Life Easier

Another factor contributing to indifference toward environmental quality is related to materialism: the human drive to make daily life easier. Some people seem to have a need to make surviving easier, to make earning money easier, and even to make pleasure seeking easier. Modern life is easier thanks to the internal combustion engine, the electric grid, paved roads, and cell phones.

But what, in terms of human suffering and death, is the cost of preserving the maximized ease of living for those who can afford it? Conflict minerals must continue to be mined with slave labor to make cell phones and other electronic devices.[8] Ocean levels must continue to rise, inundating coastal communities all over the world. Forests, crops, and public monuments must continue to suffer damage from the effects of acid precipitation.[9] Thousands more with black lung disease, asthma, and other respiratory diseases must continue to suffer and die prematurely.[10] Future generations must be deprived of the species diversity that would otherwise exist. More people's private property must be damaged by earthquakes induced by fracking.[11] These negative consequences and more are the cost of making human life easier, especially the lives of people in the wealthiest countries. The following shaded area is about medical devices.

There are those whose health and life depend on electronic devices that utilize heavy metals, rare earth elements, or conflict minerals. I don't have any objection to the utilization of such devices. I suspect that the amounts of natural resources related to military conflicts and despotic regime support and utilized in medical devices, are probably fewer than the amounts of the same natural resources used in producing consumer electronic devices like cell phones. The "How to get free cell phone service from the government" web page notes that, as of 2014, the federal government had given away an estimated 12 to 15 million free cell phones with free service to qualified households.[12] According to www.nielsen.com, at the beginning of 2011, there were 289 million mobile phone users in the United States.[13]

Melissa McNamara wrote "Facts About Blood Diamonds."[14] Ascertaining whether any diamond is a blood diamond is no simple task. As with diamonds, so with the tantalum in one's cell phone. If one cannot ascertain the origin of either, it is possible that one's purchase of either will support abuse. I neither own nor lease a cell phone nor have I ever purchased a diamond.

I need to rant about millions of free cell phones purchased by the US government. This practice is relevant to a number of problems involving rights.

First, who came up with this idea of giving away cell phones? Probably someone who sells them for a living. How was the idea pitched to our legislators? Perhaps they all believe that instant communication must be a good thing. What if false information and blatant lies were the only things that could be communicated via cell phones? There is nothing about cell phones that prohibits that.

A cell phone certainly comes in handy in an emergency situation as long as there is coverage where one is and as long as the battery is not dead. How many emergencies do legislators think poor people encounter that they would need two hundred free minutes every month? Did any legislator ask which is likely to happen more often: someone's life is saved because of a free government cell phone, or a free government cell phone is used in criminal activity? Another possible rationale for giving away phones by the millions is that it will require a lot of workers to produce those phones. But will they be American workers, or will the phones be produced in Third World countries by people on subsistence incomes? And what about all the human telephone operators whose jobs have been replaced by cell towers?

Regardless of where these phones are made, the conflict mineral tantalum will be used in each cell phone. So the US government's purchase of free cell phones is indirectly supporting bush wars and human enslavement in tantalum-mined areas of Africa. Not a good foreign policy practice.

And what is the problem with land lines? They can certainly be cheaper than cell phones. My last land-line telephone plan cost me nothing. When I had it shut off because I wasn't using it at all, the phone company said I could still use it to contact 911 in an emergency—at no charge.

If we think overhead telephone wires are unsightly, they can be buried. What is visually pleasing about thousands of cell towers that can't be buried? Free cell phones for the financially disadvantaged also allows the phone companies to remove their pay phones from poorer neighborhoods, thus saving maintenance costs.

Last question: if the government wants to do something positive for the disadvantaged, why not purchase alternative sources of energy for those people's homes? That would promote the common good and be especially helpful for poor people with asthma and similar diseases. Congress, however, would rather cut funding for solar energy research and continue to give away billions of our tax dollars to big oil.

This may seem like a comedy of errors. In fact, it isn't funny. Just sadly pathetic.

I have nothing against cell phones as long as

1. they are safe (e.g., don't cause brain cancer);
2. they are made in the United States by American citizens earning at least a healthful living wage;
3. they are made by socially responsible companies (without conflict minerals); and
4. owners have the option of deactivating any tracking devices in their phones.

C. Responsibility

All people have a right to experience environmental quality. The quality of the environment is being threatened by humans and human indifference. The source of that indifference is related to a number of factors. The next question is "What should/can we do about it?" The answer to that is related to responsibility. Some of us have more individual responsibility for environmental destruction than others of us. If you own a coal-fired electric generating plant without the best available technology for containing mercury and sulfur emissions, you bear the responsibility for the negative effects of those elements that are emitted into the environment. If you are responsible for the dumping of toxic waste in poor neighborhoods, you are responsible for the human sickness and suffering that results from that action.

Cutting trees unnecessarily and not replacing cut trees, whether it entails cutting down a rainforest or felling a live tree in your yard, results in the destruction of valuable carbon-storing organisms. Each living tree that is destroyed makes a difference. If something killed all the fully grown trees on earth, the amount of carbon compounds in the air would immediately and dramatically increase. And, all things being equal, the carbon levels would not decrease to the former level for many years, even if new trees were planted. Healthy, older trees are generally bigger and so absorb more carbon than younger trees.

If you are a contractor or city planner, think about that before destroying older trees just because they are inconveniently placed. It's easy to rationalize that one tree does not matter. We tell ourselves that one aluminum can discarded in the trash rather than in the recycling bin is not going to make a great deal of difference. Here is the problem with that concept: Ten thousand or ten million of us are thinking the same exact thing at the same exact time. If ten million of us each decide to recycle a can, it makes a positive difference. If ten thousand of us decide to cut down a tree unnecessarily, especially without planting a new one, those ten thousand fewer trees will have a negative effect on the environment.

D. Population

Whenever I contemplate the declining environmental quality in the world, it occurs to me that if there were half as many of us in the world as there are, we might have only half as much unnecessary pollution; the hole in the ozone might be 50 percent smaller; there might be fewer species that have gone extinct; 50 percent fewer coal miners might have died from black lung disease; the cost of acid precipitation in the United States might be only $2.5 billion per year; there might be 301,500 fewer asthma attacks; only 65 million gallons of gasoline might have been consumed in the United States in 2006, resulting in the emission of only 617,500 tons of carbon dioxide; only 28 tons of mercury emissions might be being added to the air every year; there might be fewer violent superstorms, smaller forest fires, and less drought; there might be more natural habitat left and perhaps twice as many trees. It would still be, in my opinion, a dismal picture. But what is better about adding more people and with them more expense, more extinctions, more disease, less ozone, and more death and destruction?

If those people being born were environmental preservers and those people dying off were environmental abusers, that would be a positive thing. But in reality, that is not happening. If one is an environmental abuser, chances are one will teach one's children to abuse the environment.

Regardless of how well we treat the environment, more of us will need more food. Raising food requires soil. In some parts of the world, particularly the tropics, much of the soil is occupied by forests. The forests in the tropics sequester carbon all year around. To replace the carbon-sequestering capacity of a tropical tree, I suspect it would require about two mature deciduous trees in a northern climate, because northern trees uptake carbon dioxide for only about five months of the year.

According to Rhett Butler of Mongabay.com, since 1978, more than 238,000 square miles of Amazonian rainforest have been destroyed. It is estimated that 50 percent of that destruction was due to clearing forest to raise cattle for beef.[15] Restoring the lost carbon-sequestering potential of all those trees by planting trees in the Northern Hemisphere would probably require more than twice that 238,000 square miles, because rainforest trees might grow closer together and grow to a larger size than northern trees. More of us equals fewer trees and more carbon dioxide in the air.

Then there is the problem of fresh water, which is becoming scarcer in many parts of the world.[16] The more of us there are, the greater the need for fresh, safe water.

Increasing population decreases the potential for everyone to have opportunities to experience their individual inalienable rights. The best solution to overpopulation would be for enough people to recognize the problem and decide to support the common good of future generations by voluntarily limiting the number of children they propagate.

E. Conclusion

We are all created equal. That means we all have individual inalienable rights—or none of us has those rights. For those who deny that we all possess the same rights, the law of the jungle rules. They believe there is no need to be concerned about earth and its creatures. The fittest will survive. The weak will perish. Whatever happens to the environment, happens. Oh, well ...

Despite the deniers, and perhaps because of them, environmental quality, which is an aspect of the common good, is declining in many ways. If we didn't all have a right to benefit from the common good, environmental quality might seem relatively insignificant. Believing that we and our descendants deserve a quality environment and the health that goes with that necessitates our acting responsibly toward the environment, questioning the value of "easy living," voting out of office the authoritarian deniers, and supporting laws and regulations that preserve environmental quality.

Positive thinking is not going to save anything. Whether or not energy production from nuclear fusion turns out to be safe, nonpolluting, and feasible forty years from now, it won't feed people. In forty years, the bees could be extinct, and most trees could be gone. Even if we completely stopped burning fossil fuels, an increasing world population without the capacity to sequester more carbon will increase global warming.

---

[1]   US EPA, "Climate Change Indicators in the United States," November 10, 2015, http://www3.epa.gov/climatechange/science/indicators/oceans/index.html.

[2]   Louis A. Helfrich, et al., "Pesticides and Aquatic Animals: A Guide to Reducing Impacts on Aquatic Systems," Virginia Cooperative Extension, May 1, 2009, accessed May 15, 2016, https://pubs.ext.vt.edu/420/420-013/420-013.html.

3   Harvard University, "Climate Change Linked to Ozone Loss: May Result in More Skin Cancer," *Science Daily,* July 26, 2012, accessed May 15, 2016, https://www.sciencedaily.com/releases/2012/07/120726142204.htm.

4   Balloons Blow … Don't Let Them Go, "Impacts on Wildlife & the Environment," accessed May 15, 2016, http://balloonsblow.org/impacts-on-wildlife-and-environment/.

5   Ashley Schaeffer, "Species Gravely Endangered by Global Trade of Commodities like Palm Oil," 2012, accessed May 15, 2016, http://www.care2.com/causes/species-gravely-endangered-by-global-trade-of-commodities-like-palm-oil.html.

6   All Bible references are from the authorized King James Version of the Holy Bible (Cleveland, Ohio: The World Publishing Company, n.d.).

7   Pope Francis, "*Laudato Si*: On Care of Our Common Home," May 4, 2015, ch. 11, note 29, accessed January 2, 2015, http://w2.vatican.va/content/francesco/en/encyclicals/documents/papa-francesco_20150524_enciclica-laudato-si.html.

8   Tom Clynes, "Is there Such a Thing as Conflict-free-minerals?" Take Part, September 4, 2015, accessed January 5, 2016, http://www.takepart.com/feature/2015/09/04/conflict-free-minerals?cmpid=tpdaily-eml-2015-09-04.

9   Amanda Briney, "Acid Rain—The Causes, History, and Effects of Acid Rain," About.com, accessed January 5, 2016, http://geography.about.com/od/globalproblemsandissues/a/acidrain.htm.

10   "How Air Pollution Contributes to Lung Disease," Physicians for Social Responsibility, accessed January 5, 2016, http://www.psr.org/assets/pdfs/air-pollution-effects-respiratory.pdf.

11   Molly Redden, "A Scary New Study Erases Doubts That Fracking Causes Earthquakes," *New Republic,* September 6, 2013, accessed January 5, 2016, https://newrepublic.com/article/114620/fracking-and-earthquakes-new-study-provides-scary-evidence.

12   "How to Get Free Cell Phone Service from the Government," Lifeline Assistance, 2014, accessed January 5, 2016, http://www.freegovernmentcellphones.net/basics/how-do-i-get-a-free-phone.

13   "Factsheet: The U.S. Media Universe," Nielsen Company, January 5, 2011, accessed January 5, 2016, http://www.nielsen.com/us/en/insights/news/2011/factsheet-the-u-s-media-universe.html.

14   Melissa McNamara, "Facts About Blood Diamonds," *CBS News*, December 11, 2006, accessed January 5, 2016, http://www.cbsnews.com/news/facts-about-blood-diamonds/.

15   Rhett Butler, "Amazon Destruction," Mongabay, 2014, accessed January 4, 2016, ch. 12, http://rainforests.mongabay.com/amazon/amazon_destruction.html.

16   "Water Scarcity and the Importance of Water," The Water Project, 2016, accessed May 15, 2016, https://thewaterproject.org/water_scarcity.

16

RELIGION IN AMERICA AND HUMAN RIGHTS

Rights *are privileges based on law or reason. An example of rights based on reason is inalienable rights possessed by everyone by virtue of everyone being created equal. An example of a right based on law would be the right to vote in public elections.*

Religion *is a system of religious beliefs and practices, which may include rituals, evangelism, and mysticism.*

What is and what should the relationship be between religion and rights? This chapter will attempt to answer that complicated question. The chapter focuses on Christian religion and consists of the following sections:

A. Summary
B. Is the United States a Christian Country?
C. Religious Privilege
D. Should the US Legal System Be Based on the Christian Bible?
E. Separation of Church and State
F. Abuse by Religious Leaders
G. Morality
H. Conclusion

A. Summary

There are long-standing conflicts in our country involving religion. This chapter is concerned with conflicts and issues related to religion that threaten or potentially threaten individual rights. This chapter is not pro-religious or attesting that religion has no redeeming value. Without the sixteen and a half years of Catholic education I experienced by the age of twenty-three, I doubt I would be able to write this book. It would have been nice to have learned in high school or college the things I have learned since beginning this manuscript. However, that excellent Catholic education enables me to express what I have learned.

A person may identify as Christian, Jewish, Muslim, and so forth without being religious. Examples of religious behavior for Christians would include attending services occasionally or regularly, having their children baptized, giving lip service to their deity, and making financial contributions to their religious organizations. Most religious Christians are not what I would characterize as *zealous*. Zealous religious Christians may lobby their legislators for Bible-based laws, willingly die a martyr's death, carry around signs about the sin of gay marriage, or bomb an abortion clinic. Christian zealots are more apt than nonzealous Christians to behave with indifference toward human rights by

- acting like America belongs to Christians,
- using their religious convictions as justification for trying to impose their religious beliefs on others, and
- believing that their religious affiliation gives them permission to attempt to deny rights to others.

Adhering to the principle of separation of church and state would help protect every citizen's individual inalienable rights. Religious people do not adhere to that principle when they exercise an excessive influence on government without respect for everyone's inalienable rights. And religious authorities who abuse children are violators of the children's inalienable rights.

Decreasing the political power and influence of religion does not need to result in a declining standard of morality for Christians and non-Christians. This chapter presents a system of morality that might be acceptable to everyone, religious and nonreligious, Christians and non-Christians.

B. Is the United States a Christian Country?

I have often heard the expression "America is a Christian country." The problem with that statement is that it implies that the rights and concerns of religious Christians are more relevant/significant than the rights and concerns of non-Christians. It's easy for many Christians to accept the idea that the United States *must* be Christian. This section poses the question, *what makes America Christian?*

According to Frank Newport, a Gallop poll reported that 76 percent of Americans expressed a religious preference of Christian in 2014. That number includes Catholics and non-Catholic Christian denominations. Nineteen percent of Americans expressed no formal religious identity. That included those who identify as atheists and agnostics. Six percent identified as believers in non-Christian religions, such as Islam, Judaism, Hinduism, and Buddhism.[1]

Is the United States, a Christian country because the majority of Americans identify as Christian? According to "Number of Christian Denominations" at www.numberof.net, there are 1,200 different Christian denominations in the United States with the largest being Roman Catholic.[2] All Christian denominations in the country neither have the same set of beliefs nor engage in the same rituals. It seems to me that if everyone in a country belonged to the same denomination, it *might* be accurate to identify that country with that denomination. I question the validity of claiming a whole country is Christian, because most of its citizens belong to 1,200 different Christian denominations.

Another reason we think of the United States as a Christian country is that it was allegedly founded by Christians. This claim implies that all the founding fathers were Christian. Many of them probably were, but some did not identify as Christian. James Watkins's "Were U.S.

Founding Fathers Christian?" asserts that Samuel Adams, Alexander Hamilton, Patrick Henry, and John Jay claimed to be Christians. John Adams was a Unitarian, and Benjamin Franklin and Thomas Jefferson were Deists. Watkins was unable to verify the religious convictions of the other forty-nine signers of the Declaration of Independence.[3] Because we know for certain that four of the fifty-six founding fathers identified as Christian, does that make our country "Christian"?

According to Andrew Skinner's "The Influence of the Hebrew Scriptures on the Founding Fathers and Founding of the American Republic," the early American colonists and founders of the American Republic found references and allusions to the Hebrew Old Testament more inspiring than the Christian New Testament.[4] The teachings of Jesus in the New Testament have a different focus and flavor than the tenets of the Old Testament. As recorded in Matthew 5:17, Jesus said he came to fulfill (from a Greek word meaning *verify*) the law (of the Old Testament), not to destroy it. He did this by explaining the distinction between God's law (Matthew 22:37–40) and the religious laws of men from the Old Testament (Mark 3:4, 10:3–5, 8–9; Matthew 5:11).

Some people claim the country is Christian because many of its secular laws are based on the Christian Bible. The truth is that American laws are based more on the Hebrew Old Testament than on the New Testament teachings of Jesus, who seemed to think that Old Testament law needed to be verified. That many American laws were inspired by the Hebrew Old Testament seems more supportive of a theoretical claim that America is actually a *Jewish* country.

A manuscript entitled *The Way of Christ: A Guide to Christian Behavior*[5] refers to the red-letter teachings of Jesus from the King James Version of the Bible and to *Strong's Greek Dictionary of the Bible*. According to its author, James Strong, the word *Christian* comes from the Greek *Christianos*, a follower of Christ.[6]

The Way of Christ explains what "following Christ" means. It does not mean to physically walk with or to travel behind Jesus. To follow Christ is to follow his teachings. To be a true follower of Christ, one must understand what Jesus the Christ taught his disciples about living, and one must strive to live that way. How many people who identify as Christian actually follow all of Christ's teachings? How many even know all the ways a true Christian should behave?

The following is a specific example. Jesus said, "And if any man will sue thee at the law, and take away thy coat, let him have thy cloak also" (Matthew 5:40). He also said, "As you are going with your adversary to the magistrate, try hard to be reconciled to him on the way, or he may drag you off to the judge, and the judge turn you over to the officer, and the officer throw you into prison" (Luke 12:58). According to William Armstrong, the United States is the most litigious country in the world.[7] If 76 percent of Americans acted according to Matthew 5:40 and Luke 12:58, our so-called "Christian" country might not have that reputation of being so litigious. If its citizens don't act in a Christian manner, does it make sense to call their country Christian?

It seems to me that US foreign policy since World War II (see chapter 9, "Human Rights and Foreign Policy") has been aggressive rather than a "turning of the other cheek" (Matthew 5:39). Some political pundits may protest that the Constitution calls for a separation between church and state, as if that gives the state permission to act in an amoral, immoral, or unchristian manner as long as the country's best interests are served. Unfortunately, the only people whose interests have been promoted through the amoral, immoral, and unchristian actions of the American government have been the rich and powerful.

If our national government officials were truly Christian, they would do to and for others as they would have others do to and for them (Matthew 7:12). They would not preside over forty-six million citizens living in involuntary poverty. They would ensure that the twenty-two million aged eighteen to sixty-four who are able to work but unemployed, have the opportunity to earn a healthful living wage. "Inasmuch as ye did it not to one of the least of these, ye did it not to me" (Matthew 25:45). They would not permit corporations to unnecessarily poison our air, water, and land. They would not allow products to be marketed *before* determining that they are safe and healthful and environmentally harmless. The federal government acts in a consistent Christian manner neither toward its own citizens nor toward other nations. The behavior of federal government officials does not support the idea that the United States is a Christian country.

This book's chapter 3, "A Culture of Abuse," demonstrates that abuse is present in the workplace, in schools, in religious institutions, in law enforcement, in national and domestic policies of the federal government, in families, in intimate relationships, in the streets, in homes, and in offices. It is glorified in song lyrics and is portrayed in some TV shows as being justified. Abuse in America is so common that we may not always identify or think about what we witness as "abusive." Where in the Gospels does Jesus ever act abusively toward others; preach, support, or condone abusive behavior; or teach that any form of abuse is okay? Is it valid to claim that a culture full of abuse is "Christian"?

Some support their belief that America is a Christian country by pointing out that every state constitution includes the word *God*. That might be relevant if Christianity were the only religion to believe in and to worship God, and if agnostics did not acknowledge the existence of something many equate or define as God, and if Christianity possessed an exclusive trademark on the word *God*. Perhaps those who equate Christianity with a belief in God don't realize that more than 92 percent of the world's population believes in God or gods, but that only 33 percent of the world's population identifies as Christian, according to "Major Religions of the World Ranked by Adherents."[8]

Many Americans probably believe the country is Christian because that's what they were told. The question is, other than that traditional *belief*, what makes America Christian? It's not numbers. Fewer than three-quarters of its citizens identify themselves as Christian. It's not a strict adherence to Christ's teachings. Those who claim to be Christians—that is, followers of Christ's teachings—don't always behave according to those teachings. The American government does not consistently act according to Jesus's teachings either. Perhaps there is something else that makes the United States a Christian nation. I have no idea what that something could be.

C. Religious Privilege

Some Americans seem to believe that their Christian identity entitles them to special privileges and to the power to control other people's behavior. One of the principles from this book's introduction is that joining a group does not add to one's individual rights. A group has no individual rights. Churches are groups of people. A person may belong to one of the 1,200 different Christian denominations in the United States. Each and every member of every denomination may believe *that* particular denomination is the only true religion in the world. That belief does not bestow on those believers an extralegal privilege that those not belonging to that denomination lack.

Why do some people believe otherwise? The answer to this is well expressed by an article by Austin Cline, an agnosticism and atheism expert. He states that many religious believers are convinced that when the civil law fails to preserve what they consider good, the morality designated by their god should take precedence over the civil law. Cline believes that conviction underlies religious extremism and a number of conflicts involving Christian and/or non-Christian religious groups.[9]

An example of this religious conviction is the case of Kim Davis, a county clerk in Kentucky. In September 2015, the Supreme Court ruled that gay marriage was legal in every state of the Union. Davis decided it was against her Christian beliefs to issue marriage licenses to gay couples, even though her job was to issue marriage licenses. She evidently decided that gay marriage is contrary to the wishes of God and that she must obey God rather than the Supreme Court. I believe Charles Manson claimed to have heard God telling him to start a race war.

Using *God* to justify violating other people's individual rights has happened repeatedly throughout human history. Regarding the case of Kim Davis, what profession in this country continues to employ workers who refuse to carry out the duties of their jobs or permits the employees to determine which of their assigned duties are acceptable? I don't understand why Davis was not given the option of (1) doing her job, (2) quitting, (3) being terminated, or (4) being demoted.

If people are allowed to violate other people's rights because of the violators' religious beliefs, chaos will result. The First Amendment to the Constitution guarantees all Americans the freedom to believe whatever they wish to believe. It does not grant any individual the freedom to deprive other people of either their inalienable rights or their civil rights.

D. Should the US Legal System Be Based on the Christian Bible?

Those who insist that the country is Christian might think that a Bible-based American legal system is reasonable and desirable. However, there seems to be no objective reason to believe that the United States is Christian. So why would a Bible-based legal system be appropriate?

Converting the American legal system to a Bible-based, "Christian" system of laws would possibly involve consulting the country's 1,200 different Christian denominations, some of which don't believe certain other denominations are truly Christian. Each denomination would probably not want the same changes, deletions, and additions to the current system of laws.

What would change if all laws and legal practices could be amended in accordance with conventional "Christian" beliefs? Because most Christians believe the Old Testament is the "Word of God," I would suspect the amended legal system would be similar to that of Saudi Arabia, which is based on Sharia or Islamic law. Under their system of justice, there are punitive stonings, beheadings, and amputations sanctioned by the state. You may think those things would not happen under a Christian system. However, "an eye for an eye and a tooth for a tooth" is an example of Old Testament justice. Christian religious and civil authorities of the past established inquisitions to punish people for the "crime" of heresy. Then there were the Salem witch trials in this country. I believe the founding fathers did not wish to permit those abuses of human rights in the United States. The principle of separation of church and state, when followed, has the effect of preventing such abuses.

E. Separation of Church and State

The United States is a nation of religious diversity with a long-standing conflict between church and state. If I were writing this book in Saudi Arabia, the "church" I would be referring to would be Islam. Because those who identify as Christian in this country are not only a numerical majority but also possess most of the political/economic power, the church or religion that experiences the most conflict with government in this country is probably Christian.

If Congress made all laws and legal system procedures conform to the Christian Bible, I believe that would be a violation of the First Amendment to the US Constitution which prohibits Congress from making any law respecting the establishment of a religion. According to a Library of Congress webpage, Thomas Jefferson wrote,

> **I contemplate with sovereign reverence that act of the whole American people which declared that their legislature should "make no law respecting an establishment of religion, or prohibiting the free exercise thereof," thus building a wall of separation between Church & State.** (https://www.loc.gov/loc/lcib/9806/danpre.html)

What is meant by the "free exercise of religion"? Any freedom guaranteed by the Constitution has limits. For example, freedom of assembly does not mean permission to obstruct the flow of traffic through the streets without a valid legal permit. Exercising your freedom of religion means you are free to attend any church or no church, to believe in whatever or in nothing. Freedom of religion does not give those who are religious, or who are Christian, permission to break the law or to violate others' individual inalienable rights or to violate the civil rights of others. I believe "free exercise of religion" was meant to pertain to individuals rather than to whole religious institutions—that is, to groups of people. As with corporations, so with churches. Neither possesses individual inalienable rights.

Is the refusal of business owners to serve certain people that the religious owners perceive or judge to be living an "immoral lifestyle" an exercise of "religious freedom"? According to "Discrimination Law and Legal Definition" at www.U.S.Legal.com, discrimination is "the treatment or consideration of, or making a distinction in favor of or against, a person or thing based on the group, class, or category to which that person or thing belongs rather than on individual merit" (2016, http://definitions.uslegal.com/d/discrimination/). An example of discrimination would be a business owned by someone who believes homosexuality is a sin refusing to serve a person because the person is known, or suspected, to be a practicing homosexual. Freedom of religion is a civil right established by law. No law can cancel or invalidate anyone's inalienable rights. Discrimination is an abuse of inalienable rights. A business owner refusing to serve certain people based on their sexual orientation is discrimination. Freedom of religion neither legalizes nor justifies discrimination.

In regard to hiring, freedom of religion does not give a business owner the right to violate Title VII of the Civil Rights Act of 1964, which prohibits discrimination in hiring. A Christian business owner may be hard-pressed to find a minister or priest who would be willing to testify that discrimination is in agreement with the teachings of Jesus.

Some Christians think that abortion, gay marriage, and birth control should be against the law in the United States. There is no mention of any of these issues in the four Gospels. For some reason, Jesus chose not to condemn these things, whereas he did choose to condemn hypocrisy and materialism. Some Christians seem to depend on the Old Testament to justify many of the things they oppose. This opposition bears a striking semblance to the Jewish Pharisees and Scribes. Matthew 23:25–26 seems to indicate that these religious leaders were less concerned about ensuring the purity of their hearts than about appearing to be holy and obedient to the Old Testament Law.

Jesus understood that true goodness depends on our motivation rather than on our actions. That is why he instructs his disciples to love their enemies rather than to resist evil in the world (Matthew 5:39, 44–45). *The Way of Christ* states that "Jesus' teachings do not even vaguely imply that passing laws is a legitimate solution to the problem of (*moral*) evil."[10]

Some Christians help fund lobbying efforts in Congress and in state legislatures to restrict abortions, gay marriage, and birth control. Each of us has a right to attempt to influence our legislators. However, trying to get laws enacted that would force anyone to live according to what one thinks of as God's will is potentially detrimental to the common good and potentially threatening to certain inalienable and civil rights.

There are those (often non-Christians) who would like all signs of religion (most often the Christian religion) removed from public functions and institutions. Others (usually Christians) want to preserve those outward signs of faith. Those who favor keeping religion (i.e., Christianity) in public life often justify that position by claiming that this is a Christian country.

Some Christians are opposed to the teaching of any idea in public school that contradicts a literal interpretation of the Bible. They favor legislation that would outlaw such instruction for Christian and for non-Christian students. Such legislation would violate both the rights of those parents who don't believe in the Bible and the rights of those parents who want their children to learn science rather than the Bible. Those Christian parents who want their children to learn the Bible have the options of Sunday School, a certified religious school, or homeschooling their children. Non-Christian parents have similar options.

Some Christians think that science is wrong/evil because it contradicts their interpretation of the Bible. Some think it is evil to prohibit publically financed displays of the Christian religion. Jesus did not call either of these things evil. In fact, he instructed his followers not to resist evil (Matthew 5:39).

Preventing organized religion from having too much power/influence over the legislative branch of government is one aspect of the separation of church and state. There is another aspect. I remember hearing that John F. Kennedy, a Catholic, was opposed to the idea of Catholic schools accepting federal funding. I suspect the root of his concern was that accepting money from a giver makes the receiver more prone to be influenced/controlled by the giver. Separation of church and state involves not only preventing the church from having too much power over the government, like in the Inquisitions and the Salem witch trials, it also involves preventing government from having too much power or influence over religious affairs.

Is the tax-exempt status of churches and tax deductions taken by church supporters relevant to the issues of separation or of individual rights? Does the government subsidize churches, in a sense, by providing services for which churches do not pay? Law enforcement and fire protection are two such services that churches receive as needed at the expense of taxpayers.

You may rationalize that what the church contributes to society justifies its tax-exempt status. I know of no measurable requirements a church must meet in terms of bettering society. Whether or not the church helps those who are poor attain better employment opportunities, it still pays no taxes. Whether or not the church plants new trees, it still pays no taxes. Those who contribute to that church might be able to deduct their contributions from the federal income tax they pay. In one sense, it seems that all taxpayers are financially supporting America's tax-exempt churches and that nonreligious taxpayers may "contribute" proportionally more than those church supporters who itemize tax deductions.

"Are Churches Making America Poor?" by Victoria Bekiempis, reports that Ryan Cragun, associate professor of sociology at the University of Tampa, determined that, in 2012, *if* the money collected by all churches in this country was taxed at the rate of for-profit corporations, the federal government would collect an extra $71 billion.[11]

John F. Kennedy's concern about churches accepting financial assistance from the federal government is perhaps relevant to requiring religious-affiliated employers to include contraceptive coverage in the health insurance they provide to their nonreligious employees. One argument is that, when the government subsidizes the religion to which the employer is affiliated, it is reasonable for the government to expect the employer to abide by government regulations. On the other hand, the employer is not preventing its employees from attaining birth control by other means and utilizing it. In that sense, the employees' rights are not being violated. But the question is, should an employer with a religious affiliation be allowed to circumvent any law by which every other secular employer is bound? I have already answered that under the section entitled "Religious Privilege." Allowing religious privilege is not in the best interest of the common good.

In accepting financial public support from the government in the form of tax exemption, churches allow themselves to be limited by government. Internal Revenue Service regulations regarding tax-exempt nonprofit organizations, including churches, from "The Restriction of Political Campaign Intervention by Section 501(c)(3) Tax-Exempt Organizations," provide for the following:

> **Under the Internal Revenue Code, all section 501(c)(3) organizations are absolutely prohibited from directly or indirectly participating in, or intervening in, any political campaign on behalf of (or in opposition to) any candidate for elective public office. Contributions to political campaign funds or public statements of position (verbal or written) made on behalf of the organization in favor of or in opposition to any candidate for public office clearly violate the prohibition against political campaign activity. Violating this prohibition may result in denial or revocation of tax-exempt status and the imposition of certain excise taxes.** (Last reviewed December 15, 2015, accessed January 6, 2016, https://www.irs.gov/Charities-&-Non-Profits/Charitable-Organizations/The-Restriction-of-Political-Campaign-Intervention-by-Section-501%28c%29%283%29-Tax-Exempt-Organizations.)

In other words, the government won't tax religion, but religion must allow politicians to do whatever they please. I have often wondered why German Christian churches did not oppose Hitler's rise to power. Perhaps Germany had a similar tax code. Or perhaps church leaders were just afraid of the Nazis.

F. Abuse by Religious Leaders

A discussion of religion and human rights would not be complete without examining the phenomenon of abuse by religious authorities. Unnecessarily threatening or violating other people's inalienable rights in a deliberate or negligent manner is abusive. Authority figures often have the power to abuse others because of their position. Some people can't seem to handle the power that comes with a position of authority without becoming abusive.

Some religious leaders seem to be power hungry and seem to want or need to experience absolute control. There were many allegations of sexual child abuse levied against Catholic priests in the 1990s and the beginning years of the twenty-first century. How many victims were there? Let's look at a study by the John Jay College of Criminal Justice commissioned and paid for by the United States Conference of Bishops, entitled *The Nature and Scope of Sexual Abuse of Minors by Catholic Priests and Deacons in the United States, 1950–2002*. The study estimated that there were 109,964 active priests in American dioceses, eparchies (Eastern Rite Catholic parishes), and religious orders during the years 1950 to 2002. Of those, 4,392, or 4 percent, were accused of sexual abuse of minors (children under the age of eighteen) during those years without having the allegations proved false or withdrawn. The allegations against the priests were made by 10,667 individuals. One should keep in mind that not all sexual abuse victims have or will come forward.[12]

I found no research that suggests Catholic priests have a higher incidence of sexual abuse than leaders of other religious denominations. For example, a 2009 National Public Radio story by Barbara Bradley Hagerty suggests that child sexual abuse by Jewish rabbis in New York City was a serious problem.[13] Kosnoff and Fasy are Seattle attorneys who, according to their website, legally oppose the

Church of Jesus Christ of the Latter-day Saints (the Mormons) because
of a culture that enables and protects child abusers.[14]

G. Morality

Some people blame many of our social and political problems in the
twenty-first century on the general lack of morality that they associate
with fewer people going to church or with a decline in religiosity. Those
whose ideas of good and bad, wrong and right, came from what they
were taught was God's will or what was pleasing to God might think of
religion and morality as being inseparable. Moral conviction, however,
can be based purely on human reasoning.

What is moral conviction? For me, it is the moral courage to do
what is "right." American society seems more secular than religious
these days. If we must be religious to do what is right—that is, to act
morally—the decline of religion could logically account for a decline
in moral behavior. The very idea that only those who are religious act
morally, however, sounds ridiculous and is insulting to humanists,
atheists, agnostics, and others who do not regard themselves as
religious. I have wondered, from time to time, whose moral behavior
is more in agreement with the true Gospel teachings of Jesus Christ,
those who are humanists or those who are conventional Christians.

Unless one is a sociopath, one has a sense of right and wrong
and the capacity to act morally regardless of one's degree of religious
devotion or beliefs, or lack thereof. Morality and religion are two
separate concepts. Morality is concerned with what is right and wrong,
good and bad. Religion is much more complicated than that. In
addition to moral teachings, religion involves religious beliefs, rituals,
evangelism, and mysticism.

It has been said that morality is a way of controlling the masses. Who
uses morality to gain power? Some people who are in positions of
authority, like priests, ministers, and government leaders, who preach
and teach us that we should behave in certain ("moral") ways, ways

that do not threaten their power. That type of moral teaching is not the morality that comes from within each of us.

Most of us, depending on our age and mental capacity, have some ability to reason. I was taught in Catholic grade school that there is an "age of reason," which most of us reach around the age of seven. The idea is that before that age, a child is incapable of telling right from wrong. An adult does not need to be taught right from wrong. An adult can decide what is right and wrong in accordance with his or her conscience guided by reason. That is the morality that comes from within.

Your capacity to discern accurately what is right or wrong, good or bad, depends on your knowledge of the facts of a situation and your capacity to remain objective. You might be one of those people who thinks that whatever benefits or gratifies you immediately is good. That is highly subjective rather than objective and will not result in an accurate assessment of what is good.

Or you might be one of the people who thinks that what benefits your family, your friends, your religious community, your tribe, your state, or your country must be intrinsically good. This is a subjective assessment that will not necessarily lead to an accurate, reasonable conclusion.

So, what is an alternative method for accurately reasoning out what is good and bad? I suspect that most people would agree that what makes everyone happy is good and what makes everyone unhappy must be bad. We do not have to be religious to accept those definitions of good and bad. What would make all people happy and no one unhappy? According to America's Declaration of Independence, we all are created equal and are born with individual rights among which are life, liberty, and the pursuit of happiness. I suggest that the opportunities to experience those rights makes everyone happy, and being deprived of those opportunities makes people unhappy. Experiencing your individual rights is good; being deprived of that experience is bad.

A moral society, not a culture of abuse, would consist of people living together without threatening one another's inalienable rights.

H. Conclusion

Religion itself is not a threat to individual inalienable rights. According to the Newport article, 82 percent of Americans identified with particular religious affiliations in 2014; 76 percent of Americans identified as Christian. Of those Christians, about 47 percent were religious—that is, they attended religious services weekly or more often. I believe that most religious Christians do not intentionally use their religious beliefs to justify threatening the individual inalienable rights of those with other beliefs. Christian religious zealots are a much smaller percentage of that 47 percent. Of that small percentage of zealots, only a very few bomb abortion clinics, murder abortion doctors, or engage in other acts of violence for the sake of their religious beliefs. Perhaps most Christian zealots realize such behavior is the complete opposite of what Jesus taught.

Violent behavior is certainly abusive and a violation of human rights. Some nonviolent Christian zealots would like to force all American citizens, through secular legislative processes, to live according to what they believe to be Bible-based principles and practices like not using birth control, not having abortions, and disallowing LBGT behavior, including gay marriage. These efforts, if successful, would deprive many people of some rights opportunities. These zealots' efforts are in keeping with neither the letter nor the spirit of Christ's instructions to his disciples. Their efforts are also in opposition to the constitutional principle of separation of church and state.

There are Christian churches that support, financially or morally, lobbying efforts against abortion, against birth control, and against gay marriage. These churches do not pay income tax, which gives them more money to support these efforts. If zealots write off their contributions to the church on their tax returns, they have that much more money with which to threaten others' rights. If they utilize that money to threaten other people's individual rights opportunities in accordance with their religious beliefs, the government would be subsidizing those threats. This would violate the principle of separation of church and state.

Then there are a small percentage of religious leaders who use their positions of power in religious organizations to violate the rights of some who are more vulnerable. How much of the responsibility the leadership of religious institutions bear for this continuing problem of abuse is debatable. I think there needs to be a shift *from* the ineffective efforts of religious institutions to deal with abusers *to* a willingness of the institutions to report the abuse to civil authorities.

It would help if more people readily challenged the idea that America is a Christian country whenever that belief is voiced. Doing that might help discourage the belief that religious faith entitles believers to violate other people's rights.

Although morality and religion are two distinct concepts, we need a system of morality with which everyone, religious and nonreligious, can agree. If we can accept the concepts of universal equality at birth and the idea that we all are born with the same individual rights, it is logical to conclude that what supports those rights is good and what deprives or detracts from those rights is wrong.

<hr />

[1] Frank Newport, "Three-quarters of Americans Identify as Christian," Gallup, December 14, 2014, accessed January 1, 2015, http://www.gallup.com/poll/180347/three-quarters-americans-identify-christian.aspx.

[2] "Number of Christian Denominations," March 5, 2010, accessed January 6, 2015, http://www.numberof.net/number-of-christian-denominations/.

[3] James Watkins, "Were U.S. Founding Fathers Christian?" Hope and Humor—James Watkins, 2003, accessed January 6, 2016, http://www.jameswatkins.com/articles-2/heavy/foundingfathers/.

[4] Andrew Skinner, "The Influence of the Hebrew Scriptures on the Founders and Founding of the American Republic," in *Lectures on Religion and the Founding of the American Republic*, ed. John W. Welsh with Stephen J. Fleming (Provo, UT: Brigham Young University Press, 2002), 39–48.

[5] Richard Geiger, *The Way of Christ: A Guide to Christian Behavior* (Butler, Pennsylvania: Self-published, 1983).

6   James Strong, *A Concise Dictionary of the Words in the Greek Testament* (New York: Abingdon Press, 1890).

7   Williams Armstrong, "Most Litigious Nation in the World," The Hill, October 11, 2011, http://thehill.com/blogs/pundits-blog/economy-a-budget/186667-most-litigious-nation-in-the-world.

8   "Major Religions of the World Ranked by Adherents," Adherents.com, January 2000, accessed January 6, 2016, http://www.adherents.com/Religions_By_Adherents.html.

9   Austin Cline, "Religious Morality vs. Civil Law: Religious Conflicts over Neutral, Civil Laws," About.com, 2016, accessed January 6, 2016, http://atheism.about.com/od/secularismseparation/a/SecularLaw.htm.

10 Geiger, *The Way of Christ*, p. 45.

11 Victoria Bekiempis, "Are Churches Making America Poor?" *Newsweek*, October 24, 2013, accessed January 6, 2016, http://w+ww.newsweek.com/are-churches-making-america-poor-243734.

12 John Jay College of Criminal Justice, *The Nature and Scope of Sexual Abuse of Minors by Catholic Priests and Deacons in the United States, 1950–2002*, February 2004, accessed January 6, 2016, http://www.usccb.org/issues-and-action/child-and-youth-protection/upload/The-Nature-and-Scope-of-Sexual-Abuse-of-Minors-by-Catholic-Priests-and-Deacons-in-the-United-States-1950-2002.pdf.

13 Barbara Bradley Hagerty, "Abuse Scandal Plagues Hasidic Jews in Brooklyn," National Public Radio, February 2, 2009, accessed January 6, 2016, http://www.npr.org/templates/story/story.php?storyId=99913807&ft=1&f=1001.

14 "Yesterday's Children Saving Today's Children," Kosnoff/Fasy, accessed January 6, 2016, http://kosnoff.com/latterdaysaints.php.

17

GUN OWNERSHIP AND VIOLENCE IN AMERICA

Sections of this chapter include the following:

A. Summary

I did not like guns when I started writing this chapter. After finishing it, I still don't like guns. But I do have a fresh understanding of the value of private gun ownership. The Second Amendment, regardless of how we interpret it, does seem to have been designed to prevent government from banning all guns and ammunition from being possessed by any responsible, law-abiding citizen. My research uncovered no correlation between the numbers of guns in a given population and the number of intentional homicides in that population. The banning of operable firearms in our country would potentially threaten our individual inalienable rights and would possibly result in a higher rate of homicides.

Many people seem to agree that additional reasonable restrictions on gun ownership are desirable and needed. The problem with legalizing such restrictions seems to be a lack of agreement about what is reasonable. When gun legislation is proposed, rather than limiting it to stricter restrictions everyone can agree on, someone will insist on including a ban on handguns or on assault rifles or on the number of bullets in a clip. Consequently, everyone does not agree with everything in the bill, and it goes down in defeat.

This is not in the best interest of the common good. Legislative bills having to do with mental health, straw purchases (by proxy), gun show loopholes, and better background checks should include neither modifications of firearms nor proposed bans on specific types of guns or ammunition.

A future Supreme Court might decide that the Second Amendment applies only to members of state militias. Whether that ever happens, all levels of government should still respect and preserve the value of gun ownership by those who are mentally stable, responsible, law-abiding private citizens with no history of violent behavior.

It would be helpful for all citizens, including gun owners, to understand the difference between violence and self-defense. Violence is a threat to our individual inalienable rights. Self-defense is a means of protecting those rights from violent offenders. For the sake of preserving our individual inalienable rights and the common good, greater efforts need to be made to prevent violence in general and gun violence in particular. Those efforts should include keeping guns out of the hands of the mentally ill, children, and criminals.

B. My Personal Perspective

I don't like guns. Would I be willing to take up arms if the United States mainland were attacked? Yes. Would I use firearms, if available, to defend myself and/or my loved ones from attempted homicide? Yes. In general, have I and those I care about been safer because I have not possessed a firearm? Yes. I do believe so.

C. A Brief Historical Perspective

Gunpowder, without which there would be no guns, was invented around AD 85 by a Chinese alchemist seeking immortality. Not until the fifteenth century in Europe was the first reliable handgun invented. The gun has had both profound positive and negative effects on earth and on human life. For instance, if it weren't for guns, there might still be passenger pigeons darkening the skies and millions of bison roaming the prairies of North America. And Europeans would have had a harder time conquering the New World.

On December 15, 1791, the US Constitution's Bill of Rights was ratified. The Second Amendment of that bill reads, "A well regulated Militia, being necessary to the security of a free State, the right of the people to keep and bear Arms, shall not be infringed." This amendment has been interpreted by the courts in various ways since then. Does it apply only to firearms owned by members of state militias? Or was its purpose to protect the rights of citizens in general to keep firearms in their homes? According to an article by Dave Kopel, research director of the Independence Institute, one of the motivating factors for the American Revolution was the efforts of the British to control the colonies by confiscating arms and ammunition.[1]

So, the Second Amendment may have been a reaction to that British effort. Had the British succeeded in their confiscation and banning of firearms, the United States might still be known as the British Colonies of America.

D. Prohibition of Guns

Today there are American farmers and ranchers who need guns to protect their livestock from predators. Some people use guns to hunt for profit, for sport, and for food. Some believe they need to possess a gun for protection. Some people collect guns. If it weren't for those who use guns to abuse others, antigun thinking would probably be less prevalent in this country. Some American citizens seem to favor outlawing private ownership of operable guns altogether. If that ever happened, which is highly improbable, it would mean gun collectors would have to render their weapons inoperable. Hunters would have to rent rifles to hunt. Farmers would have to revert to trapping or poisoning predators of their livestock. Those who felt a need for protection would have to take self-defense classes or carry weapons like knives or mace or stun guns.

E. Numbers of Guns and Homicide Rates

Why would some people like the private ownership of guns banned completely? Perhaps because they want themselves and their families to be safe. That makes a certain amount of sense. Were there fewer guns in circulation, there would probably be less violence perpetrated with *guns*. That does not mean that fewer guns in a population results in fewer homicides, however. According to Wikipedia's "Number of guns per capita by country," in 2014, there were 112.6 personal firearms for every 100 people in the United States. This was the highest rate in the world of the 178 countries listed. The second-highest rate of private gun ownership was Serbia at 69.7 per 100 people.[2] An article by Dan Griffin puts the total personal arms in the hands of American citizens at 300 to 310 million in 2014.[3]

"United Nations Office on Drugs and Crime Global Study on Homicide" involved 218 countries. The study determined that the global average of intentional homicide rate was 6.2 per 100,000 people in 2012. The United States, with the highest rate of private gun possession, had a homicide rate of 4.7 per 100,000 people. Serbia, the country with the second-highest rate of gun possession, had an intentional homicide rate of 1.2 per 100,000. I counted 105 countries with higher homicide rates than the United States. The country with the highest rate was Honduras (90.4 per 100,000).[4]

These rankings are based on the population of each country and the total number of murders per country. Even though there were twice as many murders in 2012 in the United States (14,827) than in Honduras (7,172), the population size of Honduras is about 2.5 percent of the United States population. Put another way, *if* the US homicide rate was 90.4 per 100,000 in 2012, there would have been about 216,000 murders in the United States instead of the reported total of 14,827. The United States is not the world's most violent country in terms of intentional homicides.

In the Wikipedia list of 178 countries, Honduras ranked eighty-seventh at 6.2 firearms per 100 people. Compare that with the 112.6 per 100 in the United States. There appears to be no direct relationship between the number of private firearms in a country and the number of intentional homicides.

Of the 4.7 homicides per 100,000 of us in the United States in 2012, 3.55 per 100,000 were firearm related, according to the UN study.[5] Is there any logical reason to believe that the homicide rate would decrease to 1.15 per 100,000 if private ownership of guns was banned in the United States? Were we no longer able to use guns to kill one another, the number of homicides by stabbing, drowning, poisoning, hanging, and bombing would probably increase. Would I stand a better chance of surviving a close-in knife attack than a shooting from a distance? I would suspect so. I also think that if someone is determined to kill me, depending on the killer's skill, resources, and intelligence, there may not be a lot I can do to prevent it. Even though John F. and Robert Kennedy had Secret Service protection, they were both assassinated.

Some gun ownership advocates claim that guns do not kill, people do. I would agree that guns do not kill. It is the bullets shot from guns that actually do the damage. Bullets are only one of the many tools we can use to kill one another. Even if privately owned firearms were banned and confiscated, or if the manufacture, possession, and use of all ammunition were declared illegal, homicides would still occur.

Theoretically, the homicide rate might actually *increase*. If I was a violent person intending to hurt others, what would be my main source of power? Probably a gun. What is the most effective source of defensive power for those who are potential victims of violent human predators? Guns. Taking guns out of the equation would not make violent predators less violent. It might make them bolder.

F. Protecting Individual Rights

Banning the private possession of guns would not stop intentional homicides. Some people, rightly or wrongly, believe that gun possession is necessary to protect our inalienable rights to life, liberty, and the pursuit of happiness. This might have been the everyday reality for more individual American frontiersmen back in the day than it is for us modern dwellers of suburbia.

Most of us don't need guns to protect ourselves from attacks by wild animals and Native Americans. But how long would our rights opportunities and our civil rights remain intact if private ownership of operable firearms were prohibited in this country? I don't believe that it would be impossible for some future president to declare martial law with the hidden motive of discouraging dissent and increasing the power of large corporations and the upper 1 percent. The success of such an effort would be more probable in the absence of legal private gun ownership.

Another potential threat to individual rights related to firearms is terrorism in this country. If a group of ISIS sympathizers were to invade my neighborhood, I would probably be grateful to any of my neighbors who owned military-style assault weapons that could be used to defend the neighborhood. On the other hand, what if a terrorist breaks and enters my neighbor's house, steals an assault weapon, and uses it on a killing rampage? I would support a law that would require all assault-type weapons, weapons with rapid fire capacity, and those using large ammunition clips to be equipped with biometric gun locks before being sold.[6] That would hopefully decrease the potential unauthorized use of these weapons.

G. Reasonable Gun Regulations

The possibility of an American dictatorship is the main reason I oppose a total ban on private gun ownership in the United States. On the other hand, I do not believe that *every* one of us should be allowed to own a gun or even to handle a loaded weapon. Others share this opinion. I found the following quotation of the National Rifle Association's executive vice president, Wayne LaPierre, in "NRA in Favor of Gun Control Law" by Robin Salisian: "We've always been vigilant about protecting the rights of law-abiding citizens to purchase guns and equally vigilant about keeping the guns out of the hands of criminals and the mentally defective and people who shouldn't have them" (LawCrossing, 2016, accessed July 16, 2016, http://www.lawcrossing.com/article/3197/ NRA-in-Favor-of-Gun-Control-Law/).

According to supremecourt.gov, the Supreme Court in *District of Columbia et al. v. Heller* (6/26/08) ruled that

> **Like most rights, the Second Amendment right is not unlimited. It is not a right to keep and carry any weapon whatsoever in any manner whatsoever and for whatever purpose ... The Court's opinion should not be taken to cast doubt on longstanding prohibitions on the possession of firearms by felons and the mentally ill, or laws forbidding the carrying of firearms in sensitive places such as schools and government buildings, or laws imposing conditions and qualifications on the commercial sale of arms.** (2008, accessed January 7, 2016, http://www.supremecourt.gov/ opinions/07pdf/07-290.pdf)

So both the NRA and the Supreme Court agree that there need to be reasonable restrictions on private gun ownership. In an ideal world, unless you were a mentally stable, responsible adult with no history of violent behavior, you would not be allowed to handle a firearm. Some questions would have to be answered before that principle could be converted into effective regulations, such as the following:

- How would mental stability be defined?
- If a person's mental disorder or psychosis is moderated by prescribed medication, should the person be designated mentally stable?
- How can we determine whether people without criminal or mental treatment records are responsible, nonabusive, and mentally/emotionally stable? Might a background check questionnaire help to provide that information?

You may wonder what would motivate anyone to oppose regulations to keep guns out of the hands of violent, abusive, mentally unstable, or irresponsible people. Might such opposition be prompted by profit rather than by patriotic defense of Second Amendment rights? The more mentally ill, irresponsible, and abusive individuals who buy guns, the more money gun dealers and manufacturers will make on those sales. The more irresponsible gun sales that occur, the more/bigger guns law-abiding citizens will purchase to defend themselves and their families from those who should not possess guns.

I can think of no *good* reason why background checks should not be improved, why straw purchases should not be prohibited, and why the gun show loophole should not be closed.

H. The Second Amendment

You can find articles on the Internet claiming that the Supreme Court has never ruled that the Second Amendment supports the right to own personal firearms. Before you believe this, you should check out *District of Columbia et al. v. Heller* (2008), which states in part

Held:

1. The Second Amendment protects an individual right to possess a firearm unconnected with service in a militia, and to use that arm for traditionally lawful purposes, such as self-defense within the home. (ibid., 1)

It is the role of the Supreme Court to decide what the Second Amendment right to keep and bear arms entails. If the Supreme Court ever decides that the Second Amendment applies to states rather than to individuals or that it does not guarantee the right of those not in a militia to own and use firearms, federal, state, and local governments would have the option of outlawing personal firearms and ammunition. If that happened, I would hope those governments would still grant responsible, mentally stable adults the legal privilege of gun ownership. I suspect that many modern American citizens would be no less resistant to the attempted government confiscation of all private weapons and ammunition than were the founding fathers. That is a good thing. I also hope that the Supreme Court will always choose to uphold laws prohibiting firearm possession and use by anyone convicted of a violent crime or a crime involving violence or the threat of violence.

I. Violence and Self-Defense

If you already understand these two concepts, feel free to skip this section. I think it is important to know exactly what each concept entails, especially in regard to guns.

Violence is an act of uninvited physical aggression. Self-defense is the reaction to such aggression or the intended threat of such aggression, with the sole purpose of protecting the person being physically attacked through using reasonable (not excessive) force. There are many misconceptions about what a justified act of self-defense entails. Verbal insults, harassment, humiliation, slander, and libel, although abusive, are not forms of physical violence. An aggressive physical response to those provocations does not meet the definition of self-defense.

Some people tend to be physically aggressive toward certain persons because "they have it coming." This is not self-defense. Some people practice vigilante justice, a planned effort to punish a specific person or group they have decided is evil or undesirable. Vigilante behavior is not self-defense.

In regard to private property and self-defense, a number of questions arise.

- Is it okay to kill a trespasser?
- If someone is in one's domicile and is uninvited, is it okay to eject the person physically even though the trespasser is not posing a physical threat to the people who live there?
- What about a person attempting to break into one's home? If one has a gun, is it okay to shoot to kill even before the person has gained entry?

How we respond to intruders may be legal or illegal, moral or immoral. What if you know your life is threatened? For example, you know for certain that the intruder has a gun. In my opinion, you would be justified in killing the intruder. If you know the intruder is unarmed, killing him or her may be judged to be use of "excessive force." If the intruder is unarmed and not posing a physical threat to you or to your property, the best course of action might be to call the police for assistance in removing the "uninvited guest."

It is more difficult to determine the best course of action when you don't know the identity of a suspected intruder and when you don't know whether the intruder is armed. Take, for example, the case of Oscar Pistorius, the Blade Runner, who testified that he thought there was an intruder in his hotel bathroom in the middle of the night. He evidently decided whoever was in there was going to kill him. He shot the "intruder," without warning, through a closed bathroom door. Unfortunately, the "intruder" was his girlfriend, Reeva Steenkamp. Might it have been more prudent to call the police? He was able to use his gun; why could he not use the phone to call the police? While waiting for the police, might he not have attempted to wake his sleeping girlfriend with the intention of leaving the room? Might he have at least waited for the bathroom door to open before firing his gun?

Gun ownership advocates may attempt to downplay the significance of incidents like the shooting of Reeva Steenkamp. It might be a thousand times more probable for a person to be killed by a steam engine than by a gun wielder using poor judgment. Nevertheless, one such gun death is still one too many.

J. Preventing Gun Violence

Were 11,861 of the 14,827 people in the United States murdered in 2012 killed with firearms because guns are easier to use or more effective killing weapons than bows and arrows, knives, or garrotes? Perhaps so. The more significant question is why and how did those who killed those 14,827 people come to think that it was okay to deprive others of their right to life? Why and how did those who forcibly raped others at the rate of one victim every 6.2 seconds in 2012 come to the conclusion that rape is their right? Why and how did those responsible for the aggravated assaults that occurred at a rate of one every 41.5 seconds in 2012[7] come to think that they should have the privilege of doing that?

Alcohol and drugs are not credible explanations of how or why people commit violent crimes. Getting high or drunk does not change one's basic values. Inebriation actually tends to reveal those values.

Perhaps the only foolproof way to prevent gun violence would be to destroy all guns. Should we simply throw up our hands and do nothing because all guns will never be destroyed? Gun violence, and any other form of violence, is a threat to the individual inalienable rights of us all. Accepting violence as inevitable and uncontrollable is not a viable option. Because violence is a threat to our inalienable rights, prioritizing respect for everyone's inalienable individual rights and teaching that value to the nation's children would eventually result in a decrease in violence of all sorts. (For more on integrating individual rights instruction into schools, refer to chapter 13, "Public Education and Student Rights.") Implementing additional reasonable gun regulations would help decrease the incidence of gun violence.

There have been a number of mass killings lately, including the slaying of policemen. There are probably a number of different factors that have motivated all this killing. Then there is the Black Lives Matter movement. Some see that movement as a cause of some killings. Others realize that the movement as well as some of the killings have a common source. There is ample evidence in this book that millions of Americans are financially disadvantaged, disenfranchised recipients of abuse and inequity. They feel—and accurately so—that society, in general, does not care enough about them to prevent the unfairness and injustice that affects them. From time to time, these people naturally resent, get angry about, even rage against the system that deprives them of their rights opportunities. Some of these people will inevitably act out that anger and resentment in a violent manner. When that happens, their targets are not limited to those people who do the most to support this oppressive system.

Self-responsibility is good. We can go on thinking that we are responsible for ourselves and that we need to care only about those we consider to be our own. We can continue to justify that attitude by telling ourselves that if everyone else did that, everybody would have what they need. Unfortunately, that attitude does not end abuse. It does not keep factories from poisoning the air, water, and land. It does not prevent corporations from dumping toxic waste in poor neighborhoods. It does not prevent governments from depriving members of minorities of their right to vote. As long as there is abuse, there will be anger. As long as there is anger, some of the angry people will act out violently.

K. Violence and Severe Mental Illness

The issue of mental illness and gun violence seems a bit complicated to me. Since we all deserve the opportunity to live free of violence, we cannot ignore the association of violence with SMI (severe mental illness). On the other hand, this association can lead some people to discriminate against and to stigmatize those with mental illness. This is not something those with mental illness deserve, because they have the same inalienable rights as those without mental illness.

Improved mental health treatment might result in a decrease in violent behavior. However, how do we define *improvement*? The trend in Pennsylvania has been to close expensive publicly funded institutes for mental illness treatment and integrate those with mental illness into community living. The goal is to make people with mental illness as independent as possible. The motivation? Saving the state money. Is this a treatment improvement?

The move to close institutions for people with SMI is not limited to Pennsylvania. Dr. E. Fuller Torrey states,

> **The massive discharge of patients from state psychiatric hospitals, followed by the failure to treat many of them, was well underway by 1966. During the intervening 40 years in the U.S. there have been 742,691 total homicides, of which a minimum of 37,134 (5 percent) were attributable to individuals with severe psychiatric disorders, almost all of whom were not being treated. As such, almost all of these were preventable homicides.** ("Violence and Schizophrenia: The Violence Issue among Individuals with Schizophrenia Is a Treatment Issue, Nothing More nor Less," *Schizophrenia Research* 88: 1–3, December 2006, 3–4, doi:http://dx.doi.org/10.1016/j.schres.2006.09.010)

I worked for almost ten years caring for consumers with serious chronic mental illness. I worked with consumers living in community housing, a certain number of whom would seem fine one day but then decide to stop taking their prescribed medications the next day. A number of times I witnessed consumers who had "advanced" to independent medication status (nonmonitored) and who claimed that they were taking their medications though they had stopped without letting anyone know. Very few of these consumers ever acted violently.

There are commonly held misconceptions about mental illness and violence that give the impression that those with mental illness pose a present and serious threat to those without mental illness. However, the Mental Health Reporting website presents the following facts:

> **Fact 1: The vast majority of people with mental illness are not violent.**
>
> **Fact 2: The public is misinformed about the link between mental illness and violence.**
>
> **Fact 3: Inaccurate beliefs about mental illness and violence lead to widespread stigma and discrimination**
>
> **Fact 4: The link between mental illness and violence is promoted by the entertainment and news media.** ("School of Social Work, Facts About Mental Illness and Violence," University of Washington, School of Social Work, 2016, accessed July 16, 2016, http://depts.washington.edu/mhreport/facts_violence.php)

The consumers I worked with in community housing, who would otherwise be institutionalized, seemed to be in the company of those with mental illness much more often than they were in the presence of those without mental illness. I suspect that consumers with SMI, staff working with SMI consumers, and the relatives of violent SMI consumers are more apt to be victims of violent behavior by SMI consumers than are members of the general population.

The webpage "Violence and People with Mental Illness" on the Mentalillnesspolicy.org website lists a number of studies that supported the conclusion that "being severely mentally ill and not taking medication is a third major clinical predictor of violent behavior" (see "Summary"). The first two clinical predictors were past history of violent behavior and substance abuse (alcohol or drugs) (Mental Illness Policy Org, Dr. E. Fuller Torrey, ed., accessed January 7, 2016, http://www.mentalillnesspolicy.org/consequences/violence-statistics.html).

During my almost ten years of working with the severely mentally ill in a community setting, I became aware that the few consumers who were sent to jail for various reasons missed many doses of their regular prescribed medications while incarcerated. "Mental Illness in America's Jails and Prisons: Toward a Public Safety/Public Health Model" by Dean Aufderheide asserts that inadequate treatment for mentally ill prisoners is a chronic problem in America's prisons and jails.

> **[Fifty] percent of males and 75 percent of female inmates in state prisons, and 75 percent of females and 63 percent of male inmates in jails, will experience a mental health problem requiring mental health services in any given year. It also appears that the individuals being incarcerated have more severe types of mental illness, including psychotic disorders and major mood disorders than in the past.** (Health Affairs Blog, April 1, 2014, accessed January 7, 2016, http://healthaffairs.org/blog/2014/04/01/mental-illness-in-americas-jails-and-prisons-toward-a-public-safetypublic-health-model/)

This source suggests conceptualizing psychotic and mood disorders as chronic illnesses. Encountering these problems with that concept would enable safety and public health officials to develop more and better methods for managing inmates with mental illness while incarcerated and after they are released.

How big a problem is the violent behavior of those with SMI? "Serious Mental Illness (SMI) Among U.S. Adults," on the National Institute of Mental Health website, states, "In 2014, there were an estimated 9.8 million adults aged eighteen or older in the United

States with SMI in the past year. This number represented 4.2 percent of all U.S. adults" (United States Dept. of Health and Human Services, accessed January 7, 2016, http://www.nimh.nih.gov/health/statistics/ prevalence/serious-mental-illness-smi-among-us-adults.shtml).

In an article about violence and SMI, Dr. E. Fuller Torrey asserts that the violent behavior of those with schizophrenia is simply a treatment issue because the homicides committed by such people were executed in virtually every case by individuals not taking medication. According to Torrey, about 50 percent of all those with schizophrenia are neurologically impaired in a way that prevents them from perceiving their mental illnesses and the necessity for medication. Several studies have shown that this lack of perception correlates with violent behavior and with medication noncompliance. Torrey's view is that current civil laws governing the treatment of the mentally ill make treating individuals with these problems extremely difficult. There are also studies that suggest drug and alcohol use by those with SMI, whether taking prescribed medications or not, will increase the likelihood of them behaving violently, according to Dr. Torrey's "Violence and People with Mental Illness" (cited above).

For the purpose of protecting everyone's individual rights, altering laws to facilitate the involuntary treatment of those with SMI would be helpful. Keeping firearms, alcohol, and street drugs out of the hands of those individuals would also help. I would suspect that the majority of people with SMI have neither the interest in nor the desire to own guns. Keeping guns more secure––that is, out of the hands of children— and more difficult to steal would also be beneficial. That goal might be reached more successfully through a public education campaign than through more laws. There also needs to be an improvement in treatment for mentally ill inmates in jails and prisons.

1   Dave Kopel, "The American Revolution against British Gun Control,"
    2014, accessed January 6, 2016, http://www.davekopel.org/2A/LawRev/
    american-revolution-against-british-gun-control.html.

2   Wikipedia, "Number of Guns Per Capita by Country," accessed
    January 6, 2016, https://en.wikipedia.org/wiki/Number_of_guns_per_
    capita_by_country.

3   Dan Griffin, "Gun Ownership By The Numbers," Daily Caller,
    November 4, 2014, accessed January 6, 2016, /dailycaller.
    com/2014/11/04/gun-ownership-by-the-numbers/.

4   UNODC, "United Nations Office on Drugs and Crime Global Study
    on Homicide," 2013, accessed January 6, 2016, http://www.unodc.org/
    documents/gsh/pdfs/2014_GLOBAL_HOMICIDE_BOOK_web.pdf.

5   Ibid.

6   Issie Lapowsky, "A Biometric Gun Lock That Even the NRA Might
    Like," Wired.com, May 2, 2014, http://www.wired.com/2014/05/
    sentinl-gun-lock/.

7   FBI, "Crime in the U.S. 2012—Crime Clock Statistics," 2012, accessed
    January 7, 2016, https://www.fbi.gov/about-us/cjis/ucr/crime-in-the-
    u.s/2012/crime-in-the-u.s.-2012/offenses-known-to-law-enforcement/
    crime-clock.

18

PRIVATIZATION AND THE COMMON GOOD

T he whole subject of privatization seems pretty uninspiring to me. However, privatization as public policy is being implemented by many of this nation's political leaders at all levels of government. This chapter defines privatization, describes different forms of privatization with examples, reviews the advantages and disadvantages of privatization, speculates on the underlying motives of those promoting it at any cost, and evaluates the practice of privatization in terms of the common good.

A. Definition

What is privatization? A short answer would be contracting public services to private companies. An article by Robert Poole Jr. has a more detailed answer: "Broadly speaking, it means the shift of some or all of the responsibility for a function from government to the private sector. The term has most commonly been applied to the divestiture, by sale or long-term lease, of a state-owned enterprise to private investors" (*The Concise Encyclopedia of Economics,* 2nd ed., s.v. "privatization," 2008, http://www.econlib.org/library/Enc/Privatization.html). Poole explains that a private concern or entity building, financing, or operating a large public project under a government concession or franchise is another form of privatization. Another form is outsourcing. That is the practice of government selecting a private business to deliver a service previously produced by the government's employees.

In March 2010, Governor Chris Christie created the New Jersey Privatization Task Force to study privatization. The task force reported, "Over the last several decades, in governments at all levels throughout the world, the public sector's role has increasingly evolved from direct service provider to that of an indirect provider or broker of services; governments are relying far more on networks of public, private, and nonprofit organizations to deliver services" (report by Richard A. Zimmer, et al., May 10, 2010, 1–2, http://www.njleg.state.nj.us/OPI/Reports_to_the_Legislature/privatization_task_force_2010.pdf).

B. Examples

An example of privatization is federal and state prisoners being incarcerated in for-profit facilities. "Prisoners in 2010" by Guerino, Harrison, and Sabol states, "About 16 percent of federal prisoners (33,830) and nearly 7 percent of state prisoners (94,365) were housed in private facilities on December 31, 2010" (U.S. Department of Justice, revised February 9 2012, 7, accessed January 7, 2016, http://www.bjs.gov/content/pub/pdf/p10.pdf).

The privatization of war is another example. "Edward Snowden and Booz Allen: How Privatizing Leads to Crony Corruption" by Norm Ornstein, asserts that during the Middle East wars, the United States employed "more than 100,000 contractors in Iraq." Almost half of these were "soldiers," many of whom made $1,000 per day. This was a much higher pay than was received by US military troops serving in the Middle East wars.[1]

Related to the example above is the costly ($72 billion) barracks and classrooms "refurbished or built from scratch" by an American contractor at the Baghdad police academy. A *New York Times* article by James Glanz reports that bad sewage pipes were used in the construction. This resulted in feces and urine from upper floors leaking through the ceiling below and causing the substandard concrete used in the construction to crumble.[2]

United States intelligence agencies outsource intelligence work to numerous private contractors. Norm Ornstein wrote that Edward Snowden was one of thousands of former government employees who did security work for the federal government but who were hired later by private contractors to do the same work with higher salaries.[3]

"Inspector general casts doubt on DOE contract work by ex-congresswoman Wilson" by Steven Mufson reports that the US Energy Department's National Laboratories at Sandia and Los Alamos are managed by private contractors like Lockheed Martin and Bechtel. These contractors are able to hire private consultants and charge those fees to the Energy Department.[4]

Other specific examples of privatization mentioned by Ornstein included the following:

- private toll roads constructed and operated under state licensing
- state outsourcing of public welfare administration
- outsourcing of municipal administrative services
- opening city services like garbage collection, pothole repair, waste-water services, printing, and golf course management to competitive bidding[5]

Another form of privatization takes place when governments sell assets to the public. This could take the form of selling unclaimed property recovered by the police. A theoretical example of privatization would be vouchers in which seniors would contract with private providers for their health care (as a replacement for Medicare).

C. Advantages

Are there measurable advantages to privatizing government services? One advantage to taxpayers would be the provision of the same services for a reduced cost. According to "The Pros and Cons of Privatizing Government Functions," by Russell Nichols, "Many state and local governments have identified hundreds of millions of dollars in savings by hiring outside contractors—or a neighboring city's services—to handle tasks like trash collection, pothole repair, and water and wastewater treatment" (*Governing*, December 2010, http://www.governing.com/topics/mgmt/pros-cons-privatizing-government-functions.html).

One suggested explanation of why the private sector can do things cheaper is that government employees possess neither the motivation nor ability to work as efficiently as employees in the private sector.

You may think that shrinking the size of government and creating more jobs in the private sector are advantages of privatization. However, privatization of services is not always advantageous to government and to taxpayers. The New Jersey Privatization Task Force report (cited above) noted that in states where privatized operations were most successful, a centralized permanent government authority analyzed the projects, selected vendors, and did the procurement. The task force reported that governments that do not oversee a privatized operation with due diligence can end up with costly, disastrous outsourcing outcomes.

D. Disadvantages

Outsourcing can decrease the size of government. If the size of government shrinks, government employees will lose jobs. Also, without due diligence, there is always the possibility that government employees could do a specific job less expensively than a private contractor. For instance, the article by Poole (cited above) states, "Medicare's cost of administration as a percentage of claim dollars paid is considerably less than any private insurer—less than 2 percent historically, according to the Congressional Budget Office."

Another possible drawback to outsourcing is mentioned on Wikipedia's "Privatization" web page:

> **If a government-owned company providing an essential service (such as the water supply) to all citizens is**

privatized, its new owner(s) could lead to the abandoning of the social obligation to those who are less able to pay, or to regions where this service is unprofitable. (s.v. "privatization," last modified January 4, 2006, accessed January 7, 2016, https://en.wikipedia.org/wiki/Privatization)

Then there is the bidding process. The cheapest bidder may get the contract, but the government is not necessarily going to get the quality of work it expects and which we, the common people, deserve. Private companies operate on the profit principle rather than the principle of preserving the common good. When government outsources services, the customer and the beneficiary is the taxpaying public. But taxpayers have no control over the quality of the private contractor's work.

Government agencies don't always have the resources or ability to determine ahead of time whether an outsourced service will actually save money. Cost increases by a private supplier can surpass the cost of the government agency performing the service in-house. Government corruption and profiteering go hand in hand with poor contract oversight. According to Russel Nichols's article "The Pros and Cons of Privatizing Government Functions,"

The privatization of public services can erode accountability and transparency, and drive governments deeper into debt. "Governments at all levels are just desperate to balance their budgets, and they're grasping at privatization as a panacea," says Susan Duerksen, director of communications for In the Public Interest, a project that examines privatization and contracting. (*Governing,* December 2010, http://www.governing.com/topics/mgmt/pros-cons-privatizing-government-functions.html)

There are also negative effects of privatizing war. Of the private mercenaries hired by the United States to fight in the Middle East wars, Ornstein claims in the *Atlantic* article that some of these "soldiers" murdered and raped multiple times with impunity. When these contracted mercenaries died, their deaths were not added to the official count of dead American military combatants.[6]

E. Motivation

Considering the possible pitfalls and disadvantages of privatization, you may wonder what motivates political leaders who advocate for privatization without accurate contract analysis, carefully worded contracts, and adequate oversight. Some governments are certainly desperate to balance their budgets. But why take a chance on making things worse?

In the *Atlantic* article, Ornstein writes that the increasing privatization of government is being pushed by those who passionately believe that government is too big and too powerful. Another motive, he writes, is financial gain. This can take a number of forms, including the following:

- selling off government-held real estate in a way that financially benefits campaign contributors or one's cronies that might later give one a lucrative position in a private firm
- awarding government service contracts or consulting fees to private companies in the same way as described in the previous point
- helping the government to hide the total costs of unpopular wars[7]

F. Evaluation

Does privatization support or detract from the common good and the actualization of our individual inalienable rights? The answer might vary for different forms of privatization. One form that I think is worthwhile is selling off certain government-owned assets that are not contributing to the general welfare. An example would be selling an unneeded, abandoned government-owned building of no historical or cultural significance for its fair market value.

For privatization of government services to support rights and the common good, it must save money rather than wasting taxpayer money. One of the selling points for privatization is the idea that private companies can provide the same things that governments provide, but for less cost. One of the factors that supposedly makes that possible is that the higher wages and salaries paid by private employers attracts workers who can and do labor more efficiently than public employees. Because a major expense of any business is labor, you may wonder how much better private employees must be to accomplish the same quality and quantity of work as public employees, but in less time. The cost of labor for private contractors must be measurably less than the cost of labor for government employees doing the same task. Because the private employees are being paid more than the government employees, they should be able to work faster. Otherwise, the private contractor would have to charge the government more money to make a profit.

These sorts of issues make it imperative that due diligence be exercised in making government contracts with private enterprises. There needs to be a government agency or other authority at the appropriate level of government to oversee all outsourced projects for that level. This authority should be responsible for analyzing the project, selecting the provider, creating a good contract, procuring, and ensuring the contract is fulfilled. The expectation and requirement of *quality* service should be stipulated in the contract.

It is not in the public's best interest for private companies to recruit the most skilled government employees and to use the skills of those employees to get government contracts. Perhaps the compensation of government employees could be commensurate with their individual performance. But the impediments to that from government unions and the civil service system would have to first be overcome (see "How Tennessee Transformed the Way It Hires and Fires People" by Barrett and Greene[8]).

When prioritizing everyone's individual inalienable rights is perceived as the primary function of government, it becomes clear that the government needs to be as big and as powerful as is necessary to fulfill its primary function—and neither bigger nor more powerful than that. Privatizing is neither justified nor made worthwhile by virtue of making government smaller and weaker, particularly at the cost of human rights.

Privatizing for the sake of patronage, of personal advancement, of personal gain, of deception, or of granting favors is abusive (see chapter 3, "A Culture of Abuse") and is contrary to what we, the people of America, deserve.

---

[1] Norm Ornstein, "Edward Snowden and Booz Allen: How Privatizing Leads to Crony Corruption," *Atlantic*, June 20, 2013, accessed January 7, 2016, http://www.theatlantic.com/politics/archive/2013/06/edward-snowden-and-booz-allen-how-privatizing-leads-to-crony-corruption/277052/.

[2] James Glanz, "Iraqi Police Academy Remains Largely Unusable," *New York Times*, November 6, 2007, accessed January 7, 2016, http://www.nytimes.com/2007/11/06/world/middleeast/06police.html?_r=0.

[3] Ornstein, "Edward Snowden."

[4] Steven Mufson, "Inspector general casts doubt on DOE contract work by ex-congresswoman Wilson," *Washington Post*, June 11, 2013, accessed January 7, 2016, https://www.washingtonpost.com/business/economy/lockheed-others-billed-doe-for-undocumented-work-by-ex-rep-wilson/2013/06/11/ac7b5b6e-d1d0-11e2-8cbe-1bcbee06f8f8_story.html.

[5] Ornstein, "Edward Snowden."

[6] Ibid.

[7] Ibid.

[8] Katherine Barrett and Richard Greene, "How Tennessee Transformed the Way It Hires and Fires People," Governing Institute, November 2015, accessed January 7, 2016, http://www.governing.com/columns/smart-mgmt/gov-tennessee-civil-service-reform.html.

19

GOVERNMENT, POLITICS, AND MONEY

G overnment, politics, and money are interrelated aspects of public policy that can either support our inalienable rights and the common good or help to perpetuate the culture of abuse. The first part of this chapter analyzes government. If you feel you understand different types of governments, feel free to skip over the shaded area.

There are suggestions in this book for opposing the culture of abuse. I imagine some conservative-minded so-and-so will try to discount those suggestions on the grounds that they are socialistic and therefore undemocratic. To adequately address this objection, I must present my personal concept of government.

Governments are formed so that different individuals and families can live in close proximity in a relatively orderly fashion. The elements of governing involve the following questions:

- Who is in charge?
- What are the rules?
- Who makes and changes the rules?
- Who enforces the rules?
- Who settles disputes between citizens?

There is a whole range of different ways of structuring governments. The governing systems of different countries vary: communistic (Russia), socialistic (Sweden), and republic (the United States). None of these governing systems exists in strict or pure forms. Take communism, for an example. Karl Marx, its founder, figured it would have caught on long ago and that it would be a worldwide phenomenon by now. When communism became universal, Marx believed there would be no need for government, because everyone's needs would be met, and everyone would be living in harmony in a classless society. China, Russia, Cuba, and Vietnam are alleged to be communist countries. They not only have governments, they also have privately owned and run businesses and citizens with varying incomes (so they are not classless). This is contrary to Marx's philosophy of communism.

In a purely socialist country, all means of production would be owned by the state. The government would collect all profits and use those funds to provide for the needs of the citizens in a fair and equitable manner. Some people believe that some Scandinavian countries and England are examples of socialistic governments. In reality, there is private property and privately owned and run businesses in these countries. The corporate tax rate in these so-called socialist countries is about 15 percent lower than the corporate tax rate in the United States.[1] These countries do not even approximate pure socialism.

That leaves republican forms of government. In writing this, I had to do some research to ascertain the difference between republics and democracies. I assumed that all civil governments in the United States are democracies. That's what I hear people say all the time. One definition of *democracy* from *Merriam-Webster* is "a government in which the supreme power is vested in the people and exercised by them directly or indirectly through a system of representation usually involving periodically held free elections" (s.v. "democracy," http://www.merriam-webster.com/dictionary/democracy).

According to a number of websites, in a true democracy, the ultimate political power rests *in the majority of people* or in their representatives, rather than in a constitution—specifically a constitution designed to constrain the majority of citizens from freely violating the rights of those in the minority.[2] According to these websites, in a republic, minority rights are protected by constitutional law, whereas a democracy without such a constitution lacks that protection. There are a number of countries that call themselves republics (such as the Democratic People's Republic of Korea) that really don't have that type of government at all.

I think of a true democracy as a dictatorship by mob rule without a constitution to protect minority members. I don't know of any countries that are actually run as democracies. One example of democratic rule would be that described in the biblical book of Mark, chapter 15, in which the majority of Jews call for Jesus to be crucified. If we are not happy thinking of democracy as dictatorial mob rule, we need to define democracy as something other than a form of government in which the power resides in the majority of people.

The word *democracy* is not used in the US Constitution. The word *republic* in the "Pledge of Allegiance" refers to the United States. Rather than calling the government of the United States a democracy, I call it a republic in which the rights of members of minorities are supposed to be protected by constitutional law. The citizens of both democracies and republics can have representative types of government. If those representatives, government heads, and judges are elected in free and fair elections, the election itself is a democratic process because the outcome is determined by the numerical majority of voters. A democratically elected representative government without legal protections for minority rights would not be a republic.

It is probably a good thing, in terms of inalienable rights, that the United States is supposed to be a republic. In a pure democracy, if the majority of citizens would want a communist government or a dictatorship, they would have the legal power to vote for that change.

Another thing about government that seems a bit confusing to me is the close association in certain countries between the economic system and the form of national government. I would expect Russia and China to be associated with an economy controlled by the government. The United States has a capitalistic economy, capitalism being a system in which property, industry, and businesses are privately owned. The purpose of private ownership is to create the greatest possible profits for entrepreneurs. Some websites call capitalism a form of government. This is totally baffling to me. Since capitalism, in its purest form, would be free of government ownership, control, and influence, how could capitalism be a system of government? In other words, how can a system that is separate from government be a form of government?

LessWaiting.com describes capitalist countries as those with "widespread capitalist economic activity" and in which "the government promotes and condones capitalism" ("Capitalist Countries List," October 2011, accessed February 9, 2016, http://www.lesswaiting. com/list-capitalist-countries.shtml). I thought it interesting that Russia was listed as a capitalist country and that China was noted to have a large number of privately owned companies. The point here is that capitalism is not limited to republican forms of government. Nor is capitalism exclusively American. Depending on which party and which president is in power, the American government has promoted and condoned capitalism to varying degrees. However, the Constitution does not specifically condone capitalism nor does it condemn socialism. "Capitalist Countries List" at LessWaiting.com points out that few countries in the world have no socialism at all.

I do not favor replacing capitalism entirely with socialism. Limited capitalism benefits society in certain ways; laissez-faire, however, is absolutely unacceptable. If the programs I have proposed for dealing with poverty and taking care of the disadvantaged seem socialistic, so be it. Promoting the common good and protecting our human rights is more important than promoting capitalism for the benefit of those who already possess superior advantages.

How does the practice of contemporaneous American politics relate to our individual rights and to the common good? Even though the US Constitution, an outstanding and fine document, is designed to protect our rights and to promote the general welfare, special interests have found ways to circumvent it to promote their own best interests. A republic with a representative government and a constitution is not enough to preserve everyone's opportunities to experience their inalienable rights. Why would that be? I think a quotation by Robert C. Byrd expresses the answer. "It is money, money, money! Not ideas, not principles, but money that reigns supreme in American politics" ("Robert C Byrd Quotes & Sayings," SearchQuotes, 2016, accessed

February 7, 2016, http://www.searchquotes.com/quotes/author/Robert_C_Byrd/).

The reader probably knows about the Supreme Court decision in *Citizens United v. the Federal Election Commission.*[3] The court decided that corporations have the same First Amendment right to free speech that individual citizens have. This was in relation to expressing views either for or against particular political candidates. I believe the court decided that financial contributions are expressions of free speech. This is possibly why super-PACS and corporations can and do contribute huge sums of money to certain candidates. Some people have devoted a large amount of time and energy to get this decision repealed. If and when that happens, it will be a step in a positive direction. However, it will not solve the problem of money's negative influence on American politics.

Ending the culture of abuse depends greatly on the actions of politicians. What are Washington politicians doing?

- They spend precious time raising money for their next election campaign—time not devoted to the citizens. Some congressional representatives and senators seem to think it is more important to do what benefits the constituents of *their* districts or states than what would benefit the whole country.
- Politicians are influenced by affluence. The study "Responsiveness in an Era of Inequality" by Thomas Hayes compared the voting records of senators in the 107th through the 111th Congresses with the opinions of the senators' constituents. This study found that the senators voted in accordance with the opinions of their wealthiest constituents. The opinions of lower-class constituents did not appear to have any effect on the senators' votes.[4]
- Politicians collect large salaries and benefits. According to an About.com article, "Salaries and Benefits of US Congress Members," by Robert Longley, the 2012 annual salary for rank-and-file House and Senate members was $174,000. That put all members of Congress in the top 10 percent of earners in

2012. That amount does not include retirement and health benefits. They also receive an annual allowance to help pay for the expense of executing their congressional duties. In 2012, House members received an average allowance of $1.35 million; Senate members, $7.9 million.[5]

Keeping the above points in mind, consider the study "Wealth and the Inflated Self: Class, Entitlement, and Narcissism" by Paul K. Piff, which suggests a definite connection between narcissism and higher socioeconomic status.[6] One dictionary defines *narcissism* as "inordinate fascination with oneself; excessive self-love; vanity" (Dictionary.com Unabridged, based on the Random House Dictionary, s.v. "narcissism"," 2016, accessed July 29,2016, http://www.dictionary.com/browse/narcissism).

There is an interesting article on the Daily Beast website by Michelle Goldberg relating to narcissism in politicians. She talked with Charles V. Ford, professor of psychiatry and wrote, "Narcissistic personality disorder, Ford says, is one of the personality structures associated with chronic lying" ("Palin's Ego Trip," November 18, 2009, http://www.thedailybeast.com/articles/2009/11/18/palins-ego-trip.html?source=dictionary).

Federal congresspeople are definitely of higher socioeconomic status, which increases the likelihood that they will be narcissistic and dishonest. Ken Burns's movie *Huey Long*, about the life of the Louisiana governor and senator, is a portrayal of this phenomenon.

Money in politics is definitely a problem. But what can be done about it? There are a number of possible steps that could be taken, such as the following:

- Representatives and senators should be allowed to be reelected, but not to serve consecutive terms. That way they would have time to devote to campaigning *between* terms rather than campaigning while in office.
- The salary and financial benefits of those in Congress should be limited to the median salary of American earners. That way,

members of Congress might be more apt to view issues from the perspective of those less fortunate.

- The sources of all political campaign contributions of $1,000 or more should be disclosed to the public. If contributions are a form of speech, then so is my withholding financial support for contributors who give money to fascist candidates. I will not be free to express that form of speech if I don't know who those contributors are.

- Half the total of each of those $1,000-plus contributions should go into a special fund dedicated exclusively to paying off the national debt.

- If voters believe strongly enough that large corporate campaign contributions are detrimental to the government and the nation, they may decide not to vote for candidates accepting those contributions. If enough voters did that, it could have a positive effect.

The likelihood that these suggestions will be implemented is probably remote. That is because this country is controlled by rich people who make the rules to benefit themselves and who are too narcissistic to care about everyone else's inalienable rights.

In summary, democracy is not necessarily a good thing. If most voters were perfect and concerned with everyone's freedom and well-being, democracy might be a wonderful form of government. A contemporaneous example of democracy is ISIS. The members of this terrorist organization create and maintain majority rule by punishing or killing anyone who openly disagrees. Dictatorship by mob rule; democracy at its worst.

The United States is a republic. The political power is supposed to reside in the Constitution and the laws derived therefrom. Government, politics, and money interests combine and interrelate in ways that result in politicians prioritizing the interests of the wealthiest over the constitutionally mandated promotion of the common good. There are steps that could be taken to rectify this shortcoming.

And there are criticisms of these steps. For example, one objection to limiting salaries of federal employees is that the best and brightest will opt not to serve in government if the financial compensation is not great enough. The question is, which would be preferable: the best qualified, albeit narcissistic and dishonest, public servant receiving upper-class compensation, or an average, competent, honest, and hardworking public servant receiving compensation equivalent to the national median earnings?

Another criticism of the possible steps to rectify the problem of the negative influence of money in politics is that the suggestions are idealistic. They will be resisted by politicians who prioritize their personal self-interest above what is in the best interest of the whole country. Nevertheless, if we fail to determine and strive for idealistic goals, we are bound to be limited by what someone else has decided is pragmatic.

[1]   Wikipedia, "List of Countries by Tax Rates," 2016, accessed February 9, 2016, https://en.wikipedia.org/wiki/List_of_countries_by_tax_rates.

[2]   Kate T., et al., "Democracy vs. Republic," Diffen, accessed February 7, 2016, http://www.diffen.com/difference/Democracy_vs_Republic.

[3]   Supreme Court, *Citizens United v. Federal Election Commission*, January 21, 2010, accessed February 9, 2016, http://www.supremecourt.gov/opinions/09pdf/08-205.pdf.

[4]   Thomas J. Hayes, "Responsiveness in an Era of Inequality: The Case of the U.S. Senate," APSA 2011 Annual Meeting Paper, Social Science Research Network, last revised November 21, 2011, accessed February 7, 2016, http://ssrn.com/abstract=1900856.

[5]   Robert Longley, "Salaries and Benefits of US Congress Members: The Truth," About.com, September 24, 2015, accessed February 7, 2016, http://usgovinfo.about.com/od/uscongress/a/congresspay.htm?p=1.

[6]   Paul K. Piff, "Wealth and the Inflated Self: Class, Entitlement, and Narcissism," *Personality and Social Psychology Bulletin* (SAGE) 20, no. 10 (2013): 1–10, doi:10. 1177/0146167213501699.

20

VALUES AND HUMAN RIGHTS

What's more important than individual inalienable rights? This chapter analyzes the reluctance of many Americans to use their money in a way that would ensure rights opportunities for all citizens.

The Declaration of Independence says, "We hold these truths to be self-evident, that all men are created equal, that they are endowed by their Creator with certain unalienable Rights, that among these are Life, Liberty and the pursuit of Happiness." Why don't these words have more power and influence in the United States? I would not expect them to have any effect whatsoever in countries like Russia or China. The governments of those countries don't profess to believe in equality or in a Creator or in universal inalienable rights. If every American citizen believed that we all possess the same human rights and if they *lived* that belief, it would make a positive difference.

Why has this concept of universal inalienable rights not been accepted by all citizens of the United States? To demonstrate that it has not, I need only point to the forty-five million Americans living in poverty, according to a Congressional Research Service article by Thomas Gabe,[1] and the twenty-nine million without health insurance as of March 2015, according to an article by Amy Connolly.[2] Those who are deprived of what they need to live a healthful lifestyle lack the opportunity to experience their right to life. Those millions who are abused miss the opportunity to experience their right to the pursuit of happiness. Those who are denied the ability to choose are deprived of their opportunity to experience their right to liberty. The following sections of this chapter examine the factors related to the importance we place on individual rights:

A. Factors Related to Lack of Rights Opportunities
B. An Attitude of Indifference
C. The Self-Made Man
D. To Whom Do Natural Resources Belong?
E. Could Everyone Really Be Wealthy?
F. What Is the Answer?
G. The Alternative
H. Taxes

A. Factors Related to Lack of Rights Opportunities

There is more than one reason why some Americans passively accept the deprivation of rights opportunities. The following is a list, based on my subjective experience and perception, of some of those reasons.

• Some people lack a basic understanding of what rights opportunities entail.

• Some don't believe we are born with rights or that we are entitled to rights opportunities.

• Some people believe that certain other groups of people don't deserve the same rights as they do. White supremacists, for example, may believe blacks and homosexuals are not born with the same rights as whites and therefore don't deserve the same opportunities.

• Some people may accept the idea that all people are born with certain inalienable rights but also believe that rights opportunities should somehow be "earned." They may reason that certain people are unemployed because they haven't earned the right to work.

- There are those who are fearful victims of abusers. Abusers neither acknowledge nor respect other people's rights. Abusers believe they are entitled to do things that negatively affect others, even though those actions violate others' rights.

Child abusers, corporate abusers, bullies, criminals, and dictatorial bosses take advantage of some people's passive acceptance to increase and enhance their power and to violate those people's rights with impunity. For nonabusers to attribute any sort of legitimacy to rights abuses is not courageous and is not productive for the country.

B. An Attitude of Indifference

Another factor that allows abuse to continue and perpetuates the lack of rights opportunities for millions of Americans is an attitude of indifference to the plight of those who are abused, deprived, and so forth. Paul Piff's article in the *Personality and Social Psychology Bulletin* refers to studies that have demonstrated that those with more wealth, in general, are less caring about the plight and problems of those less fortunate.[3] Successful people, those who possess the best opportunities to experience *their* rights, may accept the self-evident truth that we all come into this world possessing the same individual inalienable rights, but perhaps they value that truth less than they value their property, their stuff, their material possessions.

The value system of materialism is often defended by the belief that those who are successful and who have the best opportunities to experience their rights are in that position because of their own self-sufficient effort. They profess to believe that anyone can accomplish what they accomplished. In other words, from a materialistic viewpoint, if you are poor, if you are unemployed, if you lack health insurance, it's your fault.

I remember being told that I could accomplish anything I put my mind to. Is that so? Don't a lot of us—or even most of us—fail more times than we succeed? Thomas Edison is said to have made ten thousand attempts to invent the light bulb before succeeding. We all benefit from his success, which was made possible by the intellectual and financial resources he possessed as well as his persistence, desire, and perhaps faith. To claim that *anyone* could have done what he did is ridiculous. The truth is that all financially disadvantaged people do not have the opportunities to hold jobs that they can handle physically or intellectually and that pay a healthful living wage. How can these people be financially responsible for themselves?

A materialist may claim that if all people would be willing to be responsible for themselves and to act accordingly, no one would be a burden to society. There would be no poverty, no human rights abuses, and no unemployment. Sounds simple and uncomplicated. The problem is that it does not work for everyone. What is supposed to happen to the disabled and the elderly in this ideal scenario? When there is a shortage of jobs in the private sector, what are those who lack the aptitude to start a successful business supposed to do? Why would a system based mainly on the principle of being responsible for oneself compel all participants to behave ethically—that is, to refrain from taking unfair advantage of or coercing others or threatening the rights of other people in the quest to make a greater profit?

I don't disagree with the idea that everyone should be responsible for himself or herself. That idea neither solves the problem of abusive behaviors nor justifies indifference toward those less fortunate. The following shaded area is a more in-depth discussion of personal responsibility.

Guiding Principle #3 from the front of this book states, "Accepting personal responsibility for one's behavior is important as is holding others accountable for the effects of their decisions and behavior."

This principle does not support those who believe the government should provide more and more to its citizens in return for those citizens contributing nothing. Some think that if one is hungry, the government should give one food. If naked, clothing. If pregnant, prenatal care. If sick, health care. If mentally disturbed, mental health treatment. The more children one has, the more money and resources one should receive from the government. If one is an illegal immigrant, no problem;

the government should support illegals who are in need. This type of "reasoning" does not motivate people to be responsible for themselves or to hold others accountable for their decisions and behavior.

This might sound like conservative-minded thinking, and it probably does occur to the conservative mind more often than to the progressive mind. To me, it is *realistic* thinking. It would be nice if earth had unlimited resources, if so many plants and animals were not on the verge of extinction, and if the ice caps weren't melting and threatening to inundate human communities at or below sea level. It would be nice if there were no negative effects to anything a human being could ever do. But humans *are* doing negative things every day that detract from the common good.

There are limits to everything, including the scope and degree to which we can maltreat the planet and still preserve any discernible quality of life. We cannot continue to use fossil fuels at the present levels of consumption indefinitely. Earth's inner core will eventually cool. The sun will burn itself out one day. There are geophysical limits. There are also limits to the economic resources of the planet. Until someone figures out a way for everyone to get by without financial resources, it is irresponsible to act with Pollyanna, utopia-is-right-around-the-corner, money-is-irrelevant abandon. Money is not for wasting, especially other people's money. Wasting taxpayer money is abusive. The highest earners contributing the most of what's wasted does not minimize the abuse. Victimization is wrong. It is wrong to violate the rights of poor, undernourished blacks. It's also wrong to violate the same rights of fat, rich white people.

The irony is that although the wealthy complain about having to support the poor, the wealthy depend on the poor to maintain their political power over the middle class. If liberals ever get power and raise tax rates on the upper 1 percent to end involuntary poverty, toxic pollution, and lack of universal health care, the upper 1 percent might stop investing in American big business. If that happens, many middle-class workers could find themselves in the lower class.

So the upper 1 percent and the middle class are willing to live with a growing national debt, with a whole class of people living without the dignity and the opportunity to earn enough to keep their families healthy, with thirty-five million Americans lacking health insurance and with millions being sickened and killed by the effects of using fossil fuels. As Upton Sinclair declared, "It is difficult to get a man to understand something when his salary depends upon his not understanding it" ("Quotations by Author," QuotationsPage, 2015, accessed May 19, 2016, http://www.quotationspage.com/quotes/Upton Sinclair/).

The rather pathetic truth that occurs to me is that our social problems are growing, and coping with them is becoming an increasingly expensive proposition. One could find studies to support or to refute the idea that having children one can't afford to raise on one's own, abusing drugs, or committing crimes is correlated with unemployment. Sometimes common sense seems to have more value than research studies. This is one of those times. Boredom or depression does not encourage responsible behavior. When one does not have forty or more hours of one's week occupied by gainful activity, one is more apt to be bored or depressed. People who are unemployed and bored or depressed are more apt to engage in crime; to overuse tobacco, alcohol, or drugs; or to engage in unprotected sex. That's not a pretty picture, but neither is living in poverty.

If society/government would give all financially disadvantaged citizens productive decent jobs instead of handouts, taxpayers could save millions that are now being wasted. The very rich have a responsibility to stop resisting higher tax rates. The government has a responsibility to give the financially disadvantaged the opportunity to act more responsibly instead of wasting tax revenue. The disadvantaged have the responsibility of making the most of the opportunities that come their way.

Not only do the very wealthy use poverty to maintain their political power and deny any responsibility for the resulting abuses of human rights, they also blame the poor for being poor.

C. The Self-Made Man

Materialists love the myth of the self-made man, the belief that anyone can, through his or her own independent efforts and energy, become financially prosperous. There are literally millions of millionaires in this world—9.63 million households in the United States alone, according to "Number of millionaires in U.S. reaches a new high" by Walter Hamilton.[4] But how many are "self-made"? How many have risen from rags to riches without a lot of help and support and reliable counsel from others?

Attaining great wealth is rarely, if ever, a simple matter of "pulling yourself up by your bootstraps." Some of the ways an individual can make a megafortune in America include winning a million-dollar lottery, founding a large illegal drug cartel, marrying a rich person, and being born into a rich family.

D. To Whom Do Natural Resources Belong?

Then there are those families that made or make fortunes by exploiting the natural resources of our country. These people are respected, admired, and envied, even though these resources don't legitimately belong to them. The following shaded area is my subjective ranting explanation of this.

From a strictly moral viewpoint, the natural resources of the American continent and its territorial waters belong to the descendants of the Native American tribes that occupied the continent when the first Europeans landed in the "New World." There was never an international legal justification for Europeans to "claim" land in the Americas for their monarchs. Their standing on it did not make it their land to claim. For kings to parcel out land in the "New World" to their favorite subjects wasn't morally legitimate. How could transfers of "ownership" of territory from Mexico or France to the United States have been legitimate, since those countries stole that territory from the original occupiers? The occupation of America by Europeans was the equivalent of China marching its army into Tibet in the 1950s and claiming that Tibet was now part of China. Nothing legitimate about it.

How many white people got richer in Georgia after President Andrew Jackson refused to enforce the Supreme Court ruling in favor of the Cherokee Indian tribe in *Worcester v. Georgia*? (See "Supreme Court History: The First Hundred Years" by Alex McBride.[5]) The Trail of Tears that followed a few years later was only one of many immoral and illegal actions taken against Native Americans—actions that financially disadvantaged Native Americans and their descendants and enriched the conquerors.[6]

Those who have made fortunes on America's natural resources that were not theirs to begin with are also responsible for millions of dead and diseased Americans (see chapter 11, "Fossil Fuels and Human Rights"). Whether those fortunes came from fossil fuels, gold, or copper, the resulting negative effects on the environment and human health have been abusive to those affected.

E. Could Everyone Really Be Wealthy?

How do megarich people justify having so much more than they need, while others do not have enough? One of their rationales is that anyone could have accomplished the same thing they have. In other words, *everyone* could be as rich as they are. How realistic is that?

Assuming that everyone was willing to do whatever it took to make a million dollars, could the 7.06 billion people in the world in 2012 possess a net worth of one million dollars each? The total private wealth in the world was reportedly 135 trillion dollars in 2012, according to "Top 1% Control 39% of World's Wealth" by Robert Frank.[7] That total wealth was only enough for every human inhabitant of the planet to possess a net worth of about $19,130. So, no, *everyone*—no matter how much they won or inherited or stole—could not have been worth a million dollars in 2012.

What was the income of people actually like? According to Gallup survey numbers collected from 131 countries from 2006 to 2012, the annual median income of the world's households was $9,733 and the median income per household member was $2,920.[8] Let me point out what this data shows. Half of the seven billion people in this world have lived in households with annual incomes of $9,733 or less. Those same 3.5 billion people made $2,920 or less per capita in a year.

There are a number of exceptional people in the world who, through a combination of patience, perseverance, networking, personality, skills, and talent are able to amass fortunes. Even if everyone had the attributes necessary to make a million dollars per year, there is simply not enough money in the world to make that a reality.

The idea that anyone and everyone can independently raise themselves from rags to riches is a convenient delusional belief for those who are indifferent to the misfortunes of others and who might otherwise feel guilty about their own good fortune. But guilt and indifference won't help solve the social problems of poverty, unemployment, and public health threats. The rags-to-riches myth needs to be relegated to the same place our childhood fantasies end up.

F. What Is the Answer?

If we could clear from our thinking the myths about making money, we could face reality. Some people are very good at making money. Other people couldn't care less about making a bundle. Both groups of people have the same inalienable rights to live healthfully and to pursue happiness. If our country ever gets to the point where we value universal inalienable rights and are willing to prioritize those rights in legislation and policy, what would that look like? My answer is the following list:

- All disabled citizens and the elderly would receive what they need to stay reasonably healthy.

- All financially disadvantaged adults who are able and willing to work would have decent jobs that pay at least a healthful living wage.
- All workers would have reasonably safe and healthful working conditions and would be treated reasonably by employers.
- All renters would live in units without any of the following due to landlord neglect: unsafe conditions, insufficient insulation, allergens, and toxins.
- All primary and secondary school students in the United States would be prepared for gainful employment or for additional education/training by high school graduation.
- We would all be able to benefit from all aspects of the publicly owned/administered common good.
- Safe, affordable quality food and untainted, nontoxic affordable water would be available to us all.
- All man-made additives, genetically modified ingredients and organisms (GMOs), and known allergens in any food produced in and sold in the United States would be publicly disclosed.
- No product or service marketed in the United States would endanger physical health when used as directed.
- None of us would be exposed to any health-threatening emissions from any source when such emissions could be controlled by the best available technology.
- Information about any man-made chemicals (including proprietary formulas) that could threaten anyone's physical health would be disclosed.
- We would be served by government employees (at all levels of government) whose duties are confined within defined boundaries. When a government employee would violate those boundaries and a citizen suffer harm, the citizen would have the right to just and reasonable compensation for any financial loss from the employer of the government employee.
- We would be served by a debt-free federal government.

- We would be served by a fully funded federal government able to financially ensure that everyone possesses rights opportunities without having to borrow money to do so.

- We would be served by a federal government that does not **waste** money.

- We would be served by a federal government that does not use revenue to threaten the opportunities of foreign citizens to actualize inalienable rights and by a government that neither condones nor supports the threatening of those same rights by any American citizen or group, including businesses.

- We would be served by a federal government that neither condones nor supports foreign governments that deny their citizens opportunities to experience their individual inalienable rights.

- We would be served by a federal government that does not condone, support, or in any way favor foreign governments that have invaded or attacked another country without first being attacked, until such governments rectify their actions.

- Federal, state, and local governments would stop giving tax breaks to and would stop subsidizing the fossil fuel industry. All levels of government would lead the country toward decreasing dependence on fossil fuels by switching to alternative (nonnuclear), American-produced sources of fuel and electricity. (See chapter 12, "Fossil Fuels and Human Rights, II.")

G. The Alternative

We can let sleeping dogs lie, which means that one out of every thirty people who is good at making money will be allowed to keep much more of their income than they actually need while six out of every thirty people will not even be able to afford a healthful lifestyle. I do not advocate pure socialism in which the means of production are owned by the government. A regulated, private capitalistic system has a lot of potential value if it can be made to support the common good and our individual inalienable rights. If *support* is too high an expectation, perhaps capitalism could, at the very least, be restrained from threatening those values. (For some ideas about how this could be done, refer to chapters 5 and 6, "Poverty and Capitalism, I and II.")

The present economic system in the United States tends to reward the most talented, the boldest, the most influential, the best personalities, the smartest, the most boldly innovative, the luckiest, and the most admirable. Simultaneously, the same system tends to deprive everyone to varying degrees—but especially those with the least power, talent, influence, and so forth—of their rights opportunities.

I suspect that few people deny that those with the best deserve success. That's one sentiment. I also sense that many people feel that those with the least do not deserve the same rights opportunities as those who possess "the best that money can buy." That is another sentiment. When one combines those two sentiments, it seems reasonable for millionaires and billionaires with asthma to live comfortably in parts of the world with the best scenery and cleanest air while at the same time they make money from investing in or owning polluting industries— industries whose unnecessary pollution causes lower-class people with asthma to suffer and die.

Anyone with a 401k or a pension may be dependent on the success of those polluting factories that make people sick. If the publicly traded stocks of polluting factories in which their retirement money is invested decreases in value, so might their retirement savings. Which is more significant, a more comfortable retirement for those who can indiscriminately invest in Wall Street or the rights opportunities of the financially disadvantaged?

This valuing of Wall Street for the sake of retirement security brings to mind two very similar-sounding terms: automaton and autonomous. *Automaton* refers to "a person who acts in a mechanical or machinelike way" (*Merriam-Webster*, s.v. "automaton," accessed July 22, 2016, http:// www.merriam-webster.com/dictionary/automaton). *Autonomous*, on the other hand, at least to me, means self-determined, aware, conscious actively reasoning. It may not be reasonable for us modern Americans to be complete nonautomatons. It may be that modern life is so complex that we cannot prevent, at times, allowing others to make decisions for us or accepting advice in an automatic fashion.

How much should we give in and allow others to determine the way we live, to allow others to influence the automatic daily choices we make? Of course, it is easier to be an automaton than to be autonomous. In movies and on TV, the robots that become self-aware sometimes have enough gumption to rebel. Perhaps human automatons have that capacity as well.

We could at least choose to be self-aware, to question, to seek answers, and to share those answers with others. We really don't have to mindlessly march to the phone store every time a new model appears. We are capable of deciding if the increased convenience of a new phone justifies the suffering of people in Africa forced to mine the conflict minerals that allow that phone to function. We have the power to decide if we want to support military violence in the African bush with our purchases. We can explore retirement savings options that don't support corporate bullies.

H. Taxes

Should business owners, the very rich, or any earner be permitted to keep as much of their earnings as they choose? Some people believe taxing of income by a government is extortion and a threat to their property rights. According to Wikipedia's "Tax protester" web page, there is a distinction between the terms *tax protester* and *tax resister.*

> **A tax protester is someone who refuses to pay a tax on constitutional or legal grounds, typically because he or she claims that the tax laws are unconstitutional or otherwise invalid. Tax protesters are different from tax resisters, who refuse to pay taxes as a protest against the government or its policies, not out of a belief that the tax law itself is invalid.**

(s.v. "tax protester," last modified December 15 2015, accessed January 6, 2016, https://en.wikipedia.org/wiki/Tax_protester)

According to an article by Stephen Fishman, "Tax Protesters Never Win," the IRS "estimates that every year it receives 20,000 to 30,000 frivolous tax returns—that is, returns in which the taxpayer refuses to pay taxes on invalid grounds" (Nolo.com, 2015, accessed January 7, 2016, http://www.nolo.com/legal-encyclopedia/tax-protesters-never-win.html).

The following is a rant regarding tax protesters.

I tend to have more sympathy for tax resisters, like those who refuse to support unjust wars financially, than I have for tax protesters. The latter seem to be motivated by self-interest rather than by concern for social injustice. I would not object to tax protesters occupying an island in the middle of the ocean. In that way, we Americans who do pay taxes would not have to finance the protesters' water supply, their roads and bridges, their street lights, their garbage collections and disposal, their public library use, and their police protection. Ironically, tax protesters are probably some of the same people who complain that poor people receive economic good from the government without having to pay taxes.

I suspect the thinking of tax protesters goes something like this: "This is my money. I earned it. No one has the right to take it away from me and use it to benefit someone else." Perhaps the desire to control one's economic good by withholding taxes is inherent in human nature. If everyone did that and no one paid taxes or fees to the government, the government would have to borrow money to provide law enforcement, jurisprudence, national defense, and financial regulation. Borrowing money in the absence of income is a solution doomed to fail. No sane lender would continue lending money with no chance of repayment. This would result in the end of government—that is, anarchy. Those American citizens who believe they could cope quite nicely without government assistance might not mind a state of anarchy. They might be perfectly happy—that is, until the Russians or Chinese or ISIS invaded the United States.

Governments need economic good to protect our civil rights, our property rights, and our rights opportunities. It may be impossible for the government to provide for the common good in the absence of available revenue.

Is it fair for someone making $50,000 per year to be required to pay taxes while someone making $500,000 dollars has to pay nothing? We have a progressive tax system in this country, which means that those who make more are supposed to pay a higher tax rate.

There is enough money in this country to establish a just society in which everyone is able to actualize their inalienable rights. In an ideal world, earners would willingly pay enough taxes to create and maintain, without waste, a quality common good from which we could all benefit.

[1] Thomas Gabe, "Poverty in the United States: 2013," Summary, Congressional Research Service, January 15, 2015, accessed January 7, 2016, http://fas.org/sgp/crs/misc/RL33069.pdf.

[2] Amy R. Connolly, "Federal Report Finds Uninsured Americans on the Decline," United Press International, August 12, 2015, accessed January 7, 2016, http://www.upi.com/Top_News/US/2015/08/12/Federal-report-finds-uninsured-Americans-on-the-decline/2681439373746/.

[3] Paul K. Piff, "Wealth and the Inflated Self: Class, Entitlement, and Narcissism," *Personality and Social Psychology Bulletin* (SAGE) 20, no. 10 (2013): 1–10, doi:10. 1177/0146167213501699.

[4] Walter Hamilton, "Number of Millionaires in U.S. Reaches a New High," *Los Angeles Times*, March 13, 2014, accessed January 10, 2016, http://articles.latimes.com/2014/mar/13/business/la-fi-mo-number-of-millionaires-in-us-reaches-a-new-high-20140313.

[5] Alex McBride, "Supreme Court History: The First Hundred Years," PBS, December 2006, accessed January 10, 2016, http://www.pbs.org/wnet/supremecourt/antebellum/landmark_cherokee.html.

6   "Trail of Tears," Cherokee Nation, 2016, accessed May 19, 2016, http://
    www.cherokee.org/AboutTheNation/History/TrailofTears.aspx.

7   Robert Frank, "Top 1% Control 39% of World's Wealth," CNBC, May 31,
    2013, accessed January 10, 2016, http://www.cnbc.com/id/100780163.

8   Glenn Phelps and Steve Crabtree, "Worldwide, Median Household
    Income About $10,000," Gallup, December 16, 2013, accessed January
    10, 2016, http://www.gallup.com/poll/166211/worldwide-median-
    household-income-000.aspx.

21

WHAT CAN WE DO?

L ike many other countries, America has a culture of abuse in which abuses of and threatening attitudes toward inalienable rights seem almost commonplace. This chapter is for those who acknowledge that problem and would like to do something about it. What actions will help discourage abuse and promote individual rights?

If we all respected one another's individual rights, there would be less abuse. One answer, then, is for you and me to value, to teach, and to promote individual rights and to encourage others to do the same.

We could also develop a thorough understanding of individual rights and the common good and observe what is happening in the world through that lens of insight. Most of what we see on the evening hour of daily TV news other than accidents and natural disasters, are incidents of abusive behavior that violate individual rights or threaten the common good. For example:

- church funds embezzled—abuse
- electric wheelchair stolen—abuse
- student raped—abuse
- store windows broken in rioting—abuse
- child abducted—abuse
- mother pushes child off bridge—abuse
- football player hits girlfriend—abuse
- ISIS beheads another journalist—abuse
- Saudi men stone woman to death—abuse

- company fined for excessive toxic emissions—abuse
- policeman shot at traffic stop—abuse
- old trees cut down for right-of-way—abuse, in my opinion
- police found guilty of brutality—abuse
- occupied apartment filled with black mold due to landlord neglect of leaking pipes—abuse
- government agency aware of lead contamination, but does nothing—abuse

Realistically, can all abuse be stopped? Not while humans remain imperfect. We are all less than perfect, but imperfection does not preclude improvement. We can be sure that if we don't try to progress, the culture of abuse will persist.

Increasing your awareness of abuse and sharing that awareness is a proactive approach. Encouraging the desired behavior (i.e., respect for everyone's individual rights) has value. Some people believe in being friendly to abusive individuals and organizations. Neville Chamberlain made concessions to Hitler prior to World War II—a friendly, albeit unproductive, gesture. Discouraging the undesirable behavior (i.e., abuse) may be more productive than friendliness.

William Lloyd Garrison wrote, "With reasonable men, I will reason; with humane men I will plead; but to tyrants I will give no quarter, nor waste arguments." Giving support, especially economic support, to abusive groups is equivalent to giving quarter. I like to replace the word *tyrants* with *abusers* and *quarter* with *support*. To abusers I will give no support. If you follow the words of Garrison, you will, whenever and wherever possible, deny your support to those individuals and organizations that behave abusively or that promote abusive attitudes.

The Hitlers (abusers) of this world do not gain and maintain power and influence without a lot of support. When we support abusive groups or individuals, we fail to support everyone's rights opportunities. We can discourage abusive behavior by withholding support, especially economic support, of abusive groups and individuals. If enough people around the world boycotted goods made in China because of China's illegal occupation of and cultural genocide in Tibet, the Chinese government might soften its tyrannical attitudes and behavior. If millions of people and businesses boycotted the products and services of a certain international corporation, that megabusiness would stop spending millions of dollars to oppose consumers' right to choose not to consume GMOs. If enough people and businesses boycotted the products and resources produced by a particular pair of billionaire brothers, they might change their plan to "purchase" the 2016 election with $900 million.[1] I believe large automotive manufacturers would stop failing to disclose dangerous defects in their vehicles if we all stopped buying the cars of the next company that did that.

People who are pragmatists, or just plain indifferent, comfort themselves with the thought that this approach to the problem of abuse is impractical—that a sufficient number of people will never be willing to participate. That supposedly justifies the pragmatist's reluctance to sacrifice one iota of his or her personal comfort or convenience.

We have the right to choose not to care, the right to not get involved, and the right to entertain abusive opinions. We also have the right, as Americans, to complain about the negative conditions that will eventually befall us and ours, thanks to our exercising those particular rights.

There might be some issues or questions about which you can comfortably sit on the fence separating those who are *for* from those who are *against*. In regard to the question of inalienable rights, as the saying goes, not to decide is to decide. If you either condone the abuse of anyone's inalienable rights or if you have not decided that everyone should have actual rights opportunities, you are siding with the abusers.

There are nonabusive people who imagine they can live in isolation, not bother other people, and escape abuse directed at themselves and theirs. Don't bother me, and I won't bother you. They certainly have the right to choose that course, which reminds me of the following quote attributed to Martin Niemöller:

In Germany, they came first for the Communists,
and I didn't speak up
because I wasn't a Communist.

Then they came for the Jews,
and I didn't speak up
because I wasn't a Jew.

Then they came for the trade unionists,
and I didn't speak up
because I wasn't a trade unionist.

Then they came for the Catholics,
and I didn't speak up
because I was a Protestant.

Then they came for me,
and by that time no one was left
to speak up for me."

Some of us are automatons—that is, people who do what is suggested to them without questioning or resisting. One has the ability to be autonomous, to consciously choose how to spend one's money. To give money to a bank or other investment institution without knowing how it is being used is not an autonomous action. Such money may help to support and perpetuate abusive activities of various large corporations. One can put one's checking account, savings account, and IRA money in a small community bank that has no direct ties to Wall Street rather than in a Wall Street investment bank. (For those who doubt the existence of such banks, check out https://www.avbpgh.com/avb-history to learn about a small community bank founded in 1900 that did not close during the Great Depression, and that doesn't invest in Wall Street.[2])

Are all Wall Street businesses a threat to the common good and people's inalienable rights? It is my understanding that socially responsible Wall Street firms do exist. Selective investment in those firms could actually benefit the common good. Likewise, indiscriminate investing can help promote those firms that prioritize profit over the common good and rights.

To terminate the American culture of abuse, political and business leaders need to adopt policy changes that prioritize the common good and everyone's individual inalienable rights. We can't depend on government and business to spontaneously initiate these changes. There are too many powerful leaders who have the traditionalist mindset described in the introduction. Their thinking helps to perpetuate the culture of abuse.

Only a widespread grassroots demand of the public will persuade our leaders to change public policy so that everyone is treated more fairly. We need to let the old traditionalist beliefs go. We need to face the facts, to confront the reality of abuse, and to start caring more about everyone. We, the consumers and citizens of the United States, need to organize and demand those positive policy changes. Once those improved policies are implemented, we need to respect and support them.

---

[1]   Nicholas Confessore, "Koch Brothers' Budget of $889 Million for 2016 Is on Par with Both Parties' Spending," *New York Times,* January 26, 2015, accessed January 10, 2016, http://www.nytimes.com/2015/01/27/us/politics/kochs-plan-to-spend-900-million-on-2016-campaign.html?_r=1.

[2]   "AVB History," Allegheny Valley Bank, 2016, accessed July 18, 2016, https://www.avbpgh.com/avb-history.

22

CONCLUDING REMARKS

History is not just facts and events. History is also a pain in the heart, and we repeat history until we are able to make another's pain our own.

This is a moving quotation by Professor Julius Lester. I think it quite relevant to the subject of abuse in America.

There are those who believe abuse is inevitable and that they can't afford the time or expense to do anything about it. They don't care enough to try to change things.

I wonder if civic and business leaders consciously or unconsciously ask themselves, "How much abuse are people willing to accept?" What they should be wondering is "Why should anyone willingly accept abuse they do not deserve?" The rich and powerful might answer that question by reframing the term *abuse* to represent willing *sacrifice* to the greater good. Why should we not give up our rights opportunities for the sake of our employer's success? Why not sacrifice our lives, liberty, and happiness for the sake of our country's greatness? That doesn't seem negative. In fact, it sounds noble.

But what makes a country like the United States great is living up to its principles of equality and inalienable rights for every citizen. The way to make the country great is not to prioritize the economy of the upper 1 percent of earners and to convince the rest of us that it is noble to accept abuse willingly so that the richest can become wealthier. The United States consists of more than 324 million citizens. Until each and every one of them has the same rights opportunities, the United States, as a whole, will be less than great.

I have demonstrated that there is a culture of abuse in this country. I have presented the idea that abuse is contrary to the values of equality and human rights for which this country allegedly stands. I have suggested practical alternatives to abuse, alternatives that can preserve everyone's rights opportunities and that can promote the common good. These alternatives do not violate the guiding principles in the introduction.

Who wouldn't want to live in a world where everyone enjoys experiencing their human rights? In a world where all can benefit from the common good? In a world where everyone respects everyone's rights? What will it take for that way of life to replace the present culture of abuse? A critical mass—that is, enough people who understand and agree with the commonsense approach to public policy described in this book and who are willing to demand and work for constructive change. A critical mass of people who realize that none of us is born with the promise of guaranteed comforts or conveniences and that their personal comfort and convenience can never justify the deprivation of anyone else's rights opportunities.

During the 2016 American presidential primary campaign, one of the Democratic nominees called for a revolution. Bernie Sanders was not referring to a violent revolution in which one group of people uses force to depose and take the place of the people currently in power. It was nonviolent revolution that I and others favor that calls for lots of people to change their attitudes and behavior and to withdraw financial and other types of support from abusers, be they individuals or organizations.

Do enough of us have enough courage and perseverance to hold abusers accountable until the abusers adequately respond with real positive changes? If we don't do it, who will? If we don't start now, when will it happen?

GLOSSARY

The following terms appear repeatedly in this book in accordance with the meanings presented on this page.

abuse (*adj.* **abusive):** An unnecessary injurious action deliberately or negligently inflicted on others. In this book, "abuse" does not refer to self-abuse nor to abusing drugs/tobacco/alcohol unless specified. (See Chapter 3, "A Culture of Abuse" for more information.)

common good: Encompasses that which is owned or administered by some level of civil government and which benefits citizens in general, but which most individual citizens could not afford. Things like the infrastructure, public libraries, public health protection, environmental preservation, the courts, law enforcement, national security, firefighting, public education, public parks, public playgrounds, public green spaces, employment security, government fiscal responsibility, caring for the disabled and retired citizens in need, responsible foreign policy are all aspects of the common good. (To understand how inalienable rights and the common good are related, read Chapter 2, "Rights and the Common Good.")

financially challenged: Inability to afford a healthful lifestyle and/ or to prevent one's health from deteriorating because of insufficient self-generated financial resources.

healthful lifestyle: For most people this includes a good balanced quality diet (minimally processed, preferably organic), physical exercise, hot running water, a warm safe healthful living space. To live a healthful lifestyle, some people require allergen-free food and living space, special diets, prescribed medications, food supplements, quality health and dental care, or the help one needs to kick health-threatening habits.

healthful living wage: The amount of money necessary for a person to afford to live a healthful lifestyle in a particular location.

inalienable rights (also referred to as **rights, individual rights, human rights):** Intrinsic powers and privileges, with which every individual is born, including the rights to life, to liberty, to the pursuit of happiness, and to benefit from the common good. (See Chapter 1, "Individual Rights" for a more in-depth explanation.)

laissez-faire: A system in which the owners of industry and business dictate the rules of competition, the conditions of labor, the negative effects of their activities on the environment and on public health, the cost and safety of products and services, and other conditions, as they please, without government regulation or control.

rights opportunities: Chances to actually experience one's rights. An example would be living without one's life and health (physical, mental and emotional) being threatened, or taken away abusively.

wasteful spending: Unnecessary expenditures by entities which are in debt, particularly any level of government. (See Chapter 8, "Wasteful Government Spending" for more detail.)

INDEX

A

abuse
- alternative to culture of, 20–21
- culture of, 20
- defined, 10, 253
- elder abuse, 13
- landlord abuse, 14
- of Native Americans, 28, 237
- poverty abuse, 26
- religious abuse, 19
- by religious leaders, 191–192
- sexual abuse, 14, 191–192
- use of term, 10–11
- violent criminal abuse, 15

abusive behavior
- conditions of, 10
- examples of, 245–246
- as not necessarily illegal, 11
- starting with Cain and Abel, xxiii
- as widespread phenomenon (US), xii

achievement gaps (in education), 158

acid mine drainage (AMD), 100

acid precipitation, 103, 105, 170, 173

acidic streams, 105

Adams, John, 181

Adherents.com, 85

"Adverse Health Effects of Heavy Metals in Children," 104

affordability, regarding healthful lifestyles, 42–49

air pollution, 103, 109, 110, 115

altered ecosystem, 117–118

alternative energy, 106, 125–126, 127, 128, 130, 134, 135–136, 138, 139, 140

Amadeo, Kathy, 93

American Dream
- achievement of, 49–51
- socialism and, 49–51
- use of expression, 49

American Laboratory, 108, 113–114

American-Israeli Alliance, 83–84

apartment rentals, costs of, 44

"Are Churches Making America Poor?" (Bekiempis), 189

"Are we sure that radon is a health risk?" (EPA), 127

Arms Control Association, 88
Armstrong, William, 182
arsenic, 103, 117, 131, 136, 166
Assad, Bashar al-, 87
Atlantic, 218, 219
Aufderheide, Dean, 211
authority, defined, 64
automation, 106, 151
automaton, 241–242, 248
autonomous, 241–242, 248

B

Bachman, Michelle, 54
Bailey, Jill, 117
bald eagle, 116, 118
Bechtel, 216
Bedard, Paul, 128
Bekiempis, Victoria, 189
benzene, 114, 115–116
Berlinger, Joshua, 85
bill of attainder, 7n2
bioaccumulation, 117
bison, near extinction of, 28
"Biting One's Own Tail: The
    History of Benzene,"
    115–116
Black Lives Matter
    movement, 208
black lung disease, 100–101, 137,
    170, 173
"Black lung surges back in coal
    country" (Hamby), 100
blood diamonds, 170
blowouts, 108–109

"Blowouts and Well Control
    Problems," 109
BPA (bisphenol-A), 112–113
Brown v. the Board of Education,
    154, 155–156
budget cuts, 70–71
budget reform, 68, 72
Buffet, Warren, xxii
Bully (documentary), 13, 161
bullying
    China as megabully, 70, 82
    corporate bullying, 169
    of people of Diego
        Garcia, 80
    Russia as megabully, 82
    school bullying, 12–13,
        159–161
    workplace bullying, 13
"Bullying Facts and Solutions"
    (van der Zande), 159
Burns, Ken, 227
Business Insider, 19, 110
business startups, failure rate
    of, 50
busing (for racial desegregation
    of schools), 155
Butler, Rhett, 133, 174
Byrd, Robert C., 225

C

Californians for Population
    Stabilization, 146
Campaign for America's
    Future, 56

G

Gabe, Thomas, 230

Gallup survey, 237

gangs, 16

Garen, John, 130

Garrison, William Lloyd, 246

gasoline, 114–115

general welfare
defined, 53
use of term, 8–9

General Welfare Clause (US Constitution), 52

Genesis 1:26, 167, 168

geothermal energy, 125, 127, 130, 139

GHG (greenhouse gasses), 102, 104, 115, 125, 137

Ghose, Tia, 111

Ghosh, Shikhar, 50

Gilpin, Kenneth, 103

Glanz, James, 215

Glatz, Julianne, 146

Glink, Ilyce, 44

global warming, 11, 36, 99, 105, 133, 135, 138, 165, 167, 175

globalization, described, 58–60

glossary, 253–254

GMOs, 29, 59, 239, 247

God, as word included in every state constitution, 183

"Gold and Economic Freedom" (Greenspan), 92

gold standard, 92–93, 94, 95

Goldberg, Michelle, 227

government contracts, 68, 71, 220

government spending, wasteful government spending, 68–77

governments
foreign hostility and overthrow of legitimate governments, 81
and politics and money, 222–229
ways of structuring, 222–223

Great Depression, 93

Greece, economic plight of, 92

green cards, 150

greenhouse effect, 102–103

greenhouse gasses (GHG), 102, 104, 115, 125, 137

Greenpeace International, 129

GreenPlastics.com, 111

Greenspan, Alan, 92, 93, 94

Greyston Bakery apprentice program, 30

Griffin, Dan, 200

Guardian, 54

Guerino, 215

guiding principles, xxiii–xxiv, 25, 33, 86, 233, 251

gun ownership
criteria for, 200
historical perspective, 199–200
numbers of guns and homicide rates, 200–202
preventing gun violence, 207–208

prohibition of, 200

protecting individual rights, 202–203

reasonable gun regulations, 203–204

Second Amendment. See US Constitution, Second Amendment

and violence in America, 197–212

H

H-2A program (legal guest worker program), 147

habeas corpus, 2, 7n1

Hagerty, Barbara Bradley, 191

Hamby, Chris, 100

Hamilton, Walter, 236

Harmalkar, Sayali, 159

Harrison, 215

hate groups, 19

Hawaii, annexation of, 80

Hayes, Thomas, 226

Head, Tom, 154

health care

single-payer, 48–49

universal, 48–49, 234

health insurance, need for, 44–45

healthful lifestyle

cost of, 44–45

defined, 253–254

deprivation of, 230

organic diet as option of, 44

healthful living wage. See wages

heavy metal pollution, 103–104, 117, 118, 135

Heinberg, Richard, 92

HFCs (hydrofluorocarbons), 112

Hirsch, Lee, 13, 161

History Is a Weapon (Zinn), 27

"History of Wind Energy," 138

Hitler, 190, 246

Hoffert, J. Raymund, 100

Hollingsworth, Barbara, 131

homelessness, 33, 39, 45, 48

homicide rates (US), 200–202

Honduras, gun ownership in, 201

honey bees, 118

Hoover Dam, 125

"How can 6 pounds of gasoline create 19 pounds of carbon dioxide?" 115

"How Crude Oil Toxins and Petrochemicals Affect Your Health," 110

"How Much U.S. Debt Does China Really Own?" (Murse), 70

"How to get free cell phone service from the government," 170

Huey Long (movie), 227

human rights

economic strategies and, 91–92

economy and, 90–95

environmental quality and, 164–175

ex-congresswoman Wilson"
(Mufson), 216
Institute for Energy
Research, 119
"Interest Expense on the Debt
Outstanding" (US Treasury
Department), 70
Internal Revenue Service, 190
international trade agreements,
88. *See also* trade agreements
intimate partner violence, 14–15
involuntary poverty, 26
Iran
and nuclear weapons, 88
overthrow of government
in, 81
Iraq
and creation of Islamic State
(IS), 86
ethnic/religious groups in, 85
religious abuse in, 19
US employment of
contractors in, 215
US invasion of, 75, 81
ISIS, 85–86, 87, 228
Islamic law, 185
Islamic State (IS), 86
Israel, creation of, 85
Israelis, 83–84
IVF (in vitro fertilization), 35

J

Jackson, Andrew, 237
Japanese Americans, internment
of, 87

Jefferson, Thomas, xx, 181, 186
Jepsen, Christopher, 130
Jesus, 181, 182, 183, 187, 188
Jewish, percent of world's
population, 85
Jim Crow laws, 154
Joaquin, Sheryl, 108, 114, 126
Jobs for the Common Good
benefits of, 74
cost of, 44–45, 46
creation of, 31–32
criteria of, 37
determining eligibility, 32
need for, 43
phases 1 and 2 of, 45–46
phases of, 33
John Jay College of Criminal
Justice, 191
Johnson, Don, 56

K

Kennedy, John F., 188, 189
Kidpower.org, 159
Killam, Galem, 111
Kochhar, Rakesh, 42, 60
Kopel, Dave, 199
Korea, 84
Kosnoff, Tim, 191
Kurds, 85

L

laissez-faire capitalism, 27, 91,
92, 254
LaMonica, Gabe, 74
land lines, 171

Medicare
    cost of administration of, 217
    payroll taxes for, 46
Mental Health Reporting, 210
"Mental Illness in America's Jails
    and Prisons: Toward a Public
    Safety/Public Health Model?
    (Aufderheide), 211
mental illness, violence and
    severe mental illness (SMI),
    209–212
mercury, 104, 116, 117, 131, 136,
    137, 166, 172, 173
MFI (median family income), 45
"Microwave-induced plasma
    gasification technology
    makes headway" (Sims),
    125–126
middle class, xviii, xxi, 42, 60–
    61, 234
Middle East conflict, 83–84
Middle East wars, 75, 215, 218
military agreements, 82
military sexual abuse, 14
military spending, eliminating
    wasteful military spending,
    74–75
Miller, Ted. R., 17
Milloy, Steven, 116
mine subsidence, 100, 105
monarch butterflies, 118
money, governments, politics,
    and, 222–229
Moorhead, Molly, 48
morality, 192–193

"More Oil Spilled from Trains
    in 2013 Than in Previous
    4 Decades, Federal Data
    Show" (Tate), 109
mountaintop mining, 99
Mufson, Steven, 102, 216
multinational corporation
    (MNC), 59
Murray, Jean, 46
Murse, Tom, 70
Muslim, percent of world's
    population, 85
mutual defense treaties, 88

N

NAFTA (North American Free
    Trade Agreement), 56–57
narcissism, 227, 228, 229
National Center for Education
    Statistics, 12–13
National Center for Law and
    Economic Justice, 38, 46
national debt, 20, 70, 91, 95, 96,
    228, 234
national defense, as part of
    common good, 74–75
National Institute of Mental
    Health, 211
National Laboratories at Sandia
    and Los Alamos, 216
National Oceanic
    and Atmospheric
    Administration, 110
National Police Misconduct
    Reporting Project, 13

obesity, 17–18

"Official USDA Food Plans," 44

oil and natural gas

blowouts, 108–109

DDT, 115–117

dioxins, 111–112

downside of, 108–109

effects of hydraulic
fracking, 110

environmental effects of oil
drilling, 109

gasoline, 114–115

oil spills, 109–110

petrochemicals, 113–114

plastic waste, 111

plastics, 110–111

polystyrene, 112

skin care products, 114

upside of, 107–108

oil spills, 109–110

OilGasGlossary.com, 108

Old Testament, 181, 185, 187

1 percent, xix, 43, 59, 82, 107,
202, 234, 250

O'Neal, Glenn, 75

organic food, 44

Ornstein, Norm, 215, 216,
218, 219

"Oversight Report of
Compaction of Coal Mine
Waste Slurry Impoundment
Embankments," 101

"Overview of the Clean Air
Act and Air Pollution"
(EPA), 103

ozone layer, 112, 165, 173, 174

"Ozone Science: The Facts
Behind the Phaseout"
(EPA), 112

P

Packman, David, 13, 64

PAIR (People for Actualizing
Individual Rights), xi

Pakistan, formation of, 84

Palestinians, 83–84

parental responsibility, 34–35

"Parents Projected to Spend
$241,080 to Raise a Child
Born in 2012" (USDA), 34

particulate matter, 104, 115,
129, 133

Passel, Jeffrey S., 144, 145, 149

passenger pigeon, extinction
of, 28

Paul, Rand, 76

peace

a more peaceful world, 81–82

right to versus national unity,
84–85

People for Actualizing Individual
Rights (PAIR), xi

"Per Pupil Spending Varies
Heavily Across the United
States," 156

"Personal income in the United
States from 1990 to 2014"
(Statistica), 43

personal responsibility, xiv, xxiv,
33, 233

petrochemicals, 98, 108, 113–114, 130

Pew Research Institute, 60

phthalates, 112–113

Physicians for a National Health Program, 48

Piff, Paul K., 227

Pipeline and Hazardous Materials Safety Administration, 109

Pistorius, Oscar, 206–207

"Plastic Biodegradation in Landfills" (Killam), 111

plastic waste, 111

plastics, 110–111

Pledge of Allegiance, 224

plutocracy, xxi, 18, 57

police conduct, and individual rights, 64–67

police misconduct, 13–14, 24, 64–65

politicians, activities of, 226–227

politics
    government, politics, and money, 222–229
    influence of wealth on, 18

PolitiFactcheck.com, 48

polystyrene, 112

Poole, Robert, Jr., 214, 217

population
    and energy production, 132–133
    impact of on environmental quality, 173–174
    problem of, 36

    of US, xix, 36, 114–115
    of world, 114

positive thinking, xiv, 175

"Potential health impacts of burning coal beds and waste banks" (Finkelman), 100

poverty
    and capitalism, 25–61
    cost of fighting, 46
    defined, 19, 23–24, 25, 42
    versus middle class, 60–61
    as not synonymous with unemployment, 26
    private enterprise as solution to, 30

poverty abuse
    example of, 26
    groups experiencing, 26

"Poverty in the U.S.: A Snapshot," 38, 46

"Prisoners in 2010" (Guerino, Harrison, and Sabol), 215

prisons, overcrowding in, 74

private enterprise
    contracts with government, 220
    government regulations of, 140
    Jobs for the Common Good as benefiting, 46
    as solution to poverty, 30, 43

private ownershipof guns, 200, 201, 202
    purpose of, 224

abuse by religious leaders, 191–192

defined, 178

free exercise of, 186

and human rights, 178–195

morality, 192–193

role of in negatively affecting environment and health, 167–168

separation of church and state, 179, 182, 185, 186–191, 194

religious abuse, 19, 85, 86–87

religious privilege, 184–185, 190

Renewable Energy, 138

republics

examples of, 222, 223, 224

US as, xx, 222, 224, 228

"Responsiveness in an Era of Inequality" (Hayes), 226

"The Restriction of Political Campaign Intervention by Section 501(c)(3) Tax-Exempt Organizations," 190

rights. *See also specific rights*

and the common good, 8–9

defined, 1, 178

example of, 178

lack of, 231–232

use of term, 5

rights abuses, frequency of, 12–19

rights opportunities

defined, 254

requirements for experiencing, 23–24

"Ripe for Retirement: The Case for Closing America's Costliest Coal Plants" (Union of Concerned Scientists), 104–105

robber barons, 27–28

Roberts, Diane, 54

Russia

as capitalist country, 225

as communistic, 222, 223

as megabully, 82

and weapons development, 76

S

Sabol, 215

safety-net benefits/programs, 26, 45, 46, 70, 74, 90, 94. *See also* public assistance

"Salaries and Benefits of US Congress Members" (Longley), 226

Salisian, Robin, 203

Sanders, Bernie, 251

Saunoris, James, 130

Scandinavian countries, 222, 223

Schaefer, Luke H., 33

school bullying, 12–13, 159–161

"School Desegregation—the Busing Debate," 155

schools. *See* public education

Scott, Robert, 56

Printed in the United States
By Bookmasters